HOW TO START AND RUN A WRITING AND EDITING BUSINESS

HOW TO START AND RUN A WRITING AND EDITING BUSINESS

Herman Holtz

JOHN WILEY & SONS, INC.

NewYork • Chichester • Brisbane • Toronto • Singapore

Copyright © 1992 HRH Communications, Inc.
Published by John Wiley & Sons, Inc.

Holtz, Herman.
    How to start and run a writing and editing business / by Herman
Holtz.
       p.   ca.
    Includes bibliographical references.
    ISBN 0-471-54832-4 (cloth).—ISBN 0-471-54831-6 (pbk.)
    1. Authorship—Marketing. 2. Editing. 3. Home-based businesses.
I. Title.
PN153.H64   1992
808',02—dc20   91-31071

ISBN 0-471-54832-4
ISBN 0-471-54831-6 (pbk.)

Printed in the United States of America.

10 9 8 7 6 5 4 3

Preface

No man but a blockhead ever wrote except for money.
—*Samuel Johnson, 1776*

Who knows what old Samuel Johnson had in mind when he denounced as blockheads those who wrote for reasons other than money? Did he mean that writing was so distasteful that only money should induce one to undergo the pain of it? Was he trying to energize other writers to work at elevating the economic status of writers, most of whom were apparently always poor, hungry wretches? Was he warning those who had not yet learned that the lot of the writer was probably going to be one of privation? Or did he have the vision to foresee a bleak future for the economic status of most writers, even into the 20th century?

Whatever his inspiration or objective, his words deserve repetition today. Fortunately—or unfortunately, depending on your orientation and despite Dr. Johnson's exhortation—writing can bring you more than one kind of reward, which is what lures many writers to settle for less than an equitable financial reward: Certain kinds of writers, those who write books and movies, for example, often find themselves regarded by their friends and relatives with respect and awe. Sometimes they even earn public honors. It tends to be gratifying to the ego, of course, to have gained a bit of prestige; unfortunately, this largesse of homage only infrequently has a matching counterpart in the material reward of money. Writing has long been a notoriously poor-paying profession for most of those who have not "arrived." Dr. Johnson was not pointing out something that was not already obvious to anyone who cared to pay attention; nor has the sense of his observation changed a great deal since his time. Today, national surveys of freelance writers and their careers invariably turn up shocking economic statistics. For example, 90 percent of freelance writers earn not much more than $5,000 annually from their writing. In fact, only a tiny fraction of freelance writers are able to write full time and support themselves with their writing; a majority hold down daytime jobs and write only in their spare time or after they have retired from their breadwinning struggles.

For those who write as an avocation or whose writing is ancillary to their careers, the monetary reward (or the *lack* of monetary reward) is probably irrelevant. Still, there is information in these pages that will be helpful even to those writers, although my main intent is to address freelance writers for whom writing is a full-time career or who aspire to make it such. That is, my main objective in writing this book is to do what I can to help change the depressing economics of freelance writing. I intend to show that it is possible to dedicate yourself to a full-time writing career and still earn at least as much as most other professionals.

Granted, if you are one of the millions who are bent on writing the Great American Novel or a play and becoming the toast of New York and Hollywood, you may have to wait awhile for your success, which is not at all guaranteed. However, that need not prevent you from being economically successful as a writer—writing for money—while you are seeking artistic success. There are numerous commercial or business writing opportunities that will pay you as much as or even more than you can make unloading trucks or waiting tables all day while you work on that novel or play at night. On the other hand, you may find creative fulfillment in an area of writing other than creative fiction. Many who started out with vague ambitions of achieving literary acclaim have found satisfaction in achieving success in advertising, industry, business, and other arenas in which the writer's skills are appreciated and rewarded.

It is a simple fact that there are many ways for today's writer to avoid the traditional hardships of the literary trade. There has never been a better market—set of markets, more accurately—for anyone with writing skills and a desire to put them to work. Let us consider a few facts.

The dismal economic statistics so often associated with a writing career do not mean that most freelance writers cannot write well. On the contrary, many write very well indeed, often *better* than required by most markets for their skills. Many still struggling for success already write more fluently and more skillfully than some writers whose works are critically acclaimed and for which they receive generous monetary rewards. Literary skills and success as a writer are not inevitably linked, for reasons that are not important here. It is enough to recognize that not every freelance writer is well suited to the solitary life of creating works of fiction and nonfiction and then selling them to publishers and that this does not reflect in any way on their skills as writers. As my Canadian friend, writer Sidney Allinson, wrote me, "Selling, Marketing, Prospecting: Those are the most important aspects of any freelance editorial service or writing enterprise. . . . No matter how proficient a writer is, if he/she does not market services aggressively, the chances of success are slim." A wise observation from an old hand at writing in a broad variety of fields. Writing talent is not especially relevant; marketing talent is. And if you can learn to write well, as I assume you have done, you can certainly learn to market well. Don't believe that ancient cliché about better mousetraps and paths beaten to your door; it won't happen unless you work at *selling* your mousetrap.

Aside from that, and as important as marketing yourself is, the disappointing economics of freelance writing do not mean that the need for writers and editors is too limited to represent a suitable opportunity for freelance writing as a career; there is a constantly growing need for competent writing and editorial services. Indeed, there is today a distinct and ever-present demand for such services to create a broad variety of written materials that are used daily in business, industry, and government. Every day, the shortage of competent professional writers drives business executives to use amateur talent for writing.

One thing the dismal economics of freelance writing suggests is that far too many writers—perhaps you too—are failing to apply their writing talents in a way that is practical in the modern world. Too many pursue the field of writing that is, for most of us, the most difficult in which to succeed, fiction and popular or general-interest nonfiction. While they struggle in this field of writing, other fields—business, industry, and government—have need of their skills and will pay well for them. In addition, far too many writers are trying to succeed in a field of writing that is limited in market size, overwhelmingly competitive, and therefore especially difficult to market in successfully: They are writing on "spec" (articles and books, primarily) and then trying to find someone to buy the products they have created. They could hardly have selected a more difficult road to success as writers.

There is another broad distinction to be made between selling products you have created—short stories, articles, book manuscripts, plays, and other scripts—and selling your services as a writer. In Edgar Allan Poe's time there was relatively little demand for writers' services beyond that of newspapers, and even then most writers were members of the newspaper's staff rather than freelancers. That has changed along with all the other changes that have come about in the second half of this century. We could paraphrase what has been said with reference to engineers and scientists: More than half of all the writers who ever lived and practiced their craft are alive and practicing their craft today, but many are writers of another genre.

The world is still full, it seems, of aspiring young writers intent on becoming literary lions. Sometimes I think that everyone in the world must have the manuscript of a half-finished novel stuffed under his or her mattress. Of course, a great many writers start out that way, and some do write fine novels and plays. Most of us do not. We wind up waiting tables, teaching in universities, driving taxicabs, and delivering babies. Some of us give up the dream of being writers, while others continue working on that novel or play in their spare time for years. Now and then one of that class proves to be a Margaret Mitchell. Most do not.

As always the truth is simple: Not all who can write are novelists and playwrights, any more than all who can play the piano are concert pianists. A few of us, however, learn that we can turn to writing and editorial services as a business. We come to writing envisioning it as a great art and finally discover that it is a profession—perhaps an art, but also a *business*. We discover that there is a great demand for the services of competent writers and editors, and that unlike the vast majority of free-lance writers, we can, if we so choose, work at our elected craft full time and earn a living at it.

This is not a compromise of principles, nor is it defeatist. Many of us are simply far better suited to the workaday world of business and industry than we are to the solitary existence of the novelist, and we find it satisfying to apply our talents to the mundane world of business. We find other advantages in this world: We do not work on spec, nor do we suffer rejection slips and all-too-familiar fat packages in the morning mail. We are still writers, we are independent freelancers, but we get paid for every word we write or hour we work at rates that we have negotiated in advance. We satisfy a distinct need, and we take pride in what we do—selling our custom services as writers and editors to clients who need professional help in writing and related editorial work.

Many of these needs of business organizations are served by in-house staff writers, who, in the larger organizations, must turn out written work regularly, often on a daily basis. Others, those who have only occasional need for written work, turn to vendors such as advertising agencies, public relations firms, and freelance writers and editors to handle their needs on a custom basis. (Even large organizations with staff writers often turn to freelance writers for reasons that we will discuss later, and they are often the best of the markets available.) Thus, many writers today enjoy full-time freelancing careers as suppliers of the written word. Many provide other editorial services, as well, including design and format of publications, proofreading, editing, typemarking, illustrating, research, review, and other chores that I shall discuss in these pages. As I have been reminded of recently, many for whom writing is an important element of what they do for a living do not think of themselves as writers per se, but as consultants, public speakers, and other kinds of specialists.

Of course, times have changed quite a lot in other ways. Poe scrawled his manuscripts on paper with an old-fashioned pen, producing what would technically be termed holographic manuscripts. These would be set into metal type by hand and eventually be printed by letterpress after he succeeded in finding a publisher. A century after Poe's death in 1849, writers worked at manual typewriters or hired stenographers to type their work, since publishers no longer accepted handwritten manuscripts. Soon after, many—perhaps most—writers had turned to electric typewriters, and printing was being done on much simpler offset lithographic presses. The change continues: Today more and more writers are working with computers, word processors, and desktop publishing systems, as great an advance over typewriters as typewriters were over the quill pen. Concurrently, over the past century, technology has produced radio, television, copiers, fax machines, satellite communications, and other advances that have changed the nature of many aspects of society. For one thing, it has increased by many orders of magnitude the demand for writers and writing. The consumption of paper in our society obliterates whole forests daily. Despite the ubiquitous computer, which has elbowed typewriters aside and spawned promises of a paperless society, we spew more paper from our printing presses today than ever before—books, magazines, brochures, newspapers, newsletters, salesletters, proposals, manuals, scripts, catalogs, news releases, training programs, correspondence courses, lecture guides, transcripts, résumés, programs, and circulars.

Freelance writing (at least for all who are not working on that great American novel or play) is a business today, making its contribution to society as do other businesses. A few paragraphs ago, I noted the difference between the traditional freelancing concept of the aspiring novelist or playwright and that of selling your services as a writer and editor. In what is, in fact, an editorial service, there are two ways to conduct business. Some freelancers are purely contract writers and editors, selling their expert services to create what clients need on a custom basis. Others create written products that they themselves sell, such as newsletters and training manuals. And, as noted, some do both. Accordingly, I am going to address both approaches to creating and building an editorial services business.

I recently attended an organization meeting of a Washington Independent Writers spin-off group of business writers. Twelve of us gathered for this initial meeting. True to form, while most of us reported that we were full-time freelance or independent writers, several reported that they were consultants for whom writing was an important, if not principal, function. But all agreed that public speaking was also an important function, if a relatively minor one, and that the three functions of consulting, writing, and speaking were mutually supportive. And so I shall have a few words to say about public speaking as it relates to the business of freelance writing and editing. For while writing is a profession and a career, freelancing is a *business*. That means it involves marketing, pricing, customer relations, and other business activities. Bear this in mind as you explore with me many of the increasingly numerous avenues open to you as a business writer. You may get a few surprises.

Herman Holtz

Trademark
Acknowledgments

Apple is a registered trademark of Apple Computer, Inc.

The Bernoulli Box is a registered trademark of the Iomega Corporation.

BetterWorking the Resume Kit is a trademark of Spinnaker Software Corporation.

CompuServe is a registered trademark of the CompuServe® Service.

Definition Plus! is a registered trademark of WordScience Corporation.

GEnie is a registered trademark of The General Electric Company.

IBM PC i; a registered trademark of International Business Machines Corporation.

Inset is a registered trademark of Inset Systems, Inc.

LEXIS is a registered trademark of Mead Data Central, Inc.

Macintosh is a registered trademark of Apple Computer, Inc.

MailList is a trademark of WordStar International Corporation.

Microsoft Word is a registered trademark of the Microsoft Corporation.

PC-Outline is a trademark of Telemarketing Resources.

PROCOMM is a registered trademark of DataStorm Technologies, Inc.

PRODIGY is a registered service mark and trademark of PRODIGY Services Company.

ProFinder is a trademark of WordStar International Corporation.

QModem is a registered trademark of Quadratron Systems, Inc.

Selectric is a registered trademark of International Business Machines Corporation.

SmartKey is a trademark of No Brainer Software.

Smith Corona is a registered trademark of SCM® Corporation.

Star Exchange is a registered trademark of Systems Compatibility Corporation.

TelMerge is a registered trademark of WordStar International Corporation.

Telix is a trademark of Exis, Inc.

WordPerfect is a registered Trademark of the WordPerfect Corporation.

WordStar is a registered trademark of WordStar International Corporation.

The Write Word is a registered trademark of the Write Word® Processing Services.

XyWrite is a registerd trademark of XyQuest, Inc.

Contents

List of Figures

FIGURE	TITLE	PAGE

Introduction

PREAMBLE

If it is not already clear—and I have tried to make it clear in my own clumsy way—this is not a book designed to help you become a successful novelist or playwright. No one would be more delighted than I should you do so, but I would not be able to claim much credit unless I had frightened you away from the business-writing world and thereby forced you to succeed as a fiction writer. At any rate, it is my objective to help you succeed in a thoroughly practical sense in an editorial services business. This is a completely respectable way to put your writing talent to work on a practical basis.

As an up-and-coming freelance business writer, you will almost surely be called on occasionally for work that is not writing, strictly speaking, but some closely related service. It may be editing, advising a client in editorial or publication matters, handling illustration or production work as part of a writing project, leading and guiding a group of writers for a client, or otherwise doing something away from the keyboard and perhaps a good bit less interesting than creating copy. And so the term *writing* is used loosely throughout this book to refer to *all* the services you may be asked to perform in the course of conducting an editorial services business.

WRITERS' NICHES AND WRITING SUCCESS

Every market has niches, small segments of the market that have been overlooked or neglected as not worthy of direct attention or too small to be bothered with by those already up to their ears in work and not interested in finding new avenues. However, a great many successful businesses have been founded on niche marketing by entrepreneurs with vision. IBM, for example, already leading the world in mainframe computers, did not at first believe there would be a large enough market for desktop computers to be worth their effort to enter that market. (In fact, Tom Watson, founder of IBM, originally thought that computers generally were not worthy of more than passing thought.) Therefore IBM was a late arrival in the desktop computer market, already cluttered with hundreds of small companies that had exploited the niche markets comprised of small businesses and individuals who wanted computers that would fit both their desktops and their budgets.

There are many individuals and small companies who require the same kinds of products and services that large companies do, but they cannot place the large orders that major suppliers find attractive and worth pursuing. Major advertising agencies, for example, provide valuable services free of charge to major clients—clients whose budgets for buying space and time make handling their accounts worthwhile. They cannot do that for small advertisers whose budgets for buying space and time are small. These small advertisers, a market niche, will pay small agencies for the services that large advertising agencies provide free of charge to large clients. To win their large accounts, the major advertising agencies write formal proposals that cost thousands of dollars to prepare, an expense the smaller agencies cannot afford. But as one small agency owner explained, there are niche markets *within* many large corporations where good, solid work is wanted without the need to spend time auditioning many agencies. That means that even small agencies can do business with the large clients when they make themselves aware of the clients' problems and offer practical solutions. These niches have produced contracts from $1,500 to $170,000—perhaps a bit small as such contracts go, but quite satisfying for the small-agency owner. It takes only a few such contracts to keep the small agency—that is, the freelance writer—alive and solvent.

The process works analogously in other businesses. For example, since the larger mailing-list brokers usually require clients to rent a minimum of 5,000 names, businesses that wish to rent only 1,000 or 2,000 names are a niche in that market, served by the smaller list brokers because they are ignored and neglected by the larger ones.

Warehouse stores such as Pace and the Price Club offer the small retailer an opportunity to buy a variety of goods at the same prices the larger retailers pay when buying directly from the prime sources, a very large niche in that market.

The success of many small businesses thus depends entirely on their ability to find suitable niches, market segments neglected by others that are small enough for them to handle but large enough to be worth handling. That does not mean that they must depend on a single niche, however; they may very well address several niches. F. W. Woolworth, creator of the famous five- and ten-cent stores, is an outstanding example. He built a large business filling a niche, that of the ordinary person who spent five or ten cents carefully. The Southland Corporation also built a major business filling a niche when they created the 7–11 stores for customers whose needs were not well served by the typical supermarket.

Freelance writing is a business. It also has niches, and the comparison with other businesses is a valid one. You are not going to become an expert writer at every kind of writing known to humankind. You must decide in what niche or niches you will focus your efforts. Dan Janal revealed, in a CompuServe conference, that he operates a public relations service from his own apartment, focusing largely on PR for computer manufacturers. He had previously worked for PR firms handling computer accounts. Jerry O'Neill, in another CompuServe conference, revealed that he stumbled into freelance writing almost by chance after starting a career in photography and being invited to write on the subject. He writes advertising and promotional copy, principally on technical subjects. David Rothman writes a monthly column on laptop computers and has written several books on computer subjects. (The opportunity to write the monthly column was the result of a book he wrote about laptop computers.) And I came from a career in technical writing, through a phase as a proposal consultant, to a full-time freelance career in writing business and professional books, because that was where most of my experience and knowledge lay. I began this career by filling a very precise niche, the market represented by those who wanted information on selling to the federal government.

Finding your niche may be the most important task facing you if you are not yet established as a freelance writer. Otherwise it is possible to waste years struggling to succeed as a writer and find that ultimately success has eluded you only because you have not found the proper niche for your talents as a writer. (I was surprised, as well as elated, to discover how rapidly I began to succeed once I focused my efforts on writing about the business and professional worlds, starting with federal government markets.)

HELP IN FINDING YOUR OWN NICHES

Finding your own niche(s) requires a great deal of disciplined thinking and analysis on your part. Never mind that your spouse or your Aunt Tillie thinks that you give awfully good advice and ought to write a "Dear Abby" column, or that your friends think you are a natural poet. You are not likely to become the new Dear Abby, and poets make even less money than fiction writers. Unless Aunt Tillie is prepared to sponsor you (that means *support* you) while you are trying to become another Dear Abby, you must be practical and take time to consider the aspects of writing most suitable for you. Ask yourself the following questions:

- In which subject areas am I most knowledgeable or most expert?
- With which subject areas am I most comfortable?
- What kinds of products do I prefer to produce?
- With what kinds of clients do I wish to work?
- Do I prefer to sell writing services or written products?

The pages to come will give you an extended look at major approaches to freelancing as a business (selling services and selling products), as well as at the other areas of concern listed here, but the decision-making will be yours alone. I will offer, however, a list of items for you to consider, and you should consider them with a pencil and paper handy, scrawling your answers to the questions. They need not be final answers. In fact, they represent only a few of the questions you should ask yourself, and you will probably think of others as you proceed.

As you read on, you will get various ideas and want to change many of your answers or even add new categories of information. By all means, do so. Do so as often as you wish. Even when you have made the last change, the worksheet that results is not chiseled in stone. If you start your freelance writing business and find that you are not happy with some of the choices you made, by all means change them again. (It is most likely that you will wind up, eventually, doing work that is quite different from the work you originally contemplated. Almost all of us do.) At any rate, it is important that you stop now and prepare a first worksheet based on the following questions. This will fix these important questions in your mind and help you analyze and apply the information in these pages. Now ask yourself:

- What three specific subjects do I know the most about?
- What in my educational and experiential background might be translated into subject matter for writing?

- What three things interest me most? (Hobbies? Favorite reading?)

- How much do I like working directly with people?
  All the time?
  Sometimes?
  From a distance?
  Not at all?

- Do I want a full-time or part-time writing/editorial business?

- What resources do I have available? (Money, equipment, know-how?)

- How important is image to me? For example, will my self-esteem be intact if I make money writing for trade journals?

- How much risk am I willing to take? (Am I a crapshooter or a blackjack player?) Do I prefer a proven type of writing or am I willing to take my chances in the more artistic/creative field?

Finally, ask yourself what is perhaps the most important question of all:

- How serious am I about being a working writer? What if I find it rarely romantic, often sheer drudgery, and always hard work?

The significance of these questions may not be entirely clear to you at this point, although it should become clearer and clearer as you proceed.

SPECIALTY PUBLISHING

The main thrust of this book is toward writing and related services, with the accent on *services*. Emphasis will be placed on discovering or identifying the best markets for the writing and related services you can provide as a freelance writer. Still, there is a companion market that many freelance writers pursue as a useful and profitable adjunct. (In fact, some writers *prefer* this activity and pursue it exclusively as a career, which is an entirely viable alternative.) This is a market for which you write and publish short pieces—monographs, also referred to as *reports*. These are usually about 1,500 to 5,000 words, published in some convenient and inexpensive form, and sold by mail. It is a form of self-publishing called *specialty publishing* and it is discussed in more detail later in this book.

The questions suggested here as a basis for analyzing your assets as a writer and finding your niche have application to this kind of writing activity as well as to editorial services in general. You will understand this better when I discuss this kind of activity and provide a closer look at marketing by mail later in the book.

OTHER COVERAGE

There are some other matters of concern that will be covered later. One is the question of equipping your office suitably. Descriptions, lists, and suggestions will be offered, as well as how-to suggestions concerning writing. This is not a how-to-write book; it is a how-to-make-writing-a-business book. Still, a few writing tips are not amiss, and some will be provided. Finally, operating a general editorial services business may require you to handle a few chores with which you may be unfamiliar, such as preparing printing dummies or running sheets for the printer. Some help will be provided with that also.

PART I

EVERY WRITER A CONSULTANT
Selling Your Services as a Writer

We live in an era of services. It was long predicted as the wave of the future in our economic system. We have seen the decline of U.S. dominance in much of the world's heavy and light industry and the growth of what has come to be called the *knowledge industry*. Third World countries have developed industrial capabilities requiring far less technological sophistication than does the knowledge industry, and with their advantages in cheaper labor they have taken over much of the world market in both heavy and light industry. It is now widely acknowledged that the U.S. economy today is more and more a service economy, based largely on information and communication services and functions. That is the essence of the knowledge industry. It is an industry that has grown rapidly and shows few signs of slowing down in the near future. Happily, we writers are an important part of that industry. In many ways, we *are* the knowledge industry; a major portion of it depends on what we do.

Another significant trend has been that of specialization, and it too has been increasing without pause, the inevitable result of a geometrically proliferating information base. Most professions have become so diversified and complex that they are necessarily divided into a variety of specialties. Many have been forced to split and subdivide further, like growing cells, into even more narrowly defined specialties. It, too, is a trend likely to continue.

Members of the writing profession have not escaped these changes. We, too, have found it necessary to specialize. We may specialize according to subject matter, the kinds of written products we create, the kinds of clients we serve, and other parameters and criteria. Our ranks include speechwriters, advertising copywriters, direct-mail writers, manual writers, fundraiser writers, training-systems writers, medical writers, audiovisual writers, scriptwriters, résumé writers, newsletter writers, technical writers, and others, and many of us specialize even further within these categories. In each of these classes, there are those who work for organizations as salaried employees and those who freelance. Those of us who freelance are writers who are available for hire to do the job on a custom basis under contract. (In a recent meeting of 12 freelance business writers, 11 of the 12 reported that their writing was primarily—indeed almost exclusively—custom writing for clients under contract, although a few occasionally submitted articles to periodicals.) However, even freelance writers specialize in many ways, sometimes in response to market opportunities or changes in markets and also as a result of personal preference and even serendipitous circumstances.

Steven Clyburn, of Kensington, Maryland, is a freelance writer who wears a tie and jacket during his normal workday. That is because he is in the office of some of his clients almost every day, as are many other freelance business writers. (Those of us who do not have to see clients very often tend to dress rather informally; we are what Paul and Sarah Edwards have dubbed "open-collar" workers.) Clyburn offers his clients a wide variety of writing services, including but not confined to ghostwriting, speeches, books, reports, catalogs, direct mail, and proposals, and he lists a diverse array of clients. However, an examination of his writings over the past few years clearly shows a strong trend in quality management and closely related subjects. (Writers are as much the captives of their personal histories as are others. The fields in which we developed our credentials, whether by chance or by choice, tend to dictate our future course of specialization.)

The business world in general has grown in many ways over recent decades. Many of today's businesses and even the industries of which they are a part are completely new, born of technological progress and other new developments in this age of computers, fax machines, and satellite communications. Many corporations have become conglomerates, straddling many fields and businesses. Freelance writers who work as custom/contract writers have often tended to specialize in terms of the kinds of clients they serve, such as government agencies, large corporations, small businesses, and individuals. Or they may specialize in terms of the businesses in which their clients are engaged, such as engineering, manufacturing, retailing, or software development. Again, there are numerous subclassifications.

Writing subjects are therefore also growing in number, complexity, and diversity. The world we live in today is as different from the world of 50 years ago as that world was different from the world of a century or two earlier. The rate of growth and change is exponential; thousands of writers today write about subjects that did not exist 50 years ago, and in some cases even as recently as 10 years ago. This leads inevitably to specialization in subject matter. Many writers have special training in or knowledge of a field other than writing, such as electronics, computers, medicine, or politics. It is not surprising, then, that such writers tend to specialize in material relating to that field, although not always by preference. This offers obvious advantages to the writer, especially if it is a field in which the need for specialized knowledge limits his or her competition. It is not always necessary to have that special technical background, however. The generalizations are true, but like all generalizations, they have their exceptions. There are medical writers and other technical writers, for example, who have no formal training in medical or other technical subjects, but who somehow manage to handle the research and write about the subjects capably.

Thus it is inevitable that most freelance writers specialize to some degree—be it a broad specialization or a narrow one. The individual's specialty is, in fact, often the reason he or she is sought, even by clients who have qualified in-house writers. In any case, serving clients by providing custom writing services is a growth industry with ample opportunity to build a sound independent venture doing the kind of work you like to do, writing and possibly related editorial functions.

One great advantage in pursuing writing services as a business is that it usually lends itself well to working from your own home, especially if you concentrate on dealing with large organizations. Marketing to clients of this nature means that you need not rely on walk-in trade, as you might with a résumé service, and therefore you do not usually need a commercial location. You need a place to work and that can be a room or even a corner of a room at home, with a desk, a telephone, and a typewriter (or, preferably, a desktop computer and printer). A copier and a fax machine are useful additions, but you can manage without them, as most of us do in our early years of building a writing practice. (I will discuss equipment more fully in a later chapter.) If you do work for large organizations you will often find yourself working on the client's premises, with access to the client's copiers and other equipment. There are also public services available for copying and faxing.

One important note regarding working from your own home: For tax purposes, you must make that office dedicated space, whether it is a separate room or only part of a room. The IRS will object vigorously to your writing off part of your kitchen table as office space. They insist that, to qualify as a write-off, the space must be used only for your work.

Chapter 1

Should You Be an Editorial Consultant?

The term *freelance writer* has come to have more than one meaning. There is always that traditional freelance writer laboring away at a novel, play, or other literary effort. There is also the freelance writer who provides custom services, including advice and counsel about editorial matters, to individuals and organizations. This is a service that may fairly be called *consulting*, and there are advantages in thinking of yourself as an editorial consultant and operating as such.

WHAT HAPPENED TO THE "PAPERLESS SOCIETY"?

I hardly need point out the ubiquity of the computer in this last decade of the century. It seems as though there is a computer on every desktop, even those of school children, while typewriters gather dust and appear to be destined for survival only as museum pieces. In fact, our progression into the knowledge or information business began before the computer shrank to desktop size and made so many of us who write for a living an intimate, almost integral part of this new era. Still, the many predictions of a paperless office and a paperless society proved to be premature, if not entirely mistaken. Today we are generating more documents on paper than ever before, and this is not accounted for entirely by the equally ubiquitous copier. Computer-driven printers are churning out words and illustrations on paper at a record rate. The computer has not driven paper out; instead, it has invited more paper in! It has accelerated our ability to process information into documents of all kinds, and it has made writing and writers more necessary than ever.

WHO DOES ALL THIS WRITING?

This swelling flow of words on paper is generated more and more by professional writers, although a great deal of it is still written by engineers, executives, and others as part of their routine duties and functions. At one time, this was the basic nature of things: Writing was an ancillary duty of executives, professionals, and others on the staff of an organization. Executives were expected to turn out annual reports, brochures, sales letters, and other literature, as engineers were expected to write the several kinds of literature required to support the products they produced. The engineer who had just designed some new device, for example, was expected to then sit down and write user instructions, parts lists, maintenance manuals, specification sheets, catalog sheets, and any other necessary documents. For most executives, engineers, and others, this was an unpleasant part of their jobs: Many found writing a tedious chore, welcoming any relief they could get from the task. But this practice is not entirely a thing of the past. In many cases it is still the order of the day, as evidenced, for example, in the documentation of computer software. Thus, it is not surprising that the writing that results is usually considerably less than inspired and often a subject of bitter complaint by users, despite much humorous reference to such documentation.

THE RISE OF THE BUSINESS WRITER

Fortunately, the economics of having engineers do documentation has tended to militate against that practice. Other factors—labor shortages in technical fields, for one—have also discouraged it. This has resulted in a steady movement over the years to have most technical manuals and other technical literature written by professional technical writers. Technical writing is a relatively new profession that reportedly was rooted in the automobile manufacturing industry, where there was a clear need for extensive documentation to guide automobile mechanics, parts suppliers, and others who required various kinds of technical information about the product. The profession of technical writing began to grow rapidly in the mid-1950s, along with and largely as a result of the federal government's multibillion dollar defense program. A great many government projects involved the most modern of high-tech technologies—radar, computers, missile control and guidance systems, satellites, and surveillance systems—and required expert writing and expert knowledge to produce the documents required by the military organizations. Economic considerations, in particular the steady rise in the cost of expert professional labor, also began to show up as a major consideration contributing to the trend toward the use of professional writing services. Employing engineers to write manuals and other technical literature is almost as wasteful of costly labor as having high-salaried executives do their own typing, filing, copying, and coffee making. The same considerations apply to executives of other organizations that need brochures, sales letters, catalogs, annual reports, newsletters, and other such items.

Oddly, those same engineers, executives, and staff professionals who so intensely dislike writing are still often reluctant to admit that a professional writer can produce a better product than they can and that there is no stigma in accepting this as a premise. (Unfortunately, many professionals and executives are even reluctant to agree that a professional editor can improve their writing. Many prefer to believe that they are simply too busy to be bothered with the trivial work of writing, much less to take the time to be grammatically correct.) However, although it is still not universally acknowledged, the need for professional writers and editors to develop business and professional literature has come to be more and more widely accepted. Still, in consideration of the problem, a writer working on a client's premises should develop the ancillary skills of tact and diplomacy in working with engineers, executives, and/or other senior staff members. It pays dividends to be respectful of the staff members' editorial judgments and opinions.

CONSULTING KEEPS PACE

Consulting, a much older activity, also grew rapidly in the mid-1950s, an era of increasingly complex technology. The business of consulting was also changed a great deal during and by the events of this era.

Consulting is not really a profession itself, although it is often treated as though it were. Consulting is a way to *practice* one's profession. Thus we have medical consultants, engineering consultants, marketing consultants, beauty consultants, security consultants, dress consultants, computer consultants, and many others, including editorial consultants. In this ever more complex world even specialists specialize, so that instead of "medical consultants" there are consultants in brain surgery, consultants in heart disease, consultants in plastic surgery, and consultants in all the other medical specialties. (The "GP" [general practitioner] has become a specialist too—a specialist in so-called "family practice," in which one of his or her chief talents is the knowledge of and ability to make a judgment as to which other medical specialist should be called in for consultation!)

The same condition applies in engineering consulting, security consulting, computer consulting, and editorial consulting. There are editorial consultants who specialize as copywriters (advertising and sales copy), those who write only fundraising letters, speechwriters, others who focus entirely on newsletters, and still others who devote all their efforts to direct-mail copy other than fundraising. In short, knowing *how* to write is one thing, but knowing *what* to write is another, and that is where writing begins to merge with consulting.

One development in that seminal period of several decades ago was that the definition of the term *consulting* changed and grew in scope. It began to encompass a new kind of employee: the technical/professional temporary.

THE TECHNICAL/PROFESSIONAL TEMPORARY

Office temporaries have been familiar for a number of years. But a variety of circumstances have given rise to a much different kind of temporary today: Many scientists, engineers, computer programmers, technical writers, and others now work as temporaries, although they often refer to themselves as "consultants" or, irreverently, as "job shoppers." That is a reference to the company that actually pays them, although they are assigned to work on the premises and under the direction of a client of the company. (The term *job shop* originally referred to small machine shops that specialized in supporting larger companies by contracting to handle their overloads and special needs as single jobs. Assigning workers to handle overloads and special needs is analogous; hence the term.) The terms of the assignments can range widely, from a few days to many months, or, in some cases, even years. Eventually, many individuals who have hired out as temporaries can avoid the job shop intermediary and contract directly with the clients as they become well known to them. For many business writers, this is one way of furnishing their specialized services as editorial consultants, although it is certainly not the only way.

A FEW OF THE NEEDS

There are other factors at work in the business world creating new and increased opportunities for writers in general and for independent or freelance writers in particular. There is a wide variety of projects requiring the development of documents and publications. Following are a few examples of the various kinds of literature writers are called on to produce:

Technical manuals	Résumés	Brochures
Audiovisual scripts	Storyboards	Advertising copy
Letters of complaint	Sales letters	Proposals
Theses	Speeches	Lecture guides
Lesson plans	Instructor guides	Student manuals
Catalog sheets	Annual reports	Progress reports
Abstracts	Indexes	Bid packages
Briefing papers	Critiques	Book manuscripts
Newsletters	Software manuals	Procedures
Policy manuals	Movie scripts	News releases
Item descriptions	Catalogs	Specifications
Product releases	Magazine articles	Indexes

This list gives an indication of the array of opportunities open to the freelance business writer. It would be a rare writer or editorial specialist who could or would want to tackle all these kinds of writing jobs. Nor is that necessary. The individuals and organizations who need such documents rarely have the in-house capabilities to create them all. They find it necessary to quest for help, *your* help if you are an editorial consultant, especially if you specialize in a few chosen areas.

WHEN DOES CUSTOM WRITING
BECOME CONSULTING?

Many freelance writers prosper by specializing in just one area, such as technical writing or copywriting (advertising copy, that is). The more you specialize, you find, the more knowledgeable you become in your specialty, and you begin to think of yourself and function as a consultant. Clients call on you to write for them on a custom basis, but the service you provide is not the mere mechanical service of writing or editing and rewriting a résumé or report. It is much more than that, a service much closer to consulting. You may start out to provide simple writing services within whatever areas you feel comfortable, but you will often discover that you must do more, encountering a wide variety of circumstances in which you must counsel and guide clients and otherwise "hold their hands." You may be called on to recommend the best type of document to suit the client's need, to design publications, to organize writing projects, to conduct research, to lead programs and in-house teams, to edit and critique, to plan and implement production, to recommend a printer, and to handle a variety of related tasks and problems.

A few anecdotes taken from my own and others' experience will illustrate quite clearly the writer's need for agility and resourcefulness, which sometimes goes beyond writing and editing skills and, I believe, fully justifies regarding yourself as a consultant and charging appropriate fees. Many of these problems are quite typical; you are likely to encounter some of them. Therefore, consider carefully how each was handled (usually successfully, but not always).

A FEW TYPICAL PROJECTS

Illustrating Something That Does Not (Yet) Exist

Sometimes a writing assignment includes a difficult research requirement. One writer, Al R., took on the writing of a brochure to describe a new piece of electronic equipment that was still in the early stages of engineering development. Not even a mockup had been built, much less a prototype. Preparing this brochure meant interviewing the design engineers and studying laboratory logs, notes, reports, and other data. He was also required to include an illustration of the equipment, and here he ran into a serious problem: No production prototype had been built, so there was nothing to photograph. (Laboratory prototypes, usually called *engineering prototypes*, are working models, but they do not usually bear even a remote physical resemblance to the finished model. A production prototype must be built to furnish a model of the final product.) Al solved the problem by interviewing the engineers who would eventually build the production prototype and taking voluminous notes on their best estimates of dimensions, controls, indicators, and other external features. He then had an artist make a sketch based on his notes and had the design engineers review the sketch and offer comments and suggestions for refinements. He passed these on to the artist as input for a final drawing, which proved later to be amazingly close in appearance to the actual production model.

This may seem to be an extreme case, but it is by no means unusual for a writer to be compelled to use imagination and persistence to overcome obstacles in getting the job done. Solving this kind of problem certainly goes well beyond mere writing and/or editing; it represents consulting services and justifies a consulting fee.

Editing a Brochure

Quite a bit different, but not at all unusual, was a project in which a federal government office called me in for help with a new brochure they had drafted. It was intended to acquaint prospective contractors with the agency's needs and their new procedures for bidding. The client explained that the manuscript was still a bit rough and needed editing before they could send it on to the Government Printing Office for typesetting and printing. They retained me to edit and polish the manuscript.

It did not take long to determine that no amount of editing, as I would define that term, would help this brochure. It was hardly intelligible or even literate; it would be far more efficient to rewrite it completely.

One writer I know, in somewhat similar circumstances, snorted when he read the manuscript he had been asked to edit and asked the client, a defense contractor, "Who wrote this awful garbage?" Of course, that interview was completed as swiftly as possible, and he was ushered out of the building with "Don't call us; we'll call you."

The right way to handle this familiar problem is to be diplomatic, to stretch the definition of editing and thus be able to agree that the manuscript will benefit from a complete and thorough edit. However, you must plan to rewrite it and price it according to the actual work required. In this way, no one's pride is injured, the client is satisfied, you do what has to be done to get a proper result, and you are paid for the service you provide. Your conscience shouldn't suffer: There is often a fine line between a rewrite and a heavy edit, so you really haven't taken much liberty with the truth when you accept the job as one of editing! At worst, it is only a white lie, and you have done your client and yourself a worthwhile service in a fair exchange.

Editing a Master's Thesis

This was a project in which the client was an individual, a graduate student who had completed his course work and was trying to write the required thesis. He came to a contemporary of mine, Betty B., in some desperation, armed with a well-detailed set of instructions, an outline of his planned project, a sheaf of data he had collected, and a rough (*very* rough) draft. He was stuck at that point. He just did not feel capable of following the detailed format instructions and handling uncertainties he might encounter in grammar and spelling. He needed the draft polished to a point where he could get preliminary comments and suggestions from his advisor so that he could prepare the final draft. This is a fairly typical assignment, one that often requires a complete reorganization of the material, as well as normal editing and polishing. It turned out in this case that the advisor and reviewers were insistent that the final manuscript follow the mandated format scrupulously in its smallest detail.

There is an ethical issue here, since the thesis must reflect the student's independent research effort. To be completely ethical, an editor must insist, as Betty did, that what is provided is normal editorial service on material supplied (i.e., data gathered, analysis made, and conclusions drawn) in its entirety by the student. That done, it is morally acceptable, I believe, to aid the student in getting the material into suitable format for review by the committee. After all, it is the graduate student's independent research that is to be reviewed by the committee, not the student's writing skills.

An Abstracting Project

A woman who had just been appointed to her county school board approached me with a somewhat unusual writing task: She was a political appointee and had no expert knowledge of education. She looked forward to the first meeting with great trepidation. In preparation, she had collected a number of professional journals dealing with the subject of schools and education. The project she awarded me was to write abstracts of those articles I thought most useful to help her prepare to assume her duties and discuss the problems of education without making some embarrassing blunder. It was left to me to judge which articles would be relevant and how to translate any professional jargon into everyday language that would be suitable for her to use in speaking to the board. I would consider this to be without question a consulting responsibility.

The Proposal Strategist

One field in which I have worked extensively as a consultant is proposal writing. This requires a mix of writing and marketing skills. It was in working in this field, in fact, that I first realized that I was more than a writer—that the nature of the work compelled me to function as a consultant. In fact, while I have often written entire proposals alone, in other cases I have done little or no writing at all. In one case, I was retained specifically to recommend a strategy for the client's proposal. He was quite prepared to write the proposal and capable of doing so, but he couldn't find a "handle" for it. I read his client's request for proposals and suggested a strategic approach that worked for him. In another case, my client had a staff of writers ready to write their proposal, but they did not know how to get started. The client retained me to lead them through a brainstorming session in which they would develop both their general approach and a working outline. In some instances, I have been retained to serve as a proposal manager to manage a staff of in-house writers who have been impressed (i.e., shanghaied) by management as members of a proposal-writing team.

Letter Writing

A few centuries ago, relatively few people, other than the clergy and professionals, were literate, and the public scribe was a common sight. The need for public scribes has not passed completely in our society, despite widespread literacy. Many individuals, although literate, seek help in writing special letters. A Chicago woman ran a small classified advertisement offering letter-writing help for individuals with special problems they wished to address via correspondence, and she was all but swamped with responses. I was once approached by an individual to write a letter for him appealing a civil service ruling that he believed was unjust. I found it necessary to help him devise the strategy of his appeal, which won him reconsideration. A second letter I wrote for him as a final follow-up helped him win his appeal. Again, this is clearly more than "wordsmithing," and it entitles the consultant to fees proportionate to the skills and services provided and, especially, to the results achieved.

Defining the Problem (Not Always Technical)

You will encounter a wide variety of needs in this line of work, and accordingly you must be flexible. Often, the client does not know just what he or she really needs, and you must first analyze and define the problem. A client's problem is not always confined to technical issues. You may have to be as resourceful in your marketing (i.e., in designing the custom service you will offer or prescribe) as you are in getting the job done.

I have frequently found it necessary to design a set of services that will satisfy the client's needs and yet be affordable; that is, I customize my services to fit the client's budget. It is not unusual for clients to tell you that, while they would like to take advantage of your services, their budget won't cover several weeks of your time. One way I have surmounted that problem has been to propose a preliminary effort to help the client organize a proposal effort with in-house staff, a review of the rough draft by me—with suggestions for rewrite and possibly writing a key page or two myself—and a review of the final draft before production. Many clients have responded well to an approach along those general lines, resulting in contracts for which I might otherwise have been too high priced. I make it a practice to explore what the client can do independently—especially when the budget is tight—and design my services so that I do only that part of the job which the client cannot or does not want to do.

THERE IS MORE TO BEING A WRITER THAN BEING A WRITER

By now you must have noted that your horizons as a writer are not defined by your knowledge of the language. They are as broad—or as limited—as your ancillary knowledge and skills. Those help identify for you the fields in which you can specialize as a writer. They need not be acquired through formal education, however; they may simply be the byproduct of earlier experience. Don't underestimate the importance of this factor or the need to consider it in finding your own specialties: The writer who has no related experience or skills is handicapped by that lack, even if he or she is an excellent wordsmith.

Related, Useful Skills and Knowledge

In my own case, my knowledge of and experience in marketing generally and marketing to government agencies in particular determined to a great degree where and how I specialized. They made me a proposal consultant first, then a more general marketing consultant, and finally a general writer on a variety of business topics. Whether you offer your services as a writer, editor, consultant, or all three, you are also a writer, editor, or consultant within some defined field or set of fields. If you study the list of kinds of things you might be called upon to write, that becomes even clearer. Some items such as brochures, sales letters, and proposals are purely marketing tools. News releases, product releases, and newsletters are public relations tools. There are items to be used in training and education, others to be used in movie-making and audiovisuals, and still others to be used in engineering fields. You thus have obvious advantages if you choose to specialize as a writer in a field in which you have experience or special training. On the other hand, you would probably have great difficulty writing material in a highly specialized and technical field in which you did not have special knowledge.

I don't discount the possibility that you may be able to perform well in a technical field about which you know little but are capable of doing adequate research. When I was assigned to write a manual for a portable air conditioner used in the space program, I faced a challenge: I knew little about refrigeration and air conditioning beyond pure principles. But with an adequate engineering background, I had little difficulty in doing the necessary research. And that is really the point: You need not be a technical expert; you need only be capable of doing the research, of understanding the source materials.

Here are just a few suggestions of possible fields to start you thinking about specialties. The terms in the following list are deliberately general. You may have (or set out to develop) a general or specialized knowledge of or experience in any of these or other fields:

Marketing	Public relations	Management
Engineering	Training/education	Audiovisual equipment
Public speaking	Politics	Fundraising
Radio/TV	Medicine/health	Food/diet
Careers	Small business	Military affairs
Advertising	Publishing	Manufacturing

These items refer to content, subjects pertaining to fields about which you may be asked to write. In cases in which highly specialized technical knowledge is not required, ordinary research is usually adequate preparation for writing documents relating to the field. On the other hand, there are many cases in which the copy pertains to technical details requiring expert knowledge of the field. This is especially the case in highly specialized and technical fields such as engineering and medicine. Therefore, your choice of subject areas and fields may be dictated or at least heavily influenced by the circumstances of your other skills and knowledge, as well as by your preferences. However, there is another area of related experience and knowledge that must be considered: What writing-related functions do you have enough knowledge of to advise clients in your role as an editorial consultant, and in which of these are you skilled enough to actually perform? What are your "editorial services?"

This is the point where we must explore the meaning of the heading

"There is more to being a writer than being a writer." The term *writer* is applied in a broad sense, especially in the milieu of the business/industrial world. There, in many cases, writing may be an ongoing activity, but the related functions of producing business documents and publications are intermittent, and these efforts are organized on an ad hoc basis, as required. Following, for example, is a list of activities that are normal and necessary functions of such work, depending on the nature of what is being written and the distribution or use to be made of it:

- Writing, including research, permissions, releases (where necessary)
- Editing, general and copy
- Composition/typesetting of galleys and/or pages
- Proofreading and corrections
- Preparing layouts, roughs, comprehensives
- Copyfitting
- Illustrating
- Makeup of page mechanicals
- Production (duplicating/printing and binding)
- Word processing
- Desktop publishing

Some writers are familiar with and experienced in all these functions, which, except for word processing and desktop publishing, are classic. Today, a great many of the functions are accomplished via desktop computers armed with word processing and desktop publishing software. The writer who has experience with these and has a fully equipped facility of his or her own enjoys an advantage as a consultant, and the writer who has mastered word processing and desktop publishing enjoys an even greater advantage.

WHERE DOES AN EDITORIAL CONSULTANT WORK?

Consultants of all kinds tend to work on their clients' premises much of the time, and a freelance business writer functioning as a consultant is no exception: It is often absolutely necessary to do so, especially when you must make use of the client's files and facilities or work closely with the client's own staff. On the other hand, it may be more practical, and probably more efficient, to work on your own premises with your own facilities as much as possible. I have worked on the premises of clients who were well equipped with computers, printers, and other resources and found that I was far more productive working in my own office with my own facilities and resources. I have found it much to my advantage and, ultimately, to the advantage of my clients to install in my own office a complete set of facilities I need for my work: computer, modem, dot matrix printer, laser printer, fax machine, copier, and suitable software. (On the other hand, if I am doing work for an engineering firm, I leave the preparation of engineering drawings to the client's drafting department.)

In many cases, especially when the client is an individual or a small organization, it is necessary to have your own complete facilities, since the client often does not have them. For example, even when the client has a computer it may not be suitable for your needs and purposes. On the other hand, if you have to maintain frequent contact with a client who is located in a distant town, you may have little choice but to manage with whatever equipment the client can provide. For example, while my office is near Washington, DC, one of my clients was in San Antonio. It was impractical to travel back and forth to handle a job that had to be consummated in one week. By bringing my own software, which was compatible with my client's computers and printers, I managed to be almost as efficient as I would have been in the familiar surroundings of my own office.

WHO ARE YOUR PROSPECTIVE CLIENTS?

As a freelance business writer or editorial services consultant, the world is your market. You can win assignments from a wide variety of clients. The basic subdivisions are individuals and organizations. This is linked to the subject areas and the types of material to be written. Normally, individuals want help in writing résumés, term papers, speeches, theses, letters, and dissertations, whereas organizations usually seek help in writing proposals, reports, newsletters, manuals, and catalogs. In the next chapter, we will explore the subject of markets more thoroughly.

Chapter 2

Where Are the Markets for Your Services?

"Markets" are people because people have needs and buy goods and services. They are people as individuals and as representatives of organizations. For the business writer, depending on what you choose to make your special niche, almost every person, as an individual or as the personification of an organization, is a potential client at some time. Writing, with its related services, is that universal a need.

CORPORATE WRITING

One BBS (electronic bulletin board system, explained more fully in Chapter 10) that I make use of is dedicated especially to writers; its correspondents include full-time professionals, part-time and occasional authors, students of writing, aspirants to writing careers. Lately, one of the correspondents, who writes situation comedy scripts for television, had taken to what he refers to as "corporate writing" when his union was on strike and he was idle. He reported that he found the work to be surprisingly lucrative. Queried by others as to just what his corporate writing consisted of, he listed writing comedy material for corporate figures who had to make speeches, helping produce industrial films, and other material not unlike the material he normally wrote for TV. He was pleasantly surprised to be assigned an $800,000 film project by a major insurance company. Another writer reported that for 20 years he has been writing and performing comedy material for corporate functions of all kinds—awards dinners, sales meetings, conventions, trade shows, press conferences, client presentations, and other occasions. Several others revealed that they also write similar material for a variety of corporate clients (e.g., "a very major division of a very large auto manufacturer" and a "large blue company"). Still others identified Merrill Lynch, GE, and Metropolitan Life as clients.

There is no doubt a substantial market for corporate writing—writing that is not greatly different from writing for the world of entertainment. However, it is only a small fraction of the total amount of writing work available from corporations and other business entities. Take a sales meeting, for example. Management may want to relax the attendees with a bit of humor, but there are also serious lectures and seminars to be delivered, manuals and handouts to be written, and other presentations to be prepared. All of these are business writing assignments that may be entrusted to freelancers. These strictly-business types of writing, with their related editorial work, make up the bulk of business writing, and that is what we shall be addressing throughout this book.

THE TWO BASIC MARKETS

At its most basic level, the market for writing and related services may be divided into two categories: individuals and organizations. Each of these may be further subdivided and classified into smaller markets, also referred to as *segments* and *niche markets*. It is helpful to make those additional subdivisions and classifications because, by identifying market segments and niches, we further define the market, its needs, and opportunities. That—especially defining needs—is a necessary measure; it is key to marketing your services effectively. Probably nothing endears you to a prospective client more than exhibiting a rapid and complete understanding of his or her needs. This should be your first objective in discussing your services with a prospective client: to get a clear understanding of the client's problem and, if necessary, to help analyze the symptoms and define the problem.

Private individuals have different needs for writing services than do organizations, which is evident from the different kinds of documents each generally requires. Following, to help you visualize some of these markets and niches, are lists relating writing tasks and/or the products involved to the most likely type of client (i.e., individual or organization). Bear in mind, as you study these lists, that the actual service you provide may be writing, editing, and/or other editorial services and that you may be writing anonymously or ghostwriting (allowing the client to byline the product as his or her own work).

Projects and Products for Individuals

Correspondence	Book manuscripts	Speeches
Dissertations	Theses	Magazine/journal
Résumés	Term papers	articles

Projects and Products for Business Organizations

Manuals, all types	Speeches	Other reports
Training materials	Abstracts	Specifications
Newsletters	Magazine/journal articles	Sales letters
Releases, all kinds	Briefing papers	Bid packages
Annual reports	Scripts, all types	Correspondence
Proposals	Catalog sheets	Direct-mail packages
Indexes	Item descriptions	Procedures
Advertising copy	Storyboards	Critiques

There are two things that should be pointed out immediately about these two lists. One is that the list of materials and projects you might normally be asked to work on for organizations is much longer than that usually required by individuals. Another is that certain items (e.g., speeches and correspondence) appear on both lists. There are several other qualifications that should be made about these lists: It is possible that certain other items might appear on both lists, although it is relatively unlikely. The terms *organization* and *individual*, as used here, need explanation: When an individual is a one-person business, he or she has business needs that are more like those of organizations than those of individuals. Finally, the lists are rough approximations and are not meant to be taken as complete or definitive. If you choose to be a business writer, even if you specialize narrowly within the confines of business writing as it is defined here, unexpected and even unusual requests and opportunities will come along. Some of your best opportunities for profitable assignments will be serendipitous ones, arising by pure chance and depending on your ability to recognize them and rise to the occasion. Serendipity is much more common than you might imagine if you are ready for it, but you must be alert and ready to recognize and seize the opportunity.

INDIVIDUALS AS CLIENTS

If you live near any kind of university you have one kind of market available immediately: students. University students, both graduate and undergraduate, are all potential clients for help with their term papers, theses, dissertations, and résumés. However, actually writing the students' papers for them is less than honorable here; there have been scandals in the past surrounding writers who have written students' papers, enabling the students to get credits and even degrees fraudulently. (In fact, there have been organizations with a large stock of model term papers, theses, and dissertations that would, for a rather large fee, customize them to the individual student's needs, a grossly unethical practice.) That does not mean, in my opinion, that it is wrong to provide editorial assistance to a student to polish a presentation when the student has done the necessary work and assembled the information required for the paper. It seems to me that the line between ghostwriting and providing normal editing services is well defined here.

Résumé-Writing and Other Writing Services

Résumé services are of interest to everyone who aspires to find a job; it has become a necessary tool in job hunting in a broad array of fields. In fact, it is the principal job-hunting tool for many individuals, and it is important to individuals in the highest executive strata, as well as those employed in more humble positions. As a result of offering résumé services via advertisements in *The Wall Street Journal*, I found myself writing résumés for the top officers of some large corporations—corporate presidents and vice-presidents seeking change.

A résumé service can be generalized or specialized. As an example, one freelance writer who happened to be heavily experienced in résumé writing met the owner of a job-placement service at a cocktail party. Such a job-placement service is not a typical employment agency, but a service devoted to the counseling and placement of executives and professionals, with résumé-writing one of the services. The writer learned that this aspect of the placement service was a problem for the owner, since it is not a simple matter to write effective résumés for people in quest of high salaries and the need did not justify a full-time writer on staff. He made a deal to spend two afternoons a week at the offices of the service, interviewing the clients and drafting their résumés.

You do not have to depend on your local area for résumé business. Many résumé services are conducted by mail. For examples, see the Help Wanted sections of such newspapers as *The Washington Post, The Wall Street Journal, The New York Times,* and *Army Times,* where you will find such services advertised. Prices vary widely, and your own research, inquiring of a few advertisers, is probably the most reliable way of gauging the market.

Letter-Writing Services

It is surprising how many people will respond to an advertisement placed by someone offering to write letters for them. Most people are not good writers, and they shy away from writing the most routine letter, much less attempting a letter that must deal with a special problem such as an affair of the heart, a bereavement, a condolence, a complaint, or a demand. Clients have paid me fees ranging upward from $15 to $25 per page for letters dealing with special problems.

Speechwriting

Individuals called on to make speeches—especially those for whom public speaking is a rare and frightening event—are likely to feel the need for help in preparing their speeches. In such cases, as in the case of writing résumés and letters, you must meet with the client to discuss the circumstances of the speech in some depth before undertaking the assignment.

Speechwriting is a rather specialized field, and for that reason it is quite lucrative; yet it is not difficult to get some guidance to help you become reasonably expert at it. Following are some references recommended by knowledgeable people:

Professional Speech Writing by Dr. Jerry Tarver, Effective Speech Writing Institute, University of Richmond, Virginia.

How to Handle Speechwriting Assignments by Douglas P. Starr, Pilot Books, 1978.

How to Make a Speech by Steve Allen (sound tape), McGraw-Hill, 1986.

Instant Eloquence by James C. Humes, Harper & Row, 1973.

Podium Humor by James C. Humes, Harper & Row, 1975.

Speechwriter's Newsletter (weekly), Chicago, IL (312)922-8245.

The Executive Speaker (monthly), Dayton, OH (513)294-604.

Executive Speechwriter Newsletter (802)748-4472.

Sharing Ideas (bimonthly), P.O. Box 1120, Glendora, CA 91740.

Public speaking is a popular subject, and there is a treasure trove of information available on the subject. What is listed here is hardly a ripple in the sea of information available.

ORGANIZATIONS AS CLIENTS

The world of business organizations, especially large corporations and government agencies, is a complex and diverse one. Actually, government agencies are also business organizations in the strictest sense, but there are enough special considerations and differences between them—the multibillion dollar procurement budgets of government agencies, for example—to justify discussing them separately, as we shall do in more detail in chapters to follow. What follows is simply a brief preview.

Business Organizations

Every business organization has its own specific functions, depending on what kind of business it is in. Some functions, such as management and administration, marketing, accounting, and production, are so basic that they are necessarily found in all organizations. However, the size of the company and the nature of business it is in may dictate certain special functions and offices. In the large organization, key functions may necessarily be embodied in separate departments or divisions. In the small organization, however, it may be inexpedient and inefficient to set up separate divisions, and several functions may be combined in a single department or even in the job of a single individual. Large manufacturing companies and retailers often do so much purchasing that they have special purchasing departments, for example, whereas service organizations that do little buying incorporate purchasing in their general administrative function.

The marketing division, which may include a separate sales department and an advertising department, is often the most promising prospect for your services, since it normally produces catalogs, proposals, advertising, direct-mail packages, and other sales literature. If there is a publications department, it probably produces reports, manuals, brochures, and perhaps even a newsletter and press releases. It may also be called on to help with other writing chores. (That definitely does not rule out the organization as a good prospect for work assignments, as you will learn later when we discuss marketing.)

Government Agencies

Government agencies at all levels—federal, state, county, and city or town—are good prospects for business-writing assignments. Most have purchasing, personnel, and public relations functions. Many have special training and publications functions also, and many have procurement programs that favor small businesses, giving you a special advantage in competing for government contracts.

You do not have to be in or near Washington, DC, to do business with the federal government. It has offices and does purchasing everywhere, with major government centers in Boston, New York, Philadelphia, Atlanta, Chicago, Kansas City, Dallas-Fort Worth, Denver, San Diego, Los Angeles, San Francisco, and Seattle. Although I am situated near Washington, DC, I have done business with government agencies in Missoula, Orlando, Topeka, Oklahoma City, Tulsa, and elsewhere, in addition to the major centers just mentioned.

In the case of state governments, purchasing is usually centralized in a supply and procurement office in the state capital. All states encourage prospective contractors to visit their procurement offices and get acquainted with the buyers first hand. With the federal government you are encouraged to file a Standard Form 129, Application for Bidders List, but it is not a requirement. With most state governments, filing their equivalent of that form is a requirement before you can qualify as a contractor. (More on this later, in detailed discussions of marketing.)

Many individuals are reluctant to even try to do business with the government, usually because they believe the myth that the paperwork and other "red tape" are impossibly complex, or that one must "know somebody" to win a contract, or that it takes forever to get paid for government work. These and other myths illustrate what author Erle Stanley Gardner meant when he had his character, Perry Mason, observe that an opponent had "found a button and sewn a vest on it." There is a trace of truth underlying the myth, but the myth is more than 90 percent untrue. In fact, in many ways it is far easier to win and perform work for the government than it is for private firms. And if the government seems to be slow in paying (usually 21 to 30 days), many private corporations are far slower (45 to 90 days).

Government agencies contract for writing work for manuals, audio-visual storyboards and scripts, movie scripts, reports, and brochures. In addition, there are special needs that arise, such as answering an agency's mail, writing advertising copy, and developing direct-mail copy.

SPECIALIZATION VERSUS GENERALIZATION

Specialization is not a highly definitive word today. Its meaning changes in accordance with context and modifiers. The electronics engineer finds the world of electronics far too broad to know, be experienced in, and practice in all its many areas. It is necessary to opt for one area—communications, avionics, instrumentation, audio, secure communications, digital communications, or any of many others. But even that often proves to be too broad. The communications engineer will probably specialize in radio, television, satellite systems, two-way radio, or some other sub-specialty. Even then there may be further specialization, with engineers focusing on only certain kinds of circuits or on military equipment versus commercial equipment.

Writing is not quite as complex a field as electronics, and so writers rarely specialize to quite so narrow a focus. The writer is typically a well-read and well-educated individual who knows how to conduct research and relies on research when planning and preparing to write. In the case of custom writing, the client normally supplies the raw material—sometimes even a rough outline of the product desired—but at least some indication that helps the writer decide where, how, and what to research. But there are exceptional cases in which certain technical knowledge is required to be able to conduct the research capably. Even the most able writer would find it difficult to write a detailed procedure on brain surgery, unless he or she were an experienced brain surgeon or had unlimited access to such an individual for research. You must always ask yourself whether the amount of research you would have to do to handle a certain writing job in a less-than-familiar field is so great that it makes it uneconomical to tackle the job. Effective marketing includes turning down jobs that are not right for you.

There are thus at least two and probably three levels or kinds of specialization in some of the writing fields, and few writers feel competent in every possible field. Take technical writing, for example. The technical writer, who is probably writing operating and maintenance manuals for the most part, is already a specialist. But he or she is also compelled to specialize in at least two other ways. One is in the kinds of equipment about which he or she feels competent to write accurately; the field has grown so that it is impossible to be knowledgeable about every kind of equipment. The average technical writer will find it difficult, perhaps impossible, to write about a technical subject in which he or she has had no prior training or experience without free access to and ample time for research. The other way in which the technical writer must specialize is in the type of writing required. There is, for example, a class of maintenance manuals requiring what is called an *illustrated parts breakdown* or *IPB*. A technical writer who lacks experience with this field will shy away from attempting to write such material. Technical writers normally specialize in a technical field such as electronics, medicine, automotive technology, or satellites in which they have related special knowledge. For example, writers in the medical field usually have some knowledge of medicine and/ or medical equipment, at least enough to handle the research capably.

There are exceptions. Some writers are able, somehow, to get enough help from available technical specialists to do a credible job of writing in specialized fields they know nothing about. This is a difficult proposition, however, and it most definitely is not the rule.

There are other writing tasks that require special knowledge or experience to work at them comfortably. Scriptwriting is one of these. The writer must understand camera techniques, staging, and many related matters to handle this kind of work well. The most skilled writer who has no experience of this kind will find it difficult to handle a scriptwriting task.

Many writers choose specialties by convenience, rather than by design, writing about the subject-matter field in which they are trained and experienced. An engineer or technician with a penchant for writing is likely to wander into technical writing, a natural marriage of interests and abilities. A TV studio technician may decide to try his or her hand at scriptwriting for the same reason. On the other hand, many writers specialize because of a deliberate, reasoned preference. Some decide to specialize in writing résumés and transmittal letters to go with them. Some prefer journalism (they may or may not have been trained for the field) and work in writing newsletters, releases, and other public relations and/or journalistic endeavors. (Public relations writing is viewed by many as an outgrowth of journalism, by others as a special domain of advertising; PR specialists thus tend to have a background in journalism, advertising, or both.) Speechwriters often specialize in that kind of writing. *Copywriter* is a term applied most often to specialists in writing advertising copy, but many copywriters specialize in writing print advertising, direct-mail copy, or PR copy, rather than all types. Some specialize even further than that, dedicating themselves to writing sales letters, and even in that select society of writers there are those who specialize in fundraising sales letters.

Not all specialization is deliberate or desired. It may be unplanned and inadvertent, the result of how you market your services. If your marketing is such that it reaches the general public, and especially if it mentions the writing services that individuals are more likely to want than companies are (e.g., résumés and correspondence), you are likely to find yourself specializing in the types of writing services that individuals need. Marketing often produces unexpected results. When I advertised résumé-writing services years ago, many individuals called to inquire whether I would help them with other kinds of writing services, and many other writing assignments resulted from those advertisements offering résumé services.

Many writers find that specializing, being largely repetitive, is a bore and unchallenging. They prefer being highly diversified, seeking and accepting writing work of any kind that does not require more specialized knowledge than that of being reasonably well educated, well read, and able to do research. They happily accept assignments to write advertising copy, speeches, résumés, newsletters, catalogs, reports, releases, abstracts, and almost any other product of the pen.

There is also the matter of serendipity—stumbling into a lucrative field through pure chance. It was not by design or special training that I wrote training materials almost exclusively for a time. By pure chance I won an assignment from a company that specialized in writing training programs, and as an indirect result of a fairly long ensuing relationship with that company, I learned that the training field had many technicians who knew how to design training programs, but it was badly in need of experienced professional writers to turn those designs into reasonably interesting (or at least coherent) presentations. There was such a large market for those services that most of the writing I did for government agencies over the next few years was in developing training materials.

THE LITTLE-KNOWN MARKET OF GHOSTWRITING

In most business writing, the literature generated is anonymous: The reader has no idea who wrote it and no doubt never even wonders about it. However, there is a practice known as *ghostwriting* or *ghosting*, in which the client presents his or her own name as the author. For example, an executive in a trade association retained me to write a small booklet about proposal writing, which he would distribute to association members under his own byline. He paid me $600, in 1977 dollars, but ghostwriting jobs can be much larger than that. Ghosting a commercially published autobiography or other book that will appear under the byline of a prominent individual can bring in many thousands of dollars.

New York writer Norman Bauman reported, in an article for the Editorial Freelancers Association, on a presentation by a panel of medical writers at a meeting of the Medical Writers Affinity Group of the association. The panel members explained that pharmaceutical manufacturers are paying writers from $300 to $700 a day to ghostwrite articles under various doctors' bylines to appear in the advertising and promotional literature published by the firms. The writers themselves do not necessarily possess directly relevant technical knowledge, but they have the ability to grasp the technical detail explained to them by the doctors in interviews and gleaned from other research. (Some writers report that they are furnished enough data with the assignment to do their work without interviewing the doctors.) Most of the assignments reported on came from the manufacturers' PR firms, rather than directly from the manufacturers. A typical piece might be priced between $1,200 and $2,500, with the writer often responsible for gathering all or much of the research and resource material, including citations, charts, and figures. Most break in to this field via the PR agencies representing the pharmaceutical firms.

There are occasional problems with this type of work. One results from the fact that the work derives from the PR function. The purpose of the project is to support sales promotion or at least to enhance the image of the PR firm's client, and the client may sometimes be entirely unabashed about urging the writer to shade the material in favor of the client or the product. If you are faced with such a case as a writer, it becomes an ethical concern that you must resolve for yourself.

Another problem is estimating costs accurately. Most of the work is on a project or flat-fee basis, and if you underestimate the amount of work required to get the job done, you will wind up working for coolie wages. Still, you cannot afford to overestimate either, for it is a competitive field.

Sometimes the opportunity arises to ghostwrite directly for the doctor, who may want to have a scholarly article or perhaps even a book ghosted. In that case you are more likely to work for an hourly rate of $30 to $50. That may total less pay than writing for the pharmaceutical or PR firm, but it is also risk-free: You will get paid for every hour.

There are many people to whom appearing as the author of some book, article, or other publication is important. Although they may be professionals or executives in their own field, they are lay individuals as far as writing is concerned. For some, appearing as an author is beneficial, even critically important, to their careers or businesses; for others, it is their egos that demand gratification. There are many individuals who believe that their life story would make a great novel and want a ghostwriter to help them. Others believe they have a great idea for a novel but don't know how to write it. Many need help in finding a subject, but the chief obstacle most face is finding a writer to ghost for them. This is because few freelance writers advertise at all, and even fewer advertise ghostwriting services. In fact, most people are unaware that there *is* such a thing as a ghostwriter, so they simply *wish* that they could somehow have something published. This can be a lucrative field of writing if you choose to market such a service. I have seen classified advertisements placed in newspapers by such individuals seeking ghostwriters.

Many professionals and executives wish to be published in their professional and trade journals, but need help in developing their information into a publishable manuscript. Here, again, is a market for ghostwriting.

There are two types of payment for ghostwriting. One is a flat price for the job, and the other royalty sharing. The latter is a possibility when what is being written is a book that will be published on a royalty basis. That is often the case when the client, whose name will appear as the author, is either some well-known personality in whom the public would be interested or is a recognized authority on the subject matter of the book. (This does not refer to the practice whereby the nominal author has not actually done any significant writing and the book is labeled "by Prominent Personality, as told to Joe Smith." That is not truly ghostwriting, since the actual author is named.) If you undertake a task such as this, you must decide for yourself whether you are willing be paid on the basis of royalties, which is usually a fairly risky proposition. A relative handful of the 40,000 to 50,000 new books published every year sell well enough to earn back their printing costs, let alone pay royalties. Even a famous name does not guarantee that the book will sell well enough to bring you significant royalty income.

FREELANCE WRITER OR EDITORIAL CONSULTANT?

Even from these few pages you can perceive the enormous diversity of potential markets for freelance business writers today. You are, indeed, justified in calling yourself a consultant and functioning as such if you prefer. There is an important psychological difference that can have a salutary effect on your income because the term *consultant* justifies a larger fee than the term *writer*. (I have had occasional difficulties with clients who perceived me as a consultant when they wanted help in solving their problems but insisted that I was "only" a writer when the matter of fees came up!) In any case, there is plenty of work to be had, whether you are a freelance writer or an editorial consultant.

Chapter 3

Marketing
to Organizations

The trick in making sales in the business world—known as *business-to-business* marketing—does not always depend on making the most persuasive sales arguments. Often, it depends far more on finding and knocking on the right doors. That means that you must understand the world of business well: the organizations that make it up, how they are organized, what they do and do not do, and what they need.

MARKETING IN AND TO
THE BUSINESS WORLD

Marketing means, or should mean, satisfying needs. Customers buy only what they perceive as satisfying their needs. And they must perceive those needs as being greater than the need to hold on to their money. The art of marketing is, therefore, the art of understanding and identifying what the customer sees as need or can be persuaded to see as a need.

As ordinary citizens, we have some basis for developing insight into the needs or perceived needs of other ordinary citizens. Many of us, however, need some help in understanding the needs of organizations in the business world. We must understand what that world is, what it does, and how it does it to understand or anticipate its needs.

WHAT IS THE BUSINESS WORLD?

There are in excess of 15 million businesses, large and small, in the United States. There are at least an equal number of other organizations such as for-profit and nonprofit corporations; associations; clubs; community groups; churches; professional societies; and government, military, and civil agencies at all levels (federal, state, and local). For me, they all comprise the business world, and I will treat them equally here as organizations to be targeted for marketing.

Most of these organizations are important to us as potential clients for our services. What we do—writing, editing, and associated functions—is necessary to every organization, whatever its purpose. Government organizations and markets, however, are exceptionally huge, diverse, and specialized, especially at the federal level. While they are mentioned here as an important segment of the population of nonprofit organizations, they require separate discussion and will be examined in more detail in the next chapter.

Although many of these organizations exist for purposes other than profit, they are almost indistinguishable from the for-profit organizations in most of the ways that make them marketing prospects. They have the same needs: writing, editing, illustrating, and other services to produce releases, correspondence, brochures, speeches, training materials, newsletters, manuals, and other such end products. In fact, the federal government alone spends well over $200 billion annually for goods and services supplied by vendors and contractors, many of them individuals who are freelancers, self-employed, or one-person businesses.

In some ways, at least, differences between government agencies and private-sector companies have shrunk. In recent years, for example, government agencies have come under great pressure to reduce deficits and even to become self-supporting. (The Postal Service is one outstanding example of this.) Many agencies have therefore curtailed rather sharply the number of books and other materials they distribute without charge, and are even charging for many items that once were free. The Government Printing Office has cut back on giveaways. The racks of brochures that once were free to the public are gone now, although they still mail out notices of their latest publications offered for sale to the public. Some agencies—the Postal Service and the Federal Supply Service, to name two—have marketing departments to encourage greater use of their services and help defray more of their costs.

You can decide to dedicate your marketing and professional efforts to serving the personal needs of individuals only, if you choose to; that is itself a substantial market, and there are many successful freelance writers who limit their work to that market. On the other hand, the world of business and organizations is a much larger (and much different) market with many more sales opportunities. Most of us who offer our services as writers, editors, and providers of related services have a far greater probability of being successful if we do not ignore or neglect this much greater array of potential clients. (Be aware, however, that you will probably have to deal with larger projects and greater frustrations in working with organizations, since you may have to satisfy committees in many cases, and wait longer to get paid.)

To market services successfully to clients in the business world, you must understand their needs. Despite the great variety of organizations that exist, each with a different mission and most with certain specialized functions, there are a few functions that are common to all. Every organization must have a financial management and accounting function, for example, plus a general or executive management function and a marketing function. The last item may come as a surprise to you: Most of us do not think of marketing as a normal function of churches, associations, military groups, political parties, and civic groups, but it is probably the most common function of all organizations.

ALL ORGANIZATIONS MUST MARKET

The marketing and sales departments of every organization you contemplate as a prospective client should be among your prime targets. That is because marketing is at the heart of what every organization does. It is what the organization is about, making it the most important of all the organization's activities. This is as true for the nonprofit organization as it is for the for-profit organization. In the case of for-profit businesses, marketing is easy to understand: It consists of all the activities necessary to get orders for the products and services the businesses sell. In other kinds of organizations, these activities are not referred to as marketing, but they are marketing activities, nevertheless. Consider just a few organizations and what they do to see the truth of this:

- Associations run recruiting campaigns ("membership drives"): They market to gain members, whether individuals or organizations. Membership is their reason for existence.

- Hospitals market—discreetly—for patients; they exist only as long as they have an influx of paying patients.

- Labor unions market to add members, much as associations do.

- Colleges market to enroll students.

- Military organizations market by running recruiting campaigns: They market to get men and women to enlist, and they market for officers too.

- The nonprofit Federal Supply Service markets, making efforts to persuade other agencies to buy from their stores rather than from outside sources.

- The U.S. Postal Service markets, trying to maximize use of postal services by business and industry, even sending representatives out to help mailers use postal services effectively and imitating private industry (e.g., by Express Mail) when it has finessed them.

- Politicians and political parties market energetically, first to get contributions and then to get votes.

- Charities also market to get donations. (They call it "fundraising" and "drives," as political organizations and other nonprofit organizations do.)

- Large corporations and associations market to members of legislatures and other law-making organizations at every level of government. (This kind of marketing is called "lobbying," which is simply trying to influence legislation to favor whoever is paying the bills for the lobbying efforts.)

- Nonprofit pressure groups and similar organizations market to get new members, bring people out to meetings, raise money, and influence legislation—to get certain laws enacted and programs authorized. (Lobbying is the main objective of most pressure groups.)

FOR-PROFIT ORGANIZATIONS

For-profit organizations are easy to understand. They are "in business to make a buck"—to pay salaries, grow, and show a profit. They range from the tiny to the great, from the neighborhood hamburger stand to the supermarket, from the "mom-and-pop" store to the supercorporation. The category includes hamburger and fried chicken emporiums, supermarkets, department stores, banks, automobile dealers, and shopping centers and malls with all their retail stores, most of them franchisees or branch stores of national chains. It all adds up to more than 15 million corporations, of which well over 97 percent are classified by the U.S. Small Business Administration as small businesses. Thus, the population represents a market of impressive size.

Retailers, for the most part, comprise a rather limited market because their needs for new literature are limited and infrequent, although the headquarters offices of major retailing firms may be an exception to this.

Behind these retailers are two other kinds of organizations: The wholesalers and distributors who supply the retailers and the franchisers or home office headquarters of the chain stores. These represent a somewhat more promising set of markets for editorial work, at least as users of marketing materials and, in the case of franchisers and chain-store home offices, procedural brochures and training materials.

The most promising kinds of for-profit business organizations for our purposes are the major corporations. For a variety of reasons having to do with their methods of operation and their missions, they are the major users of writing and related services. One major reason is that they are necessarily heavily oriented to their marketing functions.

WRITERS' MARKETING OPPORTUNITIES WITH THE FOR-PROFITS

The marketing departments and divisions of business organizations are the chief sources and users of many kinds of written materials. Of these, some are direct sales appeals such as sales letters and catalog sheets, but many are indirectly supportive materials such as newsletters and releases. In fact, the functions of marketing, at least in a formal sense, include, at a minimum, the following:

- Planning campaigns

- Advertising

- Public relations

- Sundry promotional programs

- Sales programs

These functions may or may not be assigned to separate departments, groups, or individuals in a company, and the need to recognize each of these as a proper and discrete marketing function is not universally recognized. It is important to you, as a writer, to be aware of the many functions of the marketing responsibility, although in the practical world there are many variations. The major point here is to recognize that marketing units, by whatever names they are known within the organization, should be among your prime targets as prospects for new business. However, there is another reason why marketing organizations are an excellent target. In most for-profit organizations, the manager of the marketing and/ or sales department occupies the hottest seat in the organization: That person is almost always under intense pressure, charged with getting sales in a competitive business world, and the pressure rarely lets up. This tends to make marketing and sales directors willing listeners to anyone or anything that promises help in bringing in sales. When selling custom training programs, for example, I found it helpful to urge my salespeople to be sure to call on marketing or sales managers in every company they visited. Those managers were almost always receptive to the idea of additional sales training, as they were to other prospects of help in making their marketing and sales efforts more productive.

What Is a Marketing Department?

In practice, *marketing department* turns out to be more than a generic term, and marketing is not always known by that name, nor is it truly synonymous with selling, although the two terms are often used as though they were synonyms. Marketing is more than selling. Selling is one of a complex mix of marketing activities that vary widely with the nature of the company and the business it is in; it is usually the final act of marketing: getting the order. Still, the distinction is an academic one in the practical world: If an organization chooses to use "marketing" to refer to a sales department, "marketing" means sales in that organization. Thus marketing may actually refer to a wide variety of functions and offices. On close examination, business organizations are found to vary a great deal in their makeup, due to differences in the nature of their business, management philosophy, and company politics. In some companies, marketing and sales are different departments of equal standing; in others, the sales organization is part of the marketing department. But there are several other, related functions and activities that are part of, support, or coexist with marketing. Many companies have a separate advertising department, but that also may be a part of the marketing organization, depending primarily on how much advertising the company does. Finally, the company may maintain a separate public relations office or may charge another department (e.g., marketing or advertising) with the PR functions.

Within this collection of functions there may be responsibility for a company newsletter for employees or one for customers.

Other Departments and Divisions of Interest

Although sales and marketing probably account for a great portion of the almost daily need for new writing chores, companies also need many other kinds of writing. For one thing, in some companies the marketing responsibility or some large part of it may lie elsewhere than in the nominal marketing department. For example, in an engineering firm that undertakes custom development, responsibility for generating proposals may rest only nominally with the director of marketing; it may actually be assigned to an engineering manager as a practical matter. Engineering, consulting, and manufacturing companies often have writing requirements in connection with documenting their products or services. If a company manufactures a product, it must usually produce user instructions. These may be as simple in format as a leaflet to be packed with a can opener or orange press, or they may require a multipage brochure or small manual to be packed with a VCR or dishwasher, or a thick manual to train new users of a software program or electronic organ. If the company is working on government contracts, there is likely to be an obligation to turn out a complete set of operating and maintenance manuals for whatever they are building. (The government, especially if it is a military agency, may provide detailed specifications for these.) Many contracts for major systems or large equipment include a requirement that the contractor provide training materials, often a formal training program. In many cases, large, or so-called "prime," government contractors subcontract such work. This is a major market in itself, to be discussed in more detail later.

In-House Editorial Departments

If the organization is engaged in many activities that require it to turn out a great deal of new material regularly, it may support an internal writing and editorial group of some kind. Be aware of this as you develop your marketing plans and conduct your market research. But be aware, also of the statistic mentioned earlier, that more than 97 percent of all companies in the United States are small businesses, and many of those are so small that a single administrator or manager may handle all the functions referred to here. (Later you will learn that organizations with in-house writing and editorial staffs are often the best prospects as clients for your writing and editorial services.)

Miscellaneous Functionaries and Needs

Public corporations publish annual reports for stockholders and then use those reports for a great many other purposes, including PR and marketing. A report may be done completely in house, relying on the various talents of the people who work there. It is always one of the most important and quite possibly *the* most important publication generated because it represents the image of the corporation. For this reason it is often produced using the most costly processes and materials. It is often regarded as the general, all-purpose corporate brochure.

NONPROFIT ORGANIZATIONS

Among the nonprofit organizations are associations of various kinds, characterized by their purposes and the nature of their memberships. Many are trade associations, the members of which are companies within some industry such as the National Canners Association or the Computer and Business Equipment Manufacturers Association. Most industries give rise to more than one trade association, and in many cases a company will belong to several such associations.

Another type of association is composed of individuals in a common career field such as the International Association of Fire Chiefs or the Society of Financial Examiners. Again, an individual is likely to belong to several associations related to his or her interests.

Not all associations are based on the members' professions or some other common business or professional interest. Some are based entirely on some other common interest—for example, The American Legion or other veterans organizations; groups with a shared religious belief, such as the National Council of Catholic Women; groups with a commonly shared hobby; or those with common social or recreational interests, such as a travel club.

Probably a majority of associations have their headquarters in Washington, DC, or New York City. However, there are a number of others scattered across the country, and many of the larger associations have branches or local chapters. It all adds up to thousands of associations, chapters, and branches, constituting an enormous market.

Typical Functions, Events, and Writing Needs

Associations have their own purposes and objectives. If they are trade associations, they are banded together to accomplish objectives none of them could do alone and that will benefit their entire industry. It is because Washington, DC, houses the federal government and a great many federal agencies that so many associations have established their headquarters in Washington. Many Washington-based associations include lobbying as one of their chief activities. They do what they can to influence legislation in their favor; that is, to benefit their members. But lobbying efforts are not entirely directed at members of Congress and their staffs. Many regulatory agencies (e.g., the Federal Trade Commission and the Interstate Commerce Commission) have powers to make or interpret regulations that make decision makers in those agencies almost as powerful as those elected to Congress. Associations produce a continuous volume of written materials in the form of speeches, newsletters, press releases, brochures, and correspondence. (All lobbyists, including associations, assist the lawmakers and their staffs in data gathering and other research concerning their industry; they even make specific suggestions regarding legislative matters.)

Associations vary considerably. One type, for example, constitutes a professional society, such as the American Psychological Association. Another category is the association of associations, such as the Federation of Organizations for Professional Women. However, for our purposes it is not necessary to subdivide associations to this degree. Suffice it to note that the variety is substantial.

One of the common characteristics of associations is that most of them, even some rather large and well-funded ones, have small permanent staffs. They are thus inclined to call on suppliers for services as needed, especially when there are temporary, peak demands. Associations can therefore be a major market for writers who wish to specialize in serving their needs.

Most large associations have at least one kind of periodical, such as a newsletter or magazine, and some have both. The organization may or may not have an in-house staff to produce its publications. Frequently the work is done under contract, and this is not necessarily initiated by the organization. In one case, I created a monthly newsletter on my own initiative and sold it to an association, writing it each month for a fee. That kind of arrangement is not at all unusual. However, selling the association an idea that did not occur to it first is not done nearly as often as it should be. Consider this as one of your possible marketing approaches.

All associations of any size need brochures and reports for their members. Producing such items is usually one of their regular services. Many associations have an annual event (a convention usually), which is a gala of several days duration held in a hotel or convention hall, depending on the amount of space needed. The program is likely to include any or all of the following kinds of events, depending on the nature and size of the organization:

- General meeting and keynote speech
- Seminars and lectures
- Social events—lunches, cocktail parties, and dinners, with speeches
- An exhibit or trade show
- An awards dinner

Often, there are many "sideshows," such as hospitality suites held in separate rooms by participating companies, and private dinners and parties. A great deal of literature is required to conduct such an event, and much of it is prepared under contract. There are announcement brochures needed for mailing, schedules and other handouts for attendees, and a wide variety of descriptive brochures and leaflets announcing all the events and guiding the attendees.

Fundraising Events

Some associations run fundraising events such as seminars and trade shows, inviting members of the general public who are interested, as well as members, and charging substantial fees. Of course, a great deal of sales literature is required, and this is a market in itself for your services.

Many associations—labor unions, for example—undertake contracts for the dual purposes of furthering their general aims and raising funds for their normal operation. In this they often require writing support, even in the beginning, to write proposals in pursuit of the contracts.

Of course, all associations have the marketing function mentioned earlier: the drive to recruit new members. The principles of marketing here are no different from those in the world of commerce and industry: People buy whatever they think will be of greater benefit to them than the money. In the case of joining an association, however, the cost is in time and energy, as well as in money, and so it is necessary to make prospective members see some real benefits in membership. Knowledge of how to create effective marketing materials is an asset worth having to anyone offering writing and related services.

Many nonprofit organizations exist on a local scale only. Most cities and towns of any size are likely to have a businessperson's club such as a Lion's Club or Rotary Club, a local Chamber of Commerce, and a Better

Business Bureau of some sort. These can be sources of business themselves or, perhaps more likely, avenues to business.

SALES OPPORTUNITIES WITH NONPROFITS

Ingenious and resourceful writers are greatly needed to support the marketing activities of all these organizations. Many of these activities are rather subtle, especially in membership organizations; that is, not all of the writing projects are directed at creating recruiting messages. When I ghosted a proposal-writing brochure for an association executive, the idea was to create a member service, an inducement to joining the association, and so it was a marketing tool. The same philosophy underlay the contract issued to me to create a technical manual for the members of a trade association of small companies in the heating, ventilation, and air conditioning (HVAC) industry. It was a service to members. Likewise, when I happened by chance to get a stream of information on construction opportunities, I conceived a newsletter that I was able to sell to an association as a valuable service to their members. That kind of payoff was the result of knowing what the organization was all about.

The philosophy is similar with other kinds of nonprofits. When the association dedicated to championing the interests of those who have reached Social Security age sends out its appeals for donations to keep it alive, it always bases those appeals on what it represents to be the interests of the addressee. Political organizations understand the concept too, obviously. Their appeals for donations and votes always argue the interests of readers in electing the candidate and/or party to preserve their freedoms and protect their pocketbooks.

MINI-SMALL BUSINESSES AND INDIVIDUAL CLIENTS

The point was made earlier that there is no fixed number of people that distinguishes a business as an organization. The writing needs of a one-person business are different from those of a multiperson business primarily in scope, not in kind. The smallest business needs brochures, proposals, catalog sheets, advertising copy, sales letters, and many other items, just as the large business does. Moreover, with the rapidly growing number of home-based businesses, one- and two-person businesses are coming to represent an ever-larger market for your services. So although it is true that there are certain kinds of things the one- or two-person business will not want (an annual report, for one), for most purposes it makes sense to regard such a small business as another business organization. On the other hand, the "mini-small" business (to use the term once proposed in a congressional subcommittee to refer to really tiny businesses) probably needs the help of a writing professional more urgently than does the larger business, if for no other reason than its mini-small staffing.

People often need writing services as private individuals, rather than as businesses. One common need, probably the most common one, is for résumés, referred to in an earlier chapter. Many freelance writers specialize in writing résumés and associated items (e.g., letters to accompany résumés), and their clients are usually individuals. You should be aware, however, that this is not invariably the case. Sometimes an organization such as an employment agency wishes to make arrangements to have résumés written for its own clients. There are sometimes special arrangements that can be made. One example follows.

A woman operating a résumé service did not write résumés and/or accompanying letters for her clients, but merely laid the information out attractively, set the type, using the then-new desktop composing machine marketed by IBM, and had them printed. After being asked by many clients for help in writing their résumés, she went in quest of a freelance writer to handle the writing work on a subcontract basis. The writer simply made appointments with the clients, conducted interviews, and drafted the résumés, billing the résumé service at agreed-upon rates. It was satisfactory to all parties. (More on marketing résumé-writing services in Chapter 8.)

As noted earlier, many individuals will patronize a letter-writing service, not because they are illiterate, but because they have an aversion to or fear of writing even personal correspondence. This is especially the case when the letter is to serve a special and most sensitive need (e.g., a love letter, a "Dear John" letter, a complaint, an appeal, an apology) or is required for some other unusual and probably difficult situation. Even those who will write ordinary chatty letters without hesitation often are fearful of trying to cope with special problems that require correspondence and will gratefully pay for help. It is not always an inability to express themselves that motivates such people to seek help, but an inability to find a suitable strategy for response or a reluctance to say something frank and unpleasant. It is the orientation and *content* of such letters with which they need help, I have found.

Another great aversion average people have is to speaking in public, especially making a formal speech. When they must make a speech, they are likely to want to read it aloud, rather than orate it. In any case, the majority of those making public speeches, even those who enjoy making them, prefer to have a professional writer compose their speeches for them. So great is the market for speechwriting that many writers specialize in it as a full-time occupation. (Washington, DC, with its 535 senators and congressional representatives plus hundreds of unelected officials of government and all the satellite organizations of private industry, is an especially fertile marketplace for good speech writers!)

Marketing Tools Are Mostly Written Tools

In light of this, it should be no surprise that there is an almost endless array of marketing activities among all organizations in our society. It should not be difficult to understand why new marketing and sales tools are being generated constantly, dominated by written instruments ranging from simple leaflets to thick catalogs and multivolume proposals. But writing is also necessary to selling via media other than print—to create scripts and storyboards for radio, TV, film, and other audiovisual media, as well as for face-to-face sales presentations and public relations.

Chapter 4

Writing for
Government Markets

The various governing bodies of the United States represent the world's largest market for virtually all goods and services, including writing and related services. It is possible to build and support a growing business primarily or even exclusively on government contracts; more than 250,000 companies are so based. Many of these are large corporations, but many are small companies and even one-person enterprises offering writing and related editorial services to satisfy the demand by government agencies.

THE SIZE OF THE MARKET: NEARLY
80,000 GOVERNMENTS

Government, with its hundreds of agencies and thousands of offices—34,000 U.S. government offices and other facilities scattered throughout the United States and possessions—is a multibillion-dollar market for every kind of writing conceivable. Most of an estimated $14 billion spent directly (and much more spent indirectly) for a variety of editorial services alone is paid out both to organizations of all sizes and to individuals.

Many writers do not pursue this vast market because they do not grasp its size and importance, the size and nature of government, and the ready availability of suitable work from government entities. Not many people have an accurate view of the size of the federal government alone, let alone that of the total complex of governments and their agencies in the United States. It is thus not at all surprising that few have any real grasp of the market for goods and services represented by government agencies.

First, there is the matter of defining *what* governments buy: There are exceedingly few goods or services that the governments of the United States do *not* buy. ("Governments" is used justifiably as a plural, as you will see in a moment.) Collectively, this set of markets is unparalleled in both the diversity and total amount of its purchases. The federal government represents the largest market segment, not too surprisingly. At the same time, huge though it is, the federal government represents only about one-third of the total government market. The federal agencies spend well in excess of $200 billion annually for several million purchases of goods and services, while the state and local governments collectively spend at least twice that figure every year. (There are many other billions spent every year for federal government procurement that are not reflected by this figure because they are "off-budget" expenditures or expenditures of a government corporation such as the U.S. Postal Service.)

Impressive as that total is, it is not unreasonably large, given the total number of government entities, reported as "governmental units" in the 1980 official census with the following breakdown:

Federal government	1
State governments	50
Counties	3,042
Municipalities	18,862
Townships	16,822
Local school districts	15,174
Special districts	25,962
Total	79,913

MILLIONS OF GOVERNMENT CUSTOMERS

Within each such government entity, there are many agencies and offices, many buying independently and thus multiplying that 79,913 figure many times. The federal government alone supports more than a dozen departments (inexplicably, DoD is a "department," but so are the Army, Navy, and Air Force, although they are subordinate units of DoD), and there are about 160 other independent agencies and commissions within the federal system. Most of these have their own contracting offices. Many of these have up to ten regional offices in the United States, and in most cases each of these has an independent purchasing office. Moreover, in the larger agencies and departments, there are numerous subdivisions that have their own contracting officers, act otherwise as semi-autonomous federal agencies, and in many cases are larger than some of the other, independent agencies.

To get an appreciation of the federal government market from another perspective, consider these facts: There are some 15,000 contracting officers and about 125,000 federal employees engaged in managing, administering, and conducting contracting activities. (It takes a lot of people to spend over a billion dollars a day!) That does not count the thousands of employees who initiate procurement requests. In fact, it is the latter, those responsible for administering the programs of the government agencies and providing all the services, who are the real customers. The contracting officers and other procurement people are the federal government's purchasing agents or buyers; they contact suppliers; request bids and proposals; handle all the legal, accounting, and other administrative details of contracting for the requested supplies and services; monitor contract compliance; process invoices; and close out completed contracts. However, the agency executives are the real customers and clients, deciding how to spend their budgets and what to buy. As a contractor, you deal with the contracting office in matters of delivery, invoicing, and getting paid, but you deal with the program people in matters concerning the service and product. (This does not differ greatly from large corporations, where buyers or purchasing agents and accountants handle all administrative and contract details but you deal with line people for substantive matters.)

SUPPLY GROUPS

Governments identify the goods and services they buy as *supply groups*, of which there are nearly 100, each subdivided into many subcategories. For example, the federal government's *Expert and Consultant Services* includes engineering and technical services, technical writing, economic analyses, and management services. There are 19 service supply groups, several of which include various writing and editorial services. In addition, there are 76 other supply groups; these are oriented to products, but some of them also offer opportunities to contract for editorial services. There is, for example, a group of *Training Aids and Devices*, some of which require or are based on writing and other editorial services. The supply groups most likely to present you with marketing opportunities are listed in Figure 4–1. The relevance of these supply groups to writing and other editorial services may not be readily apparent in all cases, but you will find, if you pursue this market, that it is worth keeping an eye on them.

Many procurements are made via avenues other than the formal ones represented in Figure 4–1. There are also a few government organizations that have their own procedures. One example is the U.S. Postal Service, another is the Government Printing Office, which is part of the legislative branch of government, originally established to print the *Federal Register*, the statutes, and other issue of the Congress.

SIMILARITIES AND DIFFERENCES

There are both similarities and differences among federal, state, and local governments. The similarity of chief interest here is that all are markets for the kinds of goods and services offered by writers and editors. The processes and procedures for conducting business with all governments and their many agencies are reasonably similar. The chief difference is that in the federal government system purchasing is almost totally decentralized, with most agencies doing their own buying, whereas state and local governments tend to centralize buying in their own purchasing and supply organizations. (Centralization of buying in the federal government, when it occurs at all, usually occurs within a particular agency. For example, the Department of Defense, the Postal Service, the Department of Veteran's Affairs, and the Federal Supply Service have their own centralized supply centers.)

In general, aside from the tendency to centralize purchasing, most state and local governments model their procurement methods and procedures after the federal model, which is itself modeled after the Uniform Procurement Code developed by the American Bar Association. The federal government issues a Standard Form 129, Application for Bidders List, and all who wish to do business with the government are encouraged to file a copy of this form with the procurement office of each agency considered to be a potential customer. However, there is no requirement to do so; you may contract with federal agencies without filing anything but the bid or proposal required for the specific procurement. State and local governments each have a similar form, but in most cases they require that you file it as an act of registration before you can contract with those governments.

A: Experimental, Developmental, Test, and Research Work

Medical, scientific, social research, especially advanced and sophisticated projects, studies, surveys, laboratory developments, feasibility studies, design and development, modeling, educational research.

H: Expert and Consultant Services

Engineering and technical services, R&D, surveys, technical writing, economic analyses, management consulting.

L: Technical Representative Services

Engineering and technical services, especially field engineering/maintenance of sophisticated equipment and field support of technical training.

M: Operation and Maintenance of Government Owned Facility

Operate government warehouses, plants, laboratories, computers, other.

T: Photographic, Mapping, Printing, and Publication Services

Primarily printing but includes topographic surveys and photogrammetry, technical writing, mailing and addressing, photo (ground and aerial), typesetting, copy preparation, and various related functions.

U: Training Services

Development of training materials (manuals, audiovisuals, etc) and presentation of courses.

X: Miscellaneous

Anything that does not appear to fit other categories--e.g., teleprocessing, bagging groceries, making transparencies, other odd jobs.

69: Training Aids and Devices

Training programs, text and film; test materials; scoring materials/devices; learning aids, all types; language laboratories.

76: Books, Maps, and Other Publications

Books and pamphlets, newspapers and periodicals, maps, atlases, globes, sheet and book music, drawings and specifications, microfilm, and miscellaneous printed matter.

99: Miscellaneous

Signs, advertising displays, identification plates, marker bands, cutout letters, metal tags, jewelry, collector's items, smoker's articles and matches, ecclesiastical equipment and supplies, memorials, cemetery and mortuary equipment, and other miscellaneous items.

Figure 4-1. Most relevant supply groups.

The following discussions will be based largely on experiences with federal agencies, but most of the principles derived from them are applicable to government procurement at all levels. Specific examples will be given from time to time to highlight differences and specific cases, where those are relevant.

BASIC PRINCIPLES AND PROCEDURES VERSUS MYTHS

A great deal of mythology tends to spring up around every field of activity. In the case of doing business with the government, as I mentioned earlier, one of the most prevalent myths is that an individual needs to "know someone" and "pull strings" to win government contracts. Another is that there is impossibly complex "red tape," an interminably long wait to get paid, and an unacceptably oppressive bureaucratic harassment involved in government contracting. As with most mythology, these beliefs are based on shreds of truth, but in each case they constitute a gross exaggeration or extrapolation of the truth. Here are a few of the facts:

- Really large contracts—multibillion-dollar contracts in today's economy—are sought after by large corporations that enlist the aid of high-powered lobbyists and solons: representatives and senators who do what they can to steer major contracts to their own districts and states. There is, admittedly, occasional hanky-panky in awarding contracts, but it is only occasional, and the irregularity is not always inspired for venal reasons but often for convenience (i.e., to avoid some of the delays and other burdens of formal contracting). Despite the sneers of cynics, government procurement is honest, for the most part—a truly competitive process. Even when an agency tries to favor a given supplier (called "wiring" the procurement), it is far from being a foolproof dodge. Aggressive and able marketers can and often do "unwire" the procurement and elbow out the favored parties by simply submitting the lowest bid or the best proposal.

- Bureaucratic foul-ups sometimes delay payment; this is usually the case when agencies are slow to pay. You can learn how to avoid this or at least minimize it. Keep in mind that many private-sector corporations take far longer to pay their bills than the most backsliding government agencies. There is relatively little you can do about the corporations, but much you can do about the government agencies.

- Government red tape is no worse than that of most large corporations and is less complex than that of many private organizations.

- The notion that you must "know someone" is also far more likely to be the case in the private sector than in dealing with the government. Private-sector organizations can buy what they want from whomever they want whenever they want; the only regulations controlling them are their own rules. Government agencies, on the other hand, must buy according to strict regulations that are, in fact, public laws regarding the spending of public money—your taxes and mine.

That is one major difference between marketing to the public sector and marketing to the private sector. In my opinion, it is the most important difference. The fact that the laws governing purchasing and procurement by government agencies are sometimes violated does not change the principle: As a citizen or legal resident paying taxes, you are entitled to compete for and win government contracts regardless of your size or industrial importance. I have myself won many contracts without "knowing" anyone, often to the consternation of large rival companies who had never heard of me or my company and wondered where we had come from. I have simply followed the standard procedures, using whatever marketing talents I possessed or could marshal from associates. I and others I have known have done so often enough to demonstrate that such success is not a freakish exception but can be repeated again and again by determined, hard-working marketers.

THE TWO BASIC PROCUREMENT METHODS

There are two basic ways in which governments buy: through competitive bids and through competitive proposals. As writers, editors, and suppliers of relevant services, we may find ourselves competing via either of these two methods. Therefore, it is useful to understand the rationale underlying both basic approaches.

The competitive bid, known officially as the *sealed bid*, is the preferred method from the government's viewpoint because it is by nature the simplest, least costly process, and the most price competitive. It is the procurement method that elicits the lowest bids. It is also the least complicated and most efficient method of purchasing because the successful bidder is the lowest bidder. (There are exceptions, which will be discussed later.)

Unfortunately, and to the regret of most contracting officials, the sealed bid is often an unsuitable method of procurement. Sealed bids are usually entirely suitable for buying relatively standardized commodities in both goods and services, but there are many procurements in which considerations other than price must prevail or at least be considered in choosing a contractor. It is in such cases that competitive proposals, rather than competitive sealed bids, are the basis for evaluating competitors and awarding contracts. The evaluation is twofold: a technical evaluation of the proposer and the plan proposed is followed by an evaluation of costs. *Competitive proposals* is the official description of this mode of procurement today, but it was formerly called *negotiated procurement* for a very good reason. Neither prices nor other provisions submitted with a proposal are necessarily final; they may be negotiated after proposals are submitted and reviewed.

Proposal writing is thus far more complex than is bid writing, as is marketing in general in this market. For typical writing and related service projects other than relatively small tasks, it is far more likely that you will be asked to submit a proposal than a sealed bid. The client is likely to want the opportunity to evaluate you and your proposal before considering the acceptability of your cost estimates. In a nutshell, the client evaluates your proposed program, your capability for carrying the program out successfully, your dependability as a contractor, and finally, your price. (That need not necessarily be the lowest price, but it must be "within the competitive range," which generally means within the budget the agency had established for the job and within the general range established by other proposers.)

The Exception and the Freelancer's Greatest Opportunity

In the federal government, the Small Purchases Act authorizes agencies to contract for goods and services up to $25,000 as a small purchase. (State and local governments have parallel laws, but the upper limits of small purchase regulations in these governments are always far lower than $25,000.) In terms of procedure, this means that an agency may issue a government purchase order for up to that amount. The supplier will usually be asked to submit an informal bid or proposal unless the agency has issued a request for quotations (RFQ) to find the lowest quotation. The process is an informal method of contracting, most suitable for small firms or freelancing individuals. In fact, for projects falling under the Small Purchases Act, it is entirely practicable to tour government offices and "knock on doors" in search of contracts, which are typically issued in a much-simplified procedure as government purchase orders.

THE FEDERAL GOVERNMENT SYSTEM

It is much easier to understand and work with state and local governments if you first understand and learn how to work with the federal government, and most of the examples and generalizations presented thus far are based on federal government procurement methods. This may seem complex at first, but it is in fact quite orderly and logical. Over the years, there have been many efforts to simplify the federal contracting process, and they have been quite successful. One simplification was to reduce the formal contract to a single form, a Standard Form 33, including the successful proposal by reference as the "schedule" or specification of what is contracted for. Much other required paperwork is disposed of easily with a few forms that require only check marks in appropriate places and your signature. You can learn the system quite easily, and the paperwork is not at all burdensome.

One of the most pervasive and stubborn myths about government contracts is that only large and important business organizations can contract with the government. For years I was involved in marketing to and contracting with government agencies while in the employ of both large and small companies. I was even a director of marketing and general manager for such companies before I struck out on my own.

Despite my extensive experience in contracting with the government, I felt some reluctance to pursue government contracts as an individual with no more resources than a desk, a typewriter, and knowledge of the contracting procedure. But I did know the contracting officer of the Postal Service Training and Development Institute in Bethesda, Maryland, having done business there many times while managing the Washington-area branch of a large company. I therefore sought him out to see if he had any small writing jobs I could handle as a consultant.

Chet, the contracting officer, explained first that the agency was phasing out most of their consultants in favor of permanent employees. There were no longer any consultant slots available. However, the Institute was still contracting for needed services.

"Why not bid for some of our regular contracts?" he asked me.

"I am not an organization, but only one person," I said.

"So? We have lots of small jobs, suitable for one person to do, and I know that you can probably handle most of them. Here is one open right now. I guarantee that you will get fair consideration for any contract you go after." He handed me a bid set.

I bid for it. It was a $5,000 job to evaluate the results of several projects and write the results up in a definitive report. I won it, and I spent the next few weeks working on it. Since the project required that I have regular access to the files, the agency even provided an office and desk, and I did most of the work on site.

After that, greatly encouraged, I went after and won many writing contracts from many agencies. I did a great deal of such government contract work, almost exclusively at times, for several years thereafter. Following are summaries of a few of my projects to give you a better idea of what is possible and typical in this market. Bear in mind that the figures given are in 1970s dollars. Prices would be considerably higher today.

- A $2,400 project with OSHA (Occupational Safety and Health Administration of the Department of Labor) to develop a syllabus and plan for the training of occupational health specialists. Another company had written a training program for them in the form of two manuals—a student manual and an instructor manual—but had not furnished any useful guidance for organizing the study program and using the two manuals. I was hired to overcome this problem. (This was not rare; many projects authorized by government agencies require rescue later.)

- A follow-up job with OSHA to develop a textbook on the same subject, totaling about $19,000.

- An audiovisual storyboard and script on value management for the VM office of the Public Buildings Service, for approximately $3,000.

- A storyboard to accompany a script written by someone else for the VM office of the Public Buildings Service, for $1,500.

- A storyboard and script for an audiovisual program for the U.S. Forest Service presenting the culture and history of American Indians, for approximately $11,000.

- Helping the Energy Research & Development Institute handle a huge backlog of correspondence and devising a system for handling it in the future, about $6,000.

- Writing a brochure for an office of the Public Buildings Service on how to use new standard forms for architects and engineers seeking architectural commissions and engineering contracts, $2,250.

- Writing an annual report for the Federal Aviation Administration reporting on the year's progress of 20 engineering sections of the FAA, approximately $23,000.

- Updating a rate manual for the U.S. Postal Service, $600.

- Writing a procedures manual on value management for the Public Buildings Service, approximately $4,000.

- Working as a consultant to the Environmental Protection Agency (EPA) to aid one of the contractors in speeding up the report writing necessary to an EPA program, $1,500 plus travel and per diem expenses. (The EPA contractor paid the fee; EPA paid expenses.)

Note that some of these were problem-solving tasks. In two cases the contracts were to complete unfinished jobs other contractors had been paid for. Thus, requirements vary widely, from solving raw problems to revising or reworking unsatisfactory products written by others. You may recall the anecdote in Chapter 1 of a so-called "editing" assignment in which "editing" was really a euphemism for a complete rewrite of a most unsatisfactory draft. That is by no means an isolated incident; it is a fairly common situation, and it calls for tact and restraint to handle it well.

Functions and Offices of Interest

Every federal agency has specific functions and responsibilities. Those of most immediate interest to writers and editors are the responsibilities for publications, training, and public information. In large agencies or in agencies in which one of these functions is closely related to the nature of the agency, there may be separate offices for the functions. In other cases, functions may be combined, and in the smallest agencies they may be a responsibility of the personnel office. In OSHA, for example, I found an Office of Training. Much of the work I did for the Postal Service was for the training division, itself a major element of USPS, with all technical training at the branch housed at the University of Oklahoma in Norman and other training at the Bethesda site.

USPS is not alone in maintaining a major training facility. The Internal Revenue Service (IRS) and the Department of Agriculture (USDA) also maintain extensive training establishments for their own employees. The Office of Personnel Management (OPM) has a Bureau of Training and conducts many training programs to which all federal agencies may send employees. The Office of Federal Procurement Policy (OFPP), an element of the Office of Management and Budget (OMB), operates a special facility to train contracting specialists. Military organizations require a great many technical manuals and other documentation to support their training of military personnel and the day-to-day operation and maintenance of weapons systems and related equipment. Because of this, they are by far the largest developers of publications. And, of course, the military agencies have the largest training programs of all, since that is one of their prime functions in both wartime and peacetime.

Training requirements are a rich source of writing work in government agencies generally. One reason is the great amount of training conducted by these agencies. Another is that many training programs suffer from poor writing; there is a need for the services of professional writers in the development of training systems. I found that a majority of the writing assignments I won were for the development of materials for training—manuals, audiovisual scripts and storyboards, and lecture guides.

Generating and disseminating information has always been a major function of government. Washington, DC, has gained a deserved reputation as the information center of the world, and this has made the federal government the largest publisher in the United States, perhaps even in the world. Rather few of those publications are written by federal employees. The bulk of them are written by consultants, contractors, and subcontractors. Some are contracted for directly, as when NASA (National Aeronautics and Space Administration) sought out one of the world's leading authorities on celestial mechanics to write a definitive book on the subject or when the Consumer Products Safety Commission contracted for an entire system of public information materials on product safety. Others are byproducts of contracts (e.g., a report written to satisfy a contract requirement is sometimes deemed to be of enough interest to the general public to be released as a government publication). Many publications are required in connection with contracts for other things, such as a report or a training manual on a new piece of equipment. Many of these are prepared by subcontractors. (E.g., the developer of a new night vision device for the military might contract with someone else to write the required manuals or training programs.)

There is no set standard in government organizations; each agency has a large degree of freedom in organizing itself internally and allocating necessary functions according to the needs of its own missions, size, and problems.

Writing is a custom service, and normally you would compete for a writing contract by submitting a proposal. However, because so many writing jobs qualify under the law as small purchases, they are often awarded without competition, or at least informally and with only nominal competition and/or a simple letter proposal. Direct personal contact with government officials is the best approach to obtaining this work. Seek out the various government agencies and inquire who is in charge of publications, public information, and training. Make personal calls on these people and leave business cards, brochures, and capability statements describing your background, qualifications, experience, and available resources (i.e., equipment, help, other factors that reflect the kind and volume of work you can handle, how fast you can respond and turn a job around, and other relevant factors). Become a familiar figure in these offices. Just like everyone else, people in government have problems, and they often need help. For example, they discover on Thursday that they are shorthanded for a job due on Monday, or they have been handed a hot potato by a superior and are eager to find a freelance writer who can help. That is *opportunity* for those who are prepared to handle it.

Although I am based in the Washington, DC, area, my government contracts have often been in distant places such as Missoula, Montana, and Orlando, Florida. It is not necessary, in most cases, to be near the Washington office of a federal agency. The government has offices everywhere and contracts with people everywhere. In fact, you can use the mail and telephone for your contacts; in many cases you never make a face-to-face contact with the customer, even in a long-term contractual relationship.

The most basic tool of marketing to the federal government is the government's own daily publication, the *Commerce Business Daily* (CBD). It can be ordered from the Government Printing Office, Washington, DC 20402; both six-month trial subscriptions and regular annual subscriptions are available. This publication lists hundreds of government bid and proposal opportunities every day.

You should also write to the contracting officer or Public Information Office of each major agency and request information about the agency's procurement policies and practices. Many will send you pamphlets, brochures, and even thick manuals explaining their system in detail. A starter list (not a complete one, because that would be too large for the space available here) appears a bit later on. But you can get a great deal more information from any nearby office of the Small Business Administration (SBA), Department of Commerce (DOC), or General Services Administration (GSA). Be sure to visit any GSA Business Service Center near you, or at least write the GSA office in Denver, Colorado, a major federal center. To find government offices near you, check the telephone directory under "U.S., Government of."

The Government Printing Office operates a number of bookstores in which it sells numerous government publications, including most of the procurement manuals published by the various agencies. However, as noted above, many of the agencies will furnish copies of those manuals free of charge, on request. That is one of the key reasons for writing to them. (You may request similar information from the purchasing and supply offices of state and local government offices. Many of them also publish thick manuals of instructions.)

Contract Forms

The government issues several types of contracts. The two basic categories are cost reimbursement and fixed price. The cost-reimbursement contract is a form used when it is all but impossible to predict costs. Usually, the contract specifies maximum direct and indirect rates but will reimburse the contractor for all costs within the bounds so established. There are further variations within the categories, especially within the fixed-price category. The most basic fixed-price contract is one that defines the entire job to be done and establishes a fixed price for it. Some others are of the "indefinite quantity" type, in which unit prices are fixed, but the government cannot predict how many units it will buy over the course of the contract (usually one year). For example, you may be asked to furnish hourly rates for writing and editing and per-page rates for typing and proofreading. You may also be asked to furnish unit prices for illustrating, duplicating, and other services. The client agency will then issue "task orders" for each job, as the need arises, and you will do the work at the specified rates. This type of contract, with minor variations, is also known as a *time and material* or *T&M contract*, a *basic ordering agreement* or *BOA*, or a *task order contract*.

For long-term contracts, it is possible to get interim payments by billing the customer periodically, usually on a monthly basis, as work progresses.

A Few Federal Government References

GSA Business Service Centers are located in the following cities:

Boston	New York	Philadelphia
Washington	Atlanta	Kansas City (MO)
Chicago	Houston	Fort Worth
Denver	Los Angeles	San Francisco
Seattle		

You can write to the contracting officer or public information officer of the following key agencies and offices to ask for information on procurement:

Small Business Administration
1441 L Street, NW
Washington, DC 20416

General Services
  Administration
18th & F Streets, NW
Washington, DC 20405

Department of Energy
1000 Independence Avenue,
  SW
Washington, DC 20585

Department of the Interior
18th & C Streets, NW
Washington, DC 20240

NASA HQ Contracts Division
200 Maryland Avenue, SW
Washington, DC 20546

Department of Defense
The Pentagon
Washington, DC 20301

Department of Commerce
14th & Constitution Avenue,
  NW
Washington, DC 20230

General Services
  Administration
Denver Federal Center
Denver, CO 80225

Environmental Protection
  Agency
401 M Street, SW
Washington, DC 20460

Department of Transportation
400 7th Street, SW
Washington, DC 20591

Department of Labor
200 Constitution Avenue, NW
Washington, DC 20210

Directorate for Small Business
  and Economic Utilization
  Policy
The Pentagon, Room 2A340
Washington, DC 20310

STATE AND LOCAL GOVERNMENT SYSTEMS

States have governing and management structures very much like those of the federal government. For procurement, each state government operates a centralized purchasing and supply organization in the state capital. That may be an autonomous or semi-autonomous group or a group within a larger agency.

Common-use commodities are bought by these organizations by annual supply agreements. (These are similar to the "indefinite quantity" contracts referred to earlier.) Each organization has a number of purchasing agents, each responsible for the procurement of certain categories or supply groups. Prospective suppliers are encouraged to meet the buyers responsible for procuring the goods or services they offer.

Special services such as consulting, publication management and other editorial services are bought only through this organization in some states, while in others state contracting authority for special services is delegated to other agencies within the state government. In either case, the contractor may market directly to the user organization, although the user may have to process the contract or purchase order through the central supply group. In all cases, the supply chief urges all prospective suppliers to visit the offices of the supply group personally and become acquainted with the buyers and the procurement system there. At local government levels, the principles are the same, with all or nearly all purchasing done by centralized purchasing at the county seat, town hall, or city hall.

Most of the state supply groups and many of those at county and city levels can supply you with a brochure and other literature describing the goods and services they buy, their methods and procedures, regulations, and advice to prospective suppliers. Some will also supply a complete list of all their agencies. You will be surprised to discover how many agencies even relatively small state and local governments support. You will also be surprised when you get a catalog of every item the state or local government buys; most rival the federal list of supplies and services in both diversity and numbers of items. You will receive a registration form that also serves as an application to be placed on the appropriate bidders' lists.

You may pursue contracts in other states, counties, and municipalities than those of your residence and citizenship. Some jurisdictions have special socioeconomic programs that give preference to minorities and to their own citizens, but these programs do not bar you from competing for business there.

State and local governments advertise their requirements in the daily newspaper classified columns under "Bids and Proposals." Be sure to keep an eye on those and visit procurement offices in your state capital, county seat, and city or town hall.

Chapter 5

Writing Needs of Businesses and Professionals

Look around at how many different kinds of businesses, organizations, and professional practices exist today, and you get a rough idea of how many different kinds of writing needs there are. As a business writer, you must decide which writing needs you wish to serve; no one can serve them all.

IT'S A WORLD OF SPECIALISTS

Unless you are a senior citizen, you probably cannot recall personally the age of the generalist. That was a time when you were hired because you could "do anything," and after being hired you were required to do everything. What you didn't know when you started, you learned on the job. (A standard joke used to be that to get a job as a pharmacist you had to know how to make sandwiches and milkshakes, a reference to the fact that most drugstores had luncheonette counters.)

Things have changed. Today you are expected to qualify as a specialist of some kind before you can get serious consideration as a job applicant. The standard is applied even more rigorously to consultants and contractors: Clients are most likely to retain you to do a job for them only if they perceive you as a specialist qualified for that service. Sometimes the demand for special qualifications seems extreme. For example, although some technical writers choose to specialize in whatever areas they feel most comfortable with often it is the market—what clients demand, that is—that dictates the specialty. Hence, in technical publications there are radar writers, computer writers, avionics writers, and others who are specialists in terms of the subjects or kinds of equipment about which they are best qualified to write. There are also manual writers, maintenance writers, logistics writers, and others who specialize in the types of documentation with which they are most familiar. Moreover, in the case of those who write materials destined for the military, there are specialists in the writing specifications with which they are most familiar.

Being retained as a consultant or contractor to write some manual or logistics documentation may thus depend on your ability to demonstrate knowledge of or experience with some given class of equipment, type of documentation, military manual specification, other specialized knowledge and experience, or some combination of these. Of course, this obsession with superspecialization also has its advantages: You can assemble your own special qualifications into an image or presentation that strikes a nerve with the client and gives you an advantage in winning certain assignments or contracts.

Admittedly, the demand for specialization is carried to extremes in some cases, but it does have a logical foundation: Most businesses and professional practices specialize in some way today. There are corporations that do more than one thing, but they do not disprove the rule. They are known as *conglomerates*, and they have separate divisions or companies, each of which specializes as though it were a completely separate entity. For example, the General Electric Company, a major defense contractor, has both a "heavy weapons" division and a "light weapons" division.

Even retail stores have yielded to the trend, so that we now have fewer general merchandisers. There are stores and national chains that sell only athletic footwear, retailers whose sole business is renting videotapes for home use, restaurants that specialize in sandwiches, and other organizations that have found it practicable to confine their appeal to narrow markets. Even those that still purvey general merchandise have managed to present a facade of specialization by some specialized mode of marketing and merchandising. For example, many are discounters to the general public and others have become so-called "warehouse stores," soliciting bulk buying from householders and small businesses. The practice of medicine, one of the oldest professions to spawn a rapidly growing number of specialists, has gone to an almost ludicrous extreme and made a specialty of general practice. The family doctor is no longer a "GP" or general practitioner, but has become a specialist in "family practice," a major focus of which is determining which specialists to call on after initial or tentative diagnosis!

Thus, it is not too surprising that just as today's employer will not hire a person who offers to "do anything," today's client is somewhat reluctant to retain a writer who offers to "write anything" and claims competence in all things related to writing and publications. Writers have not escaped the trend to specialization; we must accommodate ourselves to the modern world and find our own niches.

Finding a niche is not always a deliberate action; many of us fall into a niche through circumstance, as did Jerry O'Neill of Rochester, New York. He says he never set out to be a writer, but started as a photographer while attending night school. O'Neill calls himself a nonfiction writer but hastens to explain that he is referring to the writing of advertising, sales literature, and public relations, obviously all marketing material. (Perhaps he is more of a specialist than he realizes.) He focuses on technical subjects, he explains, and has developed skill in asking technical experts the right questions, which enables him to write competently about such diverse items as a train control system, bar code technology, and xerographic toner. He has written brochures, slide shows, advertisements, and trade journal articles, among other things. His clients have included both large and small companies. O'Neill adds that he works primarily in the segment of marketing known as "business-to-business" marketing, another aspect of specialization.

In Chapter 1 I presented a fairly lengthy list of items writers are called upon to create. I hastened to assure you that no one would expect you to be able to write all these things equally well, nor should you demand it of yourself. Writers have long specialized to some degree; speechwriters, novelists, playwrights, and scriptwriters are examples. But the trend to specialization continues, even in the business-writing field, because the craft of writing must follow and adapt to the new developments in all the field that rely on writing. We have become copywriters, technical writers, medical writers, and political writers, among other specialties, and even more fragmented as superspecialists within many of these general specialties.

Let's have a closer look now at the specific writing needs of various businesses and professional practices. This will begin to provide a base of information from which you can begin to judge which writing specialties you find most appealing and/or most suitable for your own efforts. (Although you may happen into a special field by chance, as many of us do, you ought to have at least a broad picture of the businesses, industries, and professions within which you might be working.)

THE BUSINESS WORLD

Many writers "came up the hard way," having served as cabin boys, short-order cooks, lumberjacks, accountants, salesmen and -women, clerks, teachers, laborers, and so forth—jobs that gave them an appreciation of government, business, and industry at many levels. Others, especially those who were reared in prosperous times and escaped the rigors of a depressed economy, may have been spared this difficult and unpleasant education. They are in some ways the poorer for it; many writers who endured hardscrabble backgrounds have found the experience useful in achieving success as business writers.

Since a writer must understand the client's needs and problems to react well to them, it is important to take at least a brief look at the world of business. Probably most people think of business as individuals and organizations selling goods and services for a profit. That is not the definition we will find most useful in our discussion of business writing. It helps, for some purposes, to divide the world of prospective customers for writing services into separate markets such as individuals, for-profit organizations, nonprofit organizations, and government agencies. However, in terms of the kinds of work you may be called on to do as a writer, editor, and consultant, there are more similarities than differences: All organizations with serious missions have similar objectives and functions—accounting, recordkeeping, reporting, marketing, and producing goods or providing services. They thus have similar needs for brochures, newsletters, reports, speeches, scripts, policy manuals, releases, and many other written items in common use today. You will also find more similarities than differences in how you must sell your services to this business world. Selling to individuals is somewhat different from selling to large organizations, but the principles do not vary greatly.

MARKETING NEEDS DOMINATE—
AND OFFER GREAT OPPORTUNITY

Peter Drucker, the guru of management, put it well when he said that the prime objective of business is to create customers. Entrepreneurial business leaders often state their goals in different terms, although they have the same broad objective. According to them, they have never been motivated by the desire to make money. Money is, in their view, only a tool to be used, not an objective. Their motivation, they claim, is to succeed in reaching the deeper goal of the enterprise, the achievement or validation of an idea. For example, the late Ray Kroc had an idea—making a national chain of McDonald's hamburger stands—that launched the new fast-food industry. Kroc had for years been searching for a new idea that he could promote, for he was essentially a promoter. He had been successful in selling real estate and had discovered McDonald's original establishment when he was successfully marketing milkshake mixers as a national sales manager. He had no notion what his new idea would be, but he was always sure that he would recognize it when he found it, and obviously he did.

Kroc wasn't the first entrepreneur to create a new business, or even a new industry, with a new idea. Many new businesses are launched because the launcher has an idea that he is compelled to promote, and it is the success of the idea that drives the entrepreneur. Monroe Milstein, with his Burlington Coat Factory stores, is currently promoting his own dream somewhat along the lines of the now defunct Robert Hall clothing stores. Lawyer Joel Hyatt, with his chain store law practice, is more intent on being successful with his idea of a new kind of law firm than he is on gaining personal wealth. Charles Revson founded the Revlon cosmetics firm with a line of nail polishes on which he focused his energies 24 hours a day, 7 days a week. The Borden corporation resulted from the struggles of Gail Borden to perfect and market canned milk. The Otis Elevator company arose from the drive of Elisha T. Otis to perfect a safety device for freight hoists so that they would be safe for human passengers. Robert Fulton also resisted the jeers and sneers of his detractors and skeptics as he labored at demonstrating the practicality of the steamboat. These and thousands of similar examples support the theory that doing what you love and are passionately dedicated to will result in success. Still, marketing is inevitably a prime requirement of all business ventures, regardless of even the noblest motives. Putting the need for income and profits aside for the moment, the creation of customers in sufficient quantity is a necessity in making any idea work, no matter how virtuous or worthy it is.

Hence, regardless of whether the corporation, entrepreneur, or professional is more intent on profit or on proving a concept and making it work, winning customers—marketing—is in most cases the primary objective and primary activity of the venture. This overwhelming need for effective marketing and the resulting need for those who can create marketing materials is the richest pasture for freelance writing. It is, in fact, so rich that many freelance business writers specialize within that field, creating materials for a variety of specialized marketing methods, including public relations functions and other more subtle marketing methods required by the ethical standards of certain professionals.

EVERYONE MARKETS—EVEN INDEPENDENT PROFESSIONALS

One of the great advantages of putting your writing talents to work in the general field of marketing is the abundance of business opportunities that results from the abundance of marketing needs and activities. Just as every organization markets (as discussed in Chapter 3), every independent professional and small business must market too, pursuing buyers of their goods and services. Some lawyers advertise quite openly today, a practice that once would have been referred to as "ambulance chasing" and would have been unethical enough (by former standards) to have them ejected from the Bar Association, if not disbarred. They are legally and ethically permitted to advertise commercially today, but most lawyers still shrink from it, as do most physicians, psychologists, dentists, and others in the medical professional field. Most medical specialists and lawyers, as well as many consultants, architects, therapists, accountants, and other professional specialists, market via far more subtle and dignified methods. They seek patients and clients through a variety of networking resources, membership in various associations, public speaking, participation in community affairs, appearances in the press, and sundry other initiatives that give them a favorable image and make them more visible in the community. Such activities tend to bring about referrals and word-of-mouth recommendations. All of these approaches require implementation, and that means the writing of articles, press releases, public statements, and other print materials, as well as speeches, radio and TV spots, and other nonprint items. Professionals especially want help in preparing speeches, proposals, professional papers, and newsletters. Sometimes they want more than mere help; they want ghostwriting.

Marketing is so diverse and widespread that it may be perceived as involving several broad areas of specialization, including advertising/copywriting, direct marketing/direct mail, and public relations, although there is considerable overlap among these functions. One area in which many freelance marketing writers specialize is the huge direct-mail industry. Not surprisingly, this is an area in which many of the most experienced freelance writers regard themselves as more than writers: They have become consultants, offering services as designers and creators of complete direct-mail packages that include sales letters, brochures, releases, lift letters, and other promotional pieces. They are often master marketing strategists, a consulting function and responsibility. Even within this specialty there are writers and consultants who specialize further, as in the case of one who calls himself "The Letter Doctor."

Some typical advertisements of freelance writers specializing in direct mail are presented in Figure 5–1. (These are advertisements that have appeared in the direct-marketing trade press. Later, you will see typical freelance writers' advertisements as they appear in the Yellow Pages and other, more general media.) Many are simple one-line notices, as shown, and some are even simpler than that, mere listings of the individual's name and telephone number, with or without a street address, under a general category heading such as "Copywriting Services." Other advertisers stress a complete spread of services, including analysis and critique of existing copy in the best consulting tradition, and some offer lettershop services too.

THE LETTERSHOP

For many freelance writers today, and especially for those working in the direct-mail field, it makes good sense to offer lettershop services. Traditionally, the lettershop was a small service business that supported other business owners by typing and duplicating letters and other materials destined for mailing and providing a mailing service, using whatever equipment and facilities were available. Today services vary somewhat from that common base, according to the individual shop. Various shops might or might not do addressing, mailing-list maintenance, artwork, design, advertising layouts, comprehensives, mechanicals, fulfillment, mailing services, and other support tasks. The nature of lettershop services has changed somewhat as a result of the capabilities of modern equipment. Only a few years ago, for example, type could be set for a client only with expensive equipment. Today, anyone equipped with a laser printer and proper software can set type that, although it is not as high in quality as that set with the more costly equipment, from a practical standpoint is useful and functional.

It is not necessary to make a major investment today to provide a spread of services for the direct-mail marketing industry. Even the modestly priced modern computers and the peripheral equipment many freelance writers own confer upon them a wide variety of functional capabilities once available only to owners of unusually well-

GET RICH

with your Product or Service!

...do you have a product or service that can be sold to millions? My direct mail & ad copy can make you rich!

BUSINESS-TO-BUSINESS COPYWRITING.

BOOST YOUR RESPONSE WITH MY 2-HOUR COPY DIAGNOSIS

High-response sales letters for limited budgets. The Letter Doctor.

WORDS THAT SELL! Winning packages by DM copy pro from copy through camera-ready art -- or get a copy critique/rewrite of your existing package.

COPYWRITING. Freelance. All media, all subjects. Seasoned pro.

CONCEPT/COPY/DESIGN

DM Packages, Space Ads, Catalogs.

25 YEARS OF COPYWRITING EXCELLENCE.

Copy & Design; Business, Circ, Consumer.

QUALITY LETTER SERVICE, "the lettersmiths."

Advice * Marketing * Creative services
*Specializing in mail order.

STRATEGIC & CREATIVE SERVICES

Figure 5-1. Freelance writing advertisements.

equipped shops. In my own modestly equipped office, for example, is rather inexpensive equipment with which I can automate mailings, print labels in quantity, set type in a variety of fonts and sizes to create camera-ready copy, and even transmit that copy via telephone lines to a printer or client.

RoseMarie Siddiqui runs what is probably the modern equivalent of a lettershop in the Virginia suburbs of Washington, DC, The Write Word® (see Figure 5–2). Here, in her own words, is how she describes what she does:

> Depending on the client, my work also includes proofreading, editing, and grammatical help. Most of my long-term clients give me editorial license as they trust me completely with altering/tailoring their work on their proposals, analytical reports, legal briefs, newsletters, books, etc.

On a significant note, RoseMarie adds, "My business card and other information are about to change from 'Word Processing Services,' because in all the years I've been in business I have never been able to limit myself to strictly word processing. Future wording will be 'Word Processing and Business Services.'"

Figure 5-3 illustrates the diversity of such services with copies of advertisements that have appeared under the heading "Lettershop" in both the direct-marketing trade press and the Yellow Pages. As in Figure 5-1, names of the individuals and/or their shops are deleted. Can you tell which are advertisements in the trade press and which in the more general Yellow Pages? You probably cannot, which proves a point: Lettershop services are more general today than ever before, due largely to the enormous technological advances of recent years.

What this means to you as a freelance writer and/or editorial services provider is entirely up to you. You must decide for yourself how to define precisely what you can do and what you wish to do for clients and prospective clients. In my own case, I do not offer all the services I am capable of providing because I simply do not wish to provide all of them. I identify myself as a writer primarily, and I choose to offer only writing and closely related editing and editorial consulting services, and even the latter only infrequently. When I get an inquiry into the possibility of providing specialized services such as copywriting and public relations, I usually refer it to some contemporary who specializes in that field and with whom I maintain a friendly relationship.

That is a matter of personal preference. However, if you opt to follow this procedure you should consider making deals with the specialists to

THe WRite WoRd®

WORD PROCESSING SERVICES
10700 Ashby Place • Fairfax, VA 22030-5113
(703) 385-8631

Effective May 1990

H O U R L Y R A T E	$20.00
I N C O R P O R A T I O N P A P E R S	
(from revised model, per set)	$55.00
(all others initial input, per hour)	$20.00
R E S U M E (first two pages **Laser** printer)	$50.00
(each add'l page or client revisions, per hour)	$20.00
W I L L (from revised model)	$50.00
(all others initial input, per hour)	$20.00
N O T A R Y (FREE for Clients of The Write Word\)	$ 3.00

O T H E R   S E R V I C E S

FACSIMILE TRANSMISSION: (for docs. already stored in ASCII on diskette):
(Minimum $4.50) (Long distance charged to Client)

Domestic 1st page	=	$4.50
International 1st page	=	$9.50
Each additional page	=	$1.50

- Documents which must be converted from your WP doc. to ASCII is charged min. 1/4 hr. plus transmission charges.

- Docs. which must be typed from hard copy or dictation charged min. 1/2 hr. plus transmission charges.

FACSIMILE RECEPTION: $1.00 per page.

PRINT FROM CLIENT DISKETTES: Minimum 1 hour at $20.00/hr.

DATA STORAGE/CONVERSION/TRANSFER VIA MODEM: est. based on Client requirement.

WORD PROCESSING, DOS or MODEM INSTRUCTION: $45.00/hr. Program based on client skill level and requirements.

BULLETIN BOARD SET UP, CONSULTING AND/OR MAINTENANCE: $45.00/hr. Min. 4 hour installation charge. Usual total set up time is between 4-6 hrs. but can be up to 10 hrs. depending on client BBS requirements. Need maximum authority of 10 hrs. for installation. $150/mo. for 5 months telephone support. Add'l on-site consulting charged at $45/hr. or by contract.

TELEPHONE ANSWERING: $50.00 per month, unlimited calls, 9:00 - 5:00 p.m.

R U S H	9 a.m. - 5 p.m.	10%
C H A R G E S	5 p.m. - midnight	25%
	midnight - 9 a.m.	50%

Daytime rush charges are applied only when work of other clients must be interrupted during normal business hours to provide faster service on your work. (Rush charge is never applied to contract clients of The Write Word\)

MINIMUM CHARGE ONE HOUR PER DAILY WORK REQUEST

Minimum is applied to daily delivery of work, **not per doc.**; does not apply to contract/retainer clients.

RETAINER

The Write Word\ is available on a retainer/contract basis for clients who anticipate heavier monthly volumes of word processing. Retainer clients receive priority service for all their work requirements. **CALL FOR ESTIMATE.**

FAST • ACCURATE • COMPETITIVE RATES
HOLIDAYS & LATE EVENING HOURS

Figure 5–2.   The Write Word® schedule of services.

DIRECT MARKETING, INC.

Full service direct mail marketing company specializing in art, mechanicals and printing; fulfillment; hand & machine mailing services; data processing, including computer letters, laser letters, merge purge, and database management.

Lettershop Priced For Any Budget

*Quality controlled hand processing * Blind matched packages* Live stamp affixing * Inserting & labeling * Optimum USPS access from our mid-continent location*

Strategic Mail
* Typed envelopes
* Laser printing
* Data processing services
* Ink jet addressing
* Full lettershop services
* Print production

(Name) Total mailing and computer services

(Name) Printing and mailing with no sales tax

Complete Direct Mail Service
* Mail management and consulting
* Mass mailing - bulk or first class
* Mailing lists to reach your market
* Print supervision and procurement
* Data processing service
* Desktop publishing
* Fulfillment

(Name) Computer Letters - Small mailing specialists

(Name) Automatic labeling - Inserting - Mailing service * Custom hand inserting - Fulfillment

Figure 5-3. Typical lettershop advertisements.

whom you refer clients so that you get referrals in return. That is a form of networking, which should be a welcome addition to your regular marketing activities.

One of the several reasons to have well-designed brochures and capability statements is so that others, your contemporaries or associates, know precisely what your specialties and preferences are and thus are able to refer clients to you when appropriate. There is an old aphorism about the shoemaker's children going barefoot, but today's freelance writer cannot afford to offer prospective clients poorly designed and poorly written promotional materials. Clients may not be able to write well for themselves, but they are sophisticated enough to recognize good and bad writing.

MARKETING MATERIALS

The freelance writer of today must have not only "wordsmithing" tools but also some knowledge of the client's special field. If you are to write marketing materials, for example, you must have at least a rudimentary knowledge of marketing. It is not possible to present anything resembling a complete course in sales and marketing here, but I will present a few basic principles to give you direction.

What People Buy and Why

Marketing is based on a knowledge of what people buy. That is not nearly as simple as it seems, but it is not really complex if you disabuse yourself of conventional wisdom. The conventional thinking is that people buy goods and services because they want them. For example, a woman buys an expensive bracelet because she wants the expensive bracelet. But we must look farther if we are to understand motivation well enough to use it effectively in advertising and marketing. It is true that the bracelet buyer wants the bracelet, but in finding sales motivators it is necessary to dig deeper into the customer's heart. It is necessary to understand *why* she wants the expensive bracelet, the emotional drive of which she may not permit herself to be fully conscious: She wants the sensation or satisfaction of knowing that she is wearing an expensive bracelet and, probably, of being able to show it off to others proudly, perhaps even to make others envious as much as to make herself feel good.

That is an *emotional drive*, not a rational one, and emotion is the principal underlying element in nearly all buying. Whether or not we are conscious of the emotions that shape our rationalizations, they do exist, and successful sales promotions are designed to take advantage of them.

This is not difficult to demonstrate. Study the most successful TV commercials. How do you know which are the "most successful"? Easy: They are the ones repeated over and over and brought back for encore performances even after they have ended. The "Ring Around the Collar" commercial is a classic example. It was based on fear of embarrassment, certainly an emotional drive. When it was discontinued after a lengthy run, sales fell off, so it was brought back for another lengthy run.

On the other hand, millions of humble citizens are swindled every day through advertising that promises more than can be reasonably expected. But they *persuade* themselves to expect the impossible dream anyway because they so badly want to believe in instant success, overnight riches, and other fantasies. Even the best educated and most sophisticated individuals often succumb to promises that are alluring enough to overcome reason.

Thus people generally do not buy what goods and services *are*; they buy what goods and services *do*—or what they are persuaded to believe they will do. And that is the essence of marketing: Promise the result—what buying the product or service will do for the buyer—and provide what the buyer will accept as convincing evidence that the promise is believable and the promiser reliable.

The promise is important; the prospect must know what benefits await, *why* he or she ought to buy what is offered. But the proof is no less important; the prospect needs help in accepting the promise. There are two factors: how badly the prospect wants to believe the promise (i.e., how grandiose the promise is) and how much help the prospect needs to believe the promise (at least partially a factor of how grandiose the promise is).

That granted, there are two basic situations that you must recognize when writing sales copy. If the service or product is a new one, you must explain it to make the promised benefits believable. However, there are services and products that are so well known that they need no explanation. An example is a new diet product. There are enough dieters in the country so that no explanation, other than a cursory one, is needed. Here, the sales message must persuade the prospect that this diet product is better than any other. That requires an explanation of "better." Since probably every reader will accept that the product will work, "better," in this case, ought to mean that it is faster, easier, more comfortable, or otherwise provides some special benefit that competitive products do not provide.

Direct-Marketing Copy

The term *direct marketing* is a broad one, encompassing all marketing that is conducted in a certain fashion. It is aggressive marketing, seeking out prospects, as contrasted with the passive mode of stocking a store and waiting for customers to visit. Technically, the term applies to a wide variety of marketing methods that meet this criterion, but in practice *direct mail* is by far the dominant method. That is, in a nutshell, what many refer to as "junk mail," those thick envelopes that have messages printed boldly on the outside and are stuffed with sales letters, brochures, circulars, coupons, order forms, and return envelopes.

Such packages are used to make sales directly and to generate sales leads for follow-up by other means. In the latter case, the order form is called a "response form" and is a means for determining which recipient should be followed up as a possible sales lead. This enables sellers to turn to direct mail to help sell items that are "big tag" (e.g., automobiles, houses, boats, and some kinds of insurance policies) and would not be purchased as a direct response to the package without follow-up.

Other Kinds of Business Copy

Every organization—profit, nonprofit, government agency, or association—has marketing copy of some kind. All have brochures, for example, explaining what they do and promoting their mission and existence. Many use sales letters, newsletters, item descriptions, catalog sheets, specifications, press releases, product releases, and other promotional materials. These will be described in Chapter 7.

Chapter 6

Individuals as Clients

> You may design writing services to serve the personal needs of individuals, but surprisingly often what seems to be of interest only to individuals proves to be of equal interest to organizations.

INDIVIDUALS AND THEIR NEEDS

I specified earlier that for the purposes of this book the independent entrepreneur operating a one-person business venture would be regarded as an organization because he or she normally has business functions and business needs that are much more like those of the large organization than of the individual. Conversely, some of the services one might normally expect to offer only to individuals prove to have application to the needs of organizations too. Before we probe that in any depth, however, let's consider the ordinary needs of John and Jane Q. Wage-Earner for the services of a professional writer.

RÉSUMÉ SERVICES

The most obvious writing need of the typical wage-earner is for help in writing a résumé, and more and more people are turning to résumé services. Many writers find résumé writing tedious and perhaps boring, but it is honorable work worthy of the effort. Many writers have made a profitable business of a résumé-writing service. Figure 6–1 illustrates just

Resume Service

AZ SELECT SERVICES
2719 Gallows Rd Vienna ----------------560-8293
Ability Group 1511 K St NW ----------------659-7676

ACE TYPING & WORD PROCESSING

RESUMES

- Type-Set Look
- SF-171'S
- Envelope Addressing
- Cover Letters
- Repetitive Letters
- Hand Addressing

WORD PROCESSING

TELEPHONE ANSWERING SERVICE
- TYPING
- LABELS
- EDITING
- PROPOSALS
- THESIS
- RESUMES & 171
- TRANSCRIPTIONS
- REPETITIVE LETTERS
- MAIL RECEIVING
- DISSERTATIONS
- PROOFREADING

OPEN MONDAY-SATURDAY
OPEN SUNDAY BY APPOINTMENT

DISCOUNT FOR STUDENTS

SPECIALIZING IN
LARGE PROJECTS
LARGE VOLUME JOBS
SAME DAY SERVICE

466-TYPE
466-8973

VISA/MC

PARKLAWN BUILDING ROOM 105

2025 I St NW ----------------466-8973

ALTERNATIVE BUSINESS SYSTEMS

● RESUMES ●

- COVER LETTERS
- REPETITIVE LETTERS
- APPLICATIONS
- LAYOUT
- WRITING
- SF 171's

WORD PROCESSOR - IBM SELECTRIC
LANIER ● IBM ● CP/M.● WANG ● DEC
ANSWERING SERVICE AVAILABLE

RUSH SERVICE
AVAILABLE

INDIVIDUAL CONSULTATION
CONFIDENTIALITY ASSURED
Copier On Premises - Student Discounts

Major Credit Cards Accepted

887-0771

2021 L ST NW SUITE 250

American Resume 601 13th St NW ----------------638-6660

AMERICAN RESUME SERVICE

JOB WINNING RESUMES

Expert Writing, Editing, Layout,
Typing/Typesetting

- **Resumes/Letters** ● SF 171's
- **Mailing Campaigns ● Military Conversions**
- **Business Proposals & Reports**
- **Same Day Printing**
  FREE CONSULTATION ● JOB GUIDANCE

7676 New Hamphire Av
Langley Park Md----------------434-1941
467 N Frederick Ave Gaithersburg Md--921-9350
515 Wythe St Oldtown Alex Va ----------------548-2171
6049 Leesburg Pk
Baileys X-Rds/Skyline Va ----------------845-9844
2025 I St NW Wash DC----------------293-5587

AVENTURE SERVICES
1725 K St NW ----------------**331-0085**

CAREER CONNECTIONS

A PROFESSIONAL RESUME SERVICE
- 171 FORMS
- MASS MAILINGS
- WORD PROCESSING
  AUDIO RESUMES
  CAREER CONNECTIONS
  A BETTER RESUME
9-5 DAILY   EVES. APPT

4853 Cordell Av Beth----------------656-2107

Career Resume Service 3355 Lenox Rd
Atlanta Ga----Washington Tel No--371-0017
CHALLENGE INC
2000 Century Plaza Columbia----------------**995-6054**

Figure 6–1. Typical résumé-service advertising.

81

a few résumé writers' advertisements in the Washington, DC, area, which are typical of other metropolitan areas as well.

Résumé writing has always been a relatively easy service to launch, with little investment and modest overhead. It is even easier today if you are equipped with a computer and a good 24-pin dot-matrix printer or, better yet, a laser printer and a copier. Even then the investment need not be excessive. You can equip an office in your home with all the equipment you need to turn out professional-looking résumés for a few thousand dollars. My own office, grown more complete over the years with a late-model computer, laser printer, dot-matrix printer, copier, fax machine, large spread of software, and sundry other accessories, represents less than $10,000 total investment. (That investment was made gradually, from a modest beginning with an improvised desk in a corner of a bedroom and a somewhat weary electric typewriter.) It is possible to make an excellent start for a great deal less than $10,000. You can buy a basic computer (that will be expandable) and a serviceable 24-pin printer for well under $1,000 today, and you do not need to have a modem immediately. Neither do you need to have your own fax machine, copier, and other accessories immediately. In fact, it is often beneficial to wait since prices for this type of equipment have been going down as the technology has become more widespread.

There is excellent résumé-writing software available also—software that enables you to produce at least a dozen different kinds of résumés, depending on your clients' needs. Listings of appropriate hardware and software will be offered later. Figures 6–2, 6–3, and 6–4 illustrate just a few of the many formats and typefaces available with résumé-writing software. (These were prepared with Spinnaker's Better Working Resume Kit software, a surprisingly inexpensive program.) Such programs offer a variety of fonts (typefaces) and formats (which you may customize as you please), and usually include facilities such as a word processor for preparing cover letters and even a mailing-list manager to print out envelopes or labels. Properly equipped, you can offer your clients a complete service, even printing dozens of copies of the résumé with your own equipment. For short printing runs, modern laser printers and office copiers are almost as efficient as a small offset press, and they are a great deal more convenient to use.

Résumé writing is profitable. Many résumé writers work at home, keeping overhead low and, at the same time, writing off part of their household expenses. Others maintain offices in commercial locations. There are two major expenses of operating such a business: One is overhead—rent, advertising, equipment depreciation, and incidentals—

Charles Bytesmith

112 Hardisk Avenue   Computer Programmer
Silicon, MA 02111
617-555-5555

GEOGRAPHICAL   Prefer local assignment (New England) but will consider any
REQUIREMENTS   location in U.S.

POSITION   Prefer scientific, statistical, engineering programming applications
OBJECTIVE   but will consider others.

GENERAL   I have limited working experience but have had broad and diverse
SUMMARY   formal and informal education in computers and related
                      applications. See education section for details.

BUSINESS
EXPERIENCE

                      Munificent Insurance Corporation, Cherry Hill, MA
                      Computer Depaertment
                      Keypunch Operator
                      Summer job, 1988, 1989

                      Janes Department Store, Pussywillow Hill, MA
                      Billing Department
                      Posting clerk
                      Summer job 1987. Posted to general ledger.

EDUCATION

                      Worthington University, Worthington, NH
                      BA Computer Science in Computer Sciences, 1990
                      Minor: English Composition
                      Courses included Discrete Probability Theory, Systems Analysis &
                      Design, Advanced Systems Management, Technical Report Writing,
                      Digital Computer Techniques.

REFERENCES   Professor George Wickersham, at the University.

                      Martin Balancesheet, Computer Systems Manager, Munificent
                      Insurance Corp.

                      Morris Weisskopf, Comptroller, Janes Department Store.

Figure 6–2.   Conventional résumé format.

which ought to be modest if you plan carefully. The other major expense is labor—your own salary, primarily, although you may soon get busy enough to require help.

Prices charged for résumé writing vary enormously. There are some who use the "bait-and-switch" tactics of offering "a complete résumé" for an unrealistically low price of $7.00 or $9.00. If pressed hard to make good on the advertised price, the operator of such a service will explain that this

HERMAN HOLTZ

P.O. Box 1731   Engineering Manager &
Wheaton, MD 20915   Marketing Director
301 649-2499
Fax: 301 649-5745

EXPERIENCE

1974 to   *Technical Sciences Corp.*, New York, NY
1988   **Manager Technical Publications**
                   Wrote proposals, leading proposal teams and managing production.
                   Developed estimates of technical publications contract requirements,
                   negotiated contracts, managed projects in technical documentation.

1959 to   *Manayunk Electronics, Inc.*, Philadelphia, PA
1973   **Design Engineer**
                   Developed communications equipment and laboratory test equipment;
                   built and tested; prototypes and production models; wrote tabular parts
                   lists, manuals, reports; made "first item" presentations to military
                   customers.

PROFESSIONAL
SKILLS

Engineering   • Lead design team of 12 engineers, 2 drafters, 2 technical writers.
Management   • Supervise wll work directly.
                   • Develop engineering and production prototypes.

Marketing   • Review leads and make bid/no-bid decisions.
                   • Lead staff in brainstorming sessions to conceive and plan proposal
                     responses.
                   • Personally participate in all proposal development.

Management   • Hire staff, all levels.
                   • Issue invoices to customers
                   • Handle all internal administrative matters

EDUCATION

                   Capital Institute of Technology, Washington, DC
                   BSEE in Electrical Engineering, 1958
                   Minor: Technical writing

REFERENCES   Available upon request

Figure 6–3.   A few flourishes added to the conventional
                   résumé format.

Millicent Zimmer

3445 Banknote Avenue
Securities, PA 17888
717 555-5555

OBJECTIVE

Banking position in consumer loans

EXPERIENCE

1988 to 1990

Midwestern Trust Co., Littletown, OH
Loan Counselor
I explained the various types of loans to applicants, discussed their needs, and made recommendations. I also helped them make out their applications and added my recommendations to the loan committee. Forced to resign when my husband was transferred.

1982 to 1988

Steeltown Savings & Trust Co.
Steeltown, PA
Chief Teller
Started as teller trainee, advanced to Chief Teller. Duties then included supervising all tellers, training new hires with lectures, demonstrations, and OJT. Forced to leave when my husband was transferred to Ohio.

EDUCATION

Pennsylvania Technology Institute
Midtown, PA
B.A. in Business Administration, 1982
Minor: Accounting

Figure 6–4.   Using attention-getting fonts in a résumé.

small fee covers only the typing of the customer's own copy and is limited to one page in whatever the operator says is his or her "standard format." More realistically, résumés are generally priced at $65 and up, depending on many variables. That normally includes formatting, light editing or minor rewriting, and perhaps a dozen copies. Whether the base price includes complete writing or rewriting of the original résumé is up to you. You can offer a package price to include this service or make it an extra service to be charged separately. Writing a cover letter to accompany a résumé can be included in the package price or charged separately depending on your marketing strategy. Making these services available only as extras, for additional fees, permits you to advertise a more modest figure as the basic price, whereas making up a package of services permits you to advertise "complete service." Each strategy has its merits.

Getting Repeat Business

Advertising expense is a major overhead cost if you must depend on getting a new customer for each sale. Although most people do not have frequent need for résumés, it *is* possible to get repeat business from résumé customers. And repeat business is profitable because no advertising dollars must be spent to get it. One way to ensure a certain amount of repeat business is to store each résumé and letter on a floppy disk so that you can re-enter it into your computer's memory and offer revision and/or updating services at reduced prices. Be sure that your customers are aware that it is in their interest to update and improve their résumés periodically and that you are keeping their computer files stored safely for future use. Also, put each customer on your mailing list.

There are some other ways to expand your business base.

A Special Tip

Many job seekers need more than one résumé because they have many qualifications and can work in more than one career specialty. They should be counseled to maintain a great deal of flexibility in their job seeking. For example, an engineer may have experience as a design engineer, a maintenance engineer, a technical writer, or an expert in another specialty, and thus can seek more than one kind of work, depending on what job opportunities are open. This requires having a different résumé for each specialty. (One engineer I knew had 12 résumés!) As a résumé writer you are expected to be expert enough to counsel clients, and you should be aware of this both as a service your clients expect and as a means of increasing your business. Counseling clients is an extra service, which makes your service more valuable over all, adds to your profits, and can be a basis for diversification and expansion into ancillary services. Counseling can take more than one form, as you will see in the following examples.

Ancillary Services

Even if you specialize in résumé writing and you advertise that service only, expansion from that base is easily possible. Some clients will be interested in retaining you for other writing services, so it is not amiss to let every client and prospective client know that you can provide other writing services. In the classified advertising section of a recent *Washington Post*, for example, there were two advertisements under the heading "Typing and Word Processing Services" that recognize this truth:

SAME DAY—Letters, résumés, etc.

(telephone number)

RÉSUMÉS—Letters, reports, etc.

On PC. Low rates. (telephone number)

Another, advertising in the "Employment Services" section under the major headline "Résumés," presents the subheading "Professional Résumé & Writing Service."

Some résumé writers expand in a different direction, offering additional job-seeking services. One uses the advertising subheading "FREE Consultation/Placement Services." Another advertises as follows:

FREE
Printing, free job search, free consulting
w/any résumé, cover letter. Starting at $30.
(telephone number)

Others offer mass mailing of résumés to "100's of employers nationwide" for $29.95, stipulating that this service is free if they prepare the client's résumé. If you are equipped with a modern computer system and suitable ancillary hardware and software, it is not difficult to set up a simple database to automate your mailing (e.g., printing labels or doing "mail merge" printing) and provide such a service. (Mail merge is a capability of modern word processors to merge names from a mailing list with a form letter and print out a copy of the letter addressed individually to each individual on the list. Those million-dollar Publisher's Clearinghouse letters you get from Ed McMahon are one example of merge mailing.)

Résumé Writing for Business Organizations

You might think that résumé writing is a service that only individuals will be interested in buying. In fact, that is not true. There are organizations such as employment agencies or employment counseling services that might retain you to write résumés for their clients. Perhaps you are actually providing the service to the individual, with the employment agency acting merely as a conduit or broker (i.e., charging their client a retail price while paying you a wholesale or discounted price). On the other hand, perhaps the organization is, in fact, paying for the résumé. It doesn't matter to you; if you are billing the organization for the work, the organization is your customer. As an example, a placement and counseling service once retained me to write an instruction brochure on résumé writing to give to their clients. Later, they retained me to conduct résumé-writing and job-seeking seminars for their clients.

There are a growing number of corporations in all fields that see it as their obligation to ease the departure of employees they must lay off in slack periods. Among the services such corporations provide is help in finding new jobs. Some even retain management consultants who specialize in counseling employees about to be let go or "furloughed" indefinitely. These corporations or consulting firms may be interested in providing résumé-writing assistance or any of the other services referred to here.

LETTER WRITING

A few hundred years ago, the public scribe was a common figure because relatively few ordinary folk were literate. They turned to the public scribe to read their letters and prepare responses. Times have changed less than you might imagine in this regard: Writers offering general letter-writing services to the public have often been surprised by the enthusiastic response. At least one writer, a Chicago woman seeking only to create a part-time enterprise, hastily canceled her small classified advertisement in a local newspaper because the response began to overwhelm her almost immediately. Don't underestimate this market for writing services. Even though most people are literate today, even some of the best educated among us have an aversion to writing. Being a modern public scribe can still be a profitable function of a writing venture.

Rates for this kind of service vary. Some writers establish a flat per-page rate. That does not make a great deal of sense to me. In my own experience in writing letters for clients I have found that the time required to complete the job varies a great deal. The job requires discussion with the client to gain an understanding of his or her need, and the amount of time required for that can vary widely. I would suggest establishing a minimum charge of $10 and estimating each job independently or charging by the hour beyond that minimum. The clients you attract are not illiterates, although occasionally one may prove to be literally incapable of writing. They are mostly individuals with a normal basic education who shrink from writing for one of two reasons. First, many people simply dislike writing. I suspect that many just do not want to make the effort to think things through and compose their thoughts, and writing does require analysis and organization of thought. There are also many individuals who simply fear that they cannot cope with the problems that they must address or explain themselves well in writing. For example, one man, a city employee, came to me because he thought he had been treated unjustly by his superior in being denied a promotion he felt he merited, and the civil service commission of his city did not support him in his initial appeal. He felt that the commission did not understand the facts, and he wanted to write to them explaining those facts as an additional appeal. I charged him what I thought was quite a modest $35 (it would be twice that in today's dollars) to write a letter of appeal and $25 for a follow-up letter he needed later. Happily, he prevailed in his appeal.

The second reason why many people shrink from writing is that they need help in dealing with bureaucracies or large organizations. One New York man made a successful business of helping individuals cope with such problems as getting licenses, chasing down records such as birth certificates and recorded deeds, and straightening out difficulties of various kinds involving officialdom in government or any other large bureaucracy. Most of his services involved writing letters, filling out forms, making telephone calls, and advising clients on procedures. *Caution:* If you enter into this kind of service, be sure to avoid giving legal advice unless you happen to be a lawyer. That is against the law. But there is a fine distinction to be made. Only a licensed lawyer can give a client advice about the law with regard to the client's own circumstances. However, anyone can explain the law or some legal procedure; that is not giving legal advice. For example, it would be a violation to prepare a client's application for incorporation, but it is not a violation for anyone to prepare his or her own documents of incorporation. It is not illegal to give someone general information on how to go about applying for or preparing documents of incorporation or even to provide "John Doe" samples of such papers, as long as the client fills out his or her own papers and files them! It is a fine distinction, perhaps, but the law is the law, and you need no license to offer special training or instruction in how to do legal work.

SPEECHWRITING

Since delivering speeches is a PR activity, speechwriting might be categorized as one of the skills of writers specializing in PR. In any case, speechwriting is a highly specialized art. To write speeches effectively, you should be able to "hear" the words and phrases as you draft them. Some writers naturally have that "ear" for the written word as it will be vocalized; others must work hard at developing it; and some never succeed in doing so. The speechwriting client is always an individual, in a sense, for a speech is always delivered by an individual. And it is the individual who finds himself or herself obligated to make a speech at the next convention of the local medical association or meat-packing institute who needs help. Most such individuals are not well suited to write their own speeches.

Despite this, probably the larger and more profitable market for speechwriting lies in the business and professional world. Speechwriting is among the most lucrative of writing assignments according to experienced freelance writer Bob Bly (*Secrets of a Freelance Writer*, Gamut Books, 1988). The major market for speechwriters is public officials, top-level executives, prominent educators, and other professionals. But, as Bly points out, elected officials tend to have their own speechwriters on staff, and executives in many organizations—small businesses and nonprofit organizations, for example—either do not have the budget to pay well or fail to appreciate the importance of and the effort required to create an effective speech. He therefore concludes, with some justification, that the large corporation represents the cream of the speechwriting market and is thus the market to address.

Speechwriting can be lucrative indeed. Writing an average 20-minute speech, which means about 2,000 words or eight double-spaced pages, should be worth at least $2,000 or $3,000, according to Bly, although some expert speechwriters get as much as $5,000 for such a speech. Fees rise proportionately for speeches of greater length, as well as in proportion to your own reputation, the demand for your speechwriting services, and the prominence or importance of the client for whom you are writing the speech.

It should be obvious that speechwriting requires working closely with the presenter. You may have a good ear for the text, and you may even read it aloud to verify that it flows and does not contain verbal boobytraps, but the presenter must check it for himself or herself. Speaking is highly individual. Your client may be uncomfortable or have difficulty with expressions that trip easily from your own lips. That usually requires getting together to iron out problems and make suitable revisions.

You can begin to see now that the fees cited earlier are not manna from heaven, but are honestly earned. Obviously, you will rarely be able to command fees of this magnitude from individuals preparing to address the monthly meeting of the Podunk Gardening Society. You will probably do some of those occasionally as *pro bono* contributions or for modest fees as part of your own continuing education in writing. It is not shameful to do so, as long as you acknowledge to yourself the reasons for doing so, but ultimately, you must school yourself in demanding the proper fees for such work.

STUDENT AND PROFESSIONAL PAPERS

Individuals need papers of various kinds at various times. Professionals, whether independent practitioners or employees of organizations, often belong to societies and are invited to prepare, submit, and present papers at annual symposia and conventions. Many, quite brilliant in their own technologies and disciplines, need editorial help in organizing and refining their papers for coherence in print and verbal presentation even before their peers. This need is even more urgent when an expert must try to explain what he or she does to a lay audience.

Both graduate and undergraduate students also need editorial help with their term papers, theses, and dissertations. In both cases, you may run into a moral dilemma: How much and what kind of help can you give and remain honest and ethical? In the case of the professional, the problem does not arise very often. Generally, the client has already drafted the paper and your work is clearly defined as editing and possibly some rewriting. (The line between "heavy editing" and "rewriting" is not well defined, however. You must set it arbitrarily for yourself.) The case of the student, especially that of the graduate student, is more troublesome.

Unfortunately—or perhaps fortunately, from a selfish point of view— academia in general appears to place as much weight on the form and format of students' papers as on the content and substance, although logic tells us that the emphasis ought to be reversed. I have been shocked at how insistent committees can be on formatting a paper to conform precisely to the most minute details of some commercial specification, while they all but disregard the quality of the content. Therefore, it is my opinion that the client ought to be solely responsible for content and substance, but it is perfectly moral for you to assume responsibility for form and format—purely editorial matters. If you keep this firmly in mind, you should have no problems of conscience. If you happen to be situated near a college campus, especially one offering graduate courses, you might well consider this kind of editorial work. However, graduate students do not necessarily work on their theses and dissertations while on campus. They often write these papers long after they have completed their course work, so you may very well find a market for this service anywhere and at any time of year.

In pricing this kind of work you have the usual dilemma of whether to charge for your time or for the job. I generally charged a fee of between $250 and $500 a dozen years ago; the prices must be adjusted for today's economy, probably about double those figures.

GHOSTWRITING

In many professions, publishing is an important tool for building a reputation and standing out from the crowd: In fact, for professionals in education the expression "publish or perish" is a serious one: Attainment of a full professorship and tenure is at stake. Publishing of any kind, including formal papers, books, and articles, is gratifying to a person's ego, but career success is also at stake, making it a serious business.

Clients seeking ghostwriting services to satisfy personal needs are thus as abundant as those seeking ghostwriting services to satisfy business needs. Both classes of clients want you to ghost papers, articles, and books for them to help them satisfy personal, career, and business goals. Your job is to write the article (Bob Bly recommends charging about $1 per word) but the client is responsible for having it published. Be sure the client understands this clearly. You cannot guarantee publication and should never suggest that you can.

Some executives and professionals who have reached a degree of prominence hire writers to ghost autobiographies for them. The late Willard Marriott, Sr., had his autobiography ghosted and sold it in his restaurants. Former Ford executive and now Chrysler CEO Lee Iacocca had writer William Novak write his autobiography. This was not truly ghosted, because Novak's name appeared on the cover, for which Novak was paid a reported $50,000. As in the case of magazine articles, getting such a book published is the client's responsibility, not yours, and you must make it plain that you assume no responsibility for publication. Of course, Iacocca had no problem finding an eager publisher, and Marriott had the means of distribution and could thus afford to publish the book himself.

Many less famous individuals who have what they think is a story of Pulitzer Prize stature seek a ghostwriter to write it for them. You will see frequent classified advertisements seeking writers to do this. In most cases the story is rather ordinary, but if the client insists on having it written and is willing to pay a reasonable price for it, why pass it up? However, I recommend that you have a clear understanding that you will be paid for your work in some clearly specified sum of cash, not in a promise of a percentage of the royalties (a most uncertain prospect!), and that you get a substantial advance as a retainer and progress payments as work proceeds. If you cannot get agreement on this, it will be a risky proposition for you. (I suggest a great deal of caution in considering doing anything "on spec." Most such propositions I have encountered are losing propositions for the writer, and I lost a great deal of money before I lost the naiveté that led me into such traps.)

MISCELLANEOUS NEEDS

The needs of individuals are not any more predictable than the needs of organizations. Individuals, whether they represent their personal needs or those of their organizations, will surprise you often with requests for services you could not have anticipated and might never have considered as part of the set of services you normally provide. This is increasingly the case as your name becomes known and word of mouth becomes a factor in your marketing. If you manage to raise your visibility generally through bylined articles in magazines and other means to be explored in Chapter 8, strangers will seek you out with work projects. Many of these requests are time-wasters, and many writers simply brush them off or ignore them. It is my own policy to respond to all serious correspondence (excluding computer-generated sales letters that purport to be addressed to me personally) promptly and to respond to all telephone calls courteously. Probably most do not produce five cents worth of income for me, but I believe that common courtesy mandates my response. Moreover, once in a while such inquiries do produce income, directly or indirectly. A few examples follow.

My name is known to many people today as a writer of books published by the major book publishers. I get frequent calls from strangers as a result, and occasionally such a call results in a work assignment. One woman called me from California to seek my advice regarding a book she and her husband were writing on a technical subject. She subsequently sent me a copy of the publishing contract they were offered and wanted me to review it, as a consultant, and advise her. I reviewed the contract and wrote her my recommendations for a suitable fee—$100 in this case. (That kind of work is what a literary agent normally does for his or her clients.)

An individual wishing to enter the mail-order business with a small training manual as his first product retained me to write the manual. It was about 20 double-spaced pages on a subject I knew so well that I did not need to do any but the most cursory research. It was thus a profitable task at $500.

A Michigan consultant, Steve W., called to solicit my support for a program he envisioned. The worthiness to me in income was uncertain at best, but I agreed to give the proposition fair consideration should it develop. It never did, but Steve and I spoke a number of times over the next year or two. Ultimately, Steve recommended me for a proposal-writing project in San Antonio that netted me over $6,000 for six days' work.

Chapter 7

Samples, Models, and How-Tos

A well-known Chinese proverb says that a picture is worth a thousand words. Here, to serve as "pictures" for our purposes, are a few "for instances," along with some explanations.

VARYING LEVELS OF DIFFICULTY

Some of the writing and related services referred to in the previous pages call for special skills or training. Despite the exceptions pointed out earlier, it is clear that it would be difficult to write a technical manual presenting a set of maintenance instructions for a radar set without a good knowledge of electronics and maintenance practices. On the other hand, it is not difficult for the professional writer to learn how to write a release, a newsletter, or many other custom materials that do not call for detailed technical knowledge. Some materials that fall between the extremes do require some special skills or knowledge (advertising and direct-mail writers are specialists of a kind, for example), but usually those skills can be mastered with a bit of effort and experience. In this chapter you will find how-to explanations and, more important, "for instances"—samples and models illustrating the how-to of advertising and direct-mail writing with both good and bad examples. These will also serve you as memory refreshers and references for the future.

UNDERSTANDING MARKETING

Marketing appears to be simple and easy to master. One need only learn by observation, needn't one? Don't we all see and hear enough advertising, sales, and related marketing activity to be familiar with the common practices?

One problem with that idea is that we all see and hear a great deal of abysmal marketing, as well as much that is excellent. How can the layperson discriminate between good and bad models? That is, how can you avoid emulating the bad models, which tend to outnumber the good models by a wide margin?

A brief explanation of advertising/sales strategy and rationale was presented in Chapter 5 and earlier chapters. Although an in-depth treatment of copywriting is beyond the scope of this book, you must understand the basic principle of selling what a product or service *does* (its most important benefit to the buyer), rather than what it *is* (grandiose claims of quality, greatness, etc). Selling the product or service means promising that benefit and validating the promise with some evidence that the product or service can and will make good on it. Be sure that you select the most important benefit as your main point. *Most important* refers to the customer's sense of what is important, not to your own. The right benefit is the one that strikes a nerve with the customer.

Look for these elements in all copy, whether it is print, TV, direct mail, or any other type. You can get a great education in copywriting by doing just that. Ask yourself two main questions whenever you study an advertisement of any kind:

1. What does this advertisement promise to *do* for me?

2. What proof does it offer that the promise is valid?

The Kurse of Kleverness in Ad Kopy

A current advertisement for the Buick® automobile, placed in periodicals read by computer users, is headlined "FREE DISK DRIVE." Not satisfied with that bad pun, the copy goes on to produce an even more labored one by referring to "trunk-loads of information" about their new models that the reader will find on the free computer disk the advertisement offers.

Let's test this copy according to the simple two-question test:

1. The promise is of a free disk. The computer user will wonder for a moment, "Why 'disk drive'?" but will soon realize that the inaccuracy of the promise (it is a free disk, not a free disk drive that is offered) was deliberate to drag the pun in by the ears. If you dig into the copy, you find that the disk also has a computer golf game on it, so the promise buried in the text includes that of a free computer game.

2. There is really no need for proof in this case. Instructions for getting the disk are given, there is no risk involved, and there is no reason to doubt that the company will keep its word and send the disk to anyone requesting it.

It isn't a very compelling advertisement, is it? (In all fairness, however, it is *inquiry advertising* and thus doesn't try to sell anything except access to more advertising via a free disk on the inquirer's computer.) The advertiser has fallen prey to the worst disease of copywriters, a disease I like to call special attention to by spelling it "Kleverness." Some copywriters delight in "klever kopy," which usually depends on a pun or other double entendre. Bad enough as a form of humor that many people find slightly offensive or at least in boringly bad taste, klever kopy distracts the copywriter from the real task of selling: He or she usually tends to sacrifice good advertising practice—a sound sales argument—for the sake of cleverness. Watch for this in advertising you see and hear, and note how often it occurs.

Tombstone Advertising

Figure 7–1 offers an example of what some people refer to as "tombstone ads," which they often resemble physically, as well as substantively. The real significance of the term, however, lies in the fact that these ads do not really do much selling; they simply make unadorned announcements with the weakest of promises, usually implied rather than expressed. Imagine that the Mountain Springs Water copy actually read "Here Lies Mountain Springs Water." It wouldn't be much different from the way it is now, would it? Its implied promise is expressed as "When you care about what you drink," which might be used just as effectively to plug whiskey or anything else that can be imbibed. The other ads make equally weak sales appeals. "A design that complements your home" may have meaning to the advertiser, but it doesn't say much to the reader. The CPA

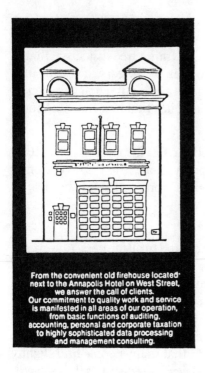

Figure 7–1.   A few tombstone ads.

firm appears to be conscious of the need to present a highly conserva-
tive image in its ad, but it has gone out of its way to make its message
exceptionally stiff and formal (as well as slightly ungrammatical). The
fine print copy is reproduced here because you may not be able to make
it out in the figure:

> Our commitment to quality work and service is manifested in all areas of
> our operation, from basic functions of auditing, accounting, personal
> and corporate taxation, to highly sophisticated data processing and
> management consulting.

It would not take much to convert some of this nonadvertising and nonsalesmanship to something more effective. Take the phrase "When you care about what you drink," for example. Think about what it implies and express that implication so that it is a statement, something *specified*, and not a cryptic hint. Even the simple change to "When you care about your health" is a vast improvement. Even better is "When you care about guarding your health." Or "When you want to be sure that the water you drink is only water."

"A design that complements your home" presents a more difficult problem because not everyone is sure what "complements" means, much less what it implies. How could anyone translate those words as promising a benefit? The copy would be much more effective if it made a specific promise to beautify the reader's home, increase its value, make it the envy of friends and relatives, or make it the outstanding home on the street. These are just a few of the possibilities.

The third piece of copy needs revolutionary change. It doesn't even imply a benefit to the customer. The author of that copy needs to do some serious thinking about what the firm has to offer that is special and likely to motivate the customer. If the firm is a long-established one and/or handles some major accounts, a possible theme might be evidence of solid dependability. If it is a small firm, the promise of the personal touch, dealing directly with the principals in the firm, might be an attractive prospect to the reader.

Bear in mind that there are two classes of motivation, fear and greed. That is, people are motivated by the fear of loss and by the prospect of gain. Some products and services are best sold by one or the other. For example, insurance and security devices are naturals for fear motivation, while investment services and bonds are naturals for gain motivation. However, a sales argument for almost anything can be based on either fear or greed.

Tombstone advertising is by no means confined to print. The same weakness is found in radio and TV commercials, signs, direct mail, and press releases.

DIRECT MARKETING

Direct marketing (DM) is a generic term used almost interchangeably with the term *direct mail*. That is because the direct-marketing industry in general *is* direct mail: Direct mail dominates the DM industry by virtue of being the dominant means of seeking out prospective customers aggressively and directly. Direct mail calls for the skills of the writer to create the literature to be mailed. That literature may include any of the following items:

Sales letters	Return envelopes	Testimonials
Brochures	Releases	Certifications
Pamphlets	Catalog sheets	Specifications
Leaflets	Article reprints	Business cards
Broadsides	Report reprints	Advertising novelties
Order forms		

Of course, no direct-mail package is going to include all of these. The obligatory items that conventional wisdom says should be in all DM packages as a minimum include a sales letter, a brochure, an order form, and a return envelope.

The sales letter is the centerpiece of the package. It is addressed, either directly or by implication, to the prospective customer, and it presents the proposition. It may be a single page or several pages. The brochure reinforces and adds to the message. The order form should be either a completely separate piece (preferably) or easily detached from the letter, brochure, or other enclosure. The return envelope should accommodate the order form without difficulty. (In some packages, the reader must figure out how to fold the order form along both its dimensions to get it into the envelope provided. That's bad planning and bad marketing.) The return envelope should be postage paid so the customer does not have to find a stamp.

The "no postage required" variety of return envelope, also known as *Business Reply Mail* or as "BRE" (for Business Reply Envelope) is a legitimate use of advertising dollars when sending direct mail to individuals in their homes. However, in business-to-business DM, it has been my experience that the return envelope is a waste. Most businesspeople do not use the envelope when they order, but turn the order over to a clerk or secretary to address and send out in the company's own envelope.

The Sales Letter

The premise underlying the DM package is that the recipient will read the sales letter first. Therefore, the sales letter ought to be introductory, explaining immediately what the proposition is and providing the motivator. All of the other elements of the package are ancillary, intended to support the message of the letter. Figure 7–2 is one example of a sales letter. It has all the basic elements. However, many direct-mail writers use a special technique with sales letters: They add comments and other emphasis in handwritten bold strokes, often in another color (see Figure 7–3). This, however, smacks of high-pressure selling tactics, and many marketers shun it. It may be appropriate to some kinds of propositions, but not to all.

I recently received a DM package from the country's principal cataloger of airline schedules, the *Official Airlines Guide*. Immediately under the company's name and logo at the head of the sales letter is an announcement in small type advising the reader that this letter is from the desk of Larry G. Honeywell, President.

That bothers me immediately. I agree with H. L. Mencken, the noted writer and late editor of the *Baltimore Sun*, in this. He refused to respond to memoranda and letters headed with "From the desk of. . . . " He said that he never corresponded with office furniture. I, too, think that correspondence ought to be to and from people, not furniture.

Aside from that, the letter addresses me as "Dear World Traveller" (sic). That bothers me too. Except for occasional business trips to Canada, I have not been out of the country since World War II. I am hardly a "world traveler." I know immediately that the letter and whatever it is selling are not for me. That is the second strike against this package, and I won't read beyond that salutation. Had the letter addressed me as "Dear Traveler," I would have read on; I do fly around the country a bit. It makes me wonder how many readers were turned off the way I was with a salutation that said, "Don't bother reading this if you are not a *world* traveler. We are not interested in you if you travel only in this country."

Perhaps this goes just a bit beyond the bounds of writing *per se* and verges into direct-mail strategy. However, if you are going to write direct-mail materials, it is necessary to understand the strategies. The ability to handle the language to express others' ideas is not enough; it is necessary to manage the content of the package. Your clients will hold you accountable for the success or failure of the package.

One of the myths about sales letters is that they must be addressed to someone. With today's technology, even a small office with a modest desktop computer can run mail-merge programs that print form letters addressing individuals by name. Before this became so easy to do, most DM packages included sales letters addressed to anonymous recipients.

EXCELSIOR ELECTRONICS, INC.
4222 Lincoln Drive   Pleasantville, OH 44444

**Never again a forgotten and burned roast or spoiled dish with this fantastic
new Cook's Helper: It takes the guesswork out of cooking and minds it for you.
(It's an AM/FM radio, kitchen clock, and alarm clock too!)**

The computer age brings this fantastic new high-tech unit to you. It minds the kitchen for
you while you are busy doing other things. You can even have the built-in radio play your
favorite music while the Cook's Helper keeps track of things and signals you when time's up.

AVAILABLE IN DECORATOR COLORS
This beautiful, compact unit is available in 7 decorator colors (white, yellow, red, blue,
green, orange, and beige). It can be placed on a counter top or fastened conveniently to the
underside of one of your kitchen cabinets or on a wall, using the special easy-mount brackets
included. It is only 4 x 5 x 8 inches; it needs practically no space, even in small kitchens. Yet
it is so modern and attractively styled that your friends will all want to know where you got it.

IT HAS FEATURES GALORE
Among its many features is a means for adjusting the kind and intensity of the signal it sends
when time is up. That is adjustable from a subtle chiming note to an insistent ring or buzz.
You can also use the timer to turn the radio on or off automatically at some future time. It also
has its own outlet that you can use to turn another appliance on or off at some preset time--to
start your coffee in the morning, for example.

FANTASTIC DISCOUNT PRICE
This is the hottest item offered in years. Supplies will not last long at the low-low price
we've set: This item was built to sell for $49.95, but we've persuaded the manufacturer to
help us introduce this new item at a special price. If you act within the next 21 days, you can
have your own Cook's Helper (only two to a customer at this price) for only $29.95.

BONUS FREE GIFTS YOURS TO KEEP
Even that is not all the good news. If your order is received within 10 days you will get two
gifts: A set of aluminum measuring spoons and a mystery gift, also useful in the kitchen.
Moreover, this unit is sold with a 100-percent money-back guarantee. You can return it within
two weeks for full refund, and you keep the free gifts.
Obviously, you can't go wrong here, no matter what you do, for our ironclad money-back
guarantee protects you completely. But you must act NOW to be sure of getting your own
Cook's Helper at this price

FAST ACTION IS A MUST
Just fill out the handy order form enclosed and get it in the mail with your check, money
order, or credit card number for immediate delivery of this marvelous new labor saver. Be
sure to tell us what color you want while we still have a complete selection of colors available.

Cordially,

Ben Carter, President

Figure 7–2.   A typical sales letter.

EXCELSIOR ELECTRONICS, INC.

4222 Lincoln Drive   Pleasantville, OH 44444

Never again a forgotten and burned roast or spoiled dish with this fantastic new Cook's Helper: It takes the guesswork out of cooking and minds it for you. (It's an AM/FM radio, kitchen clock, and alarm clock too!)
nothing like it anywhere.

The computer age brings this <u>fantastic new unit to you</u>. It minds the kitchen for you while you are busy doing other things. You can even have the built-in radio play your favorite music while the Cook's Helper keeps track of things and signals you when time's up.

AVAILABLE IN DECORATOR COLORS

This beautiful, compact unit is available in 7 decorator colors (white, yellow, red, blue, green, orange, and beige). It can be placed on a counter top or fastened conveniently to the underside of one of your kitchen cabinets or on a wall, using the special easy-mount brackets included. It is only 4 x 5 x 8 inches; it needs practically no space, even in small kitchens. Yet it is so modern and attractively styled that <u>your friends will all want to know where you got it.</u>

IT HAS FEATURES GALORE

Among its many features is a means for adjusting the kind and intensity of the signal it sends when time is up. That is adjustable from a subtle chiming note to an insistent ring or buzz. You can also use the timer to turn the radio on or off automatically at some future time. It also has its own outlet that you can use to turn another appliance on or off at some preset time--to start your coffee in the morning, for example.

FANTASTIC DISCOUNT PRICE

This is the hottest item offered in years. Supplies will not last long at the low-low price we've set: This item was built to sell for $49.95, but we've persuaded the manufacturer to help us introduce this new item at a special price. If you act within the next 21 days, you can have your own Cook's Helper (only two to a customer at this price) for only $29.95. *Limited time offer*

BONUS FREE GIFTS YOURS TO KEEP   *Bonus!*

Even that is not all the good news. If your order is received within 10 days <u>you will get two gifts</u>: A set of aluminum measuring spoons and a mystery gift, also useful in the kitchen. Moreover, this unit is sold with a 100-percent money-back guarantee. You can return it within two weeks for full refund, and you keep the free gifts.

Obviously, you can't go wrong here, no matter what you do, for our ironclad money-back guarantee protects you completely. But you must act NOW to be sure of getting your own Cook's Helper at this price

FAST ACTION IS A MUST

Just fill out the handy order form enclosed and get it in the mail with your check, money order, or credit card number for immediate delivery of this marvelous new labor saver. Be sure to tell us what color you want while we still have a complete selection of colors available.

Cordially,

Ben Carter

Ben Carter, President

Figure 7–3. An enhanced sales letter.

Even now there are sales letters that bear addresses such as the following:

Dear World Traveler:

Dear Friend: (the most frequent salutation)

Dear Subscriber:

Dear Marketer: (the second most frequent salutation)

Dear Planner:

Dear Entrepreneur:

There are a few sales letters without salutation of any kind. They just plunge directly into the message. I find them no less appealing for their lack of a salutation; in fact, they may be *more* appealing because the generic salutations ring so falsely hearty, almost patronizing. I have experimented with this in my own mailings, and I could find no significant difference resulting from using or failing to use a salutation of any kind. My vote is for skipping the salutation unless you are going to use the mail-merge approach with real names. But I doubt that you gain a great advantage even in doing that: By now, everyone knows that this is done by computer and is really no more personal than "Dear Friend."

The sales letter may be one page or more. Some are on 11- × 17-inch sheets, folded to letter size, and then folded again to fit into a regular business envelope. They are often printed in two or three colors, further negating the notion of being a personal letter. One such letter I received recently came from the Homestead Publishing Company, who wish to sell me "The Living Trust Kit" to protect my heirs from the high cost of probate. The letter bears no salutation but begins with a box at the top of the first page wherein three sad cases are summarized, showing by example how much probate costs. The letter goes on to elaborate on this evil, explain the living trust as a remedy (actually a preventive measure), and attempt to sell me the kit. The package includes two other 8 1/2- × 11-inch sheets printed on both sides and folded to fit the envelope, a separate order form, and a response envelope. It was bulk-mailed (at slightly more than one-half the cost of first class mail) in an envelope imprinted "Don't Let Them Steal Your Children's Inheritance!" This is scare advertising, using fear as the motivator by generating a "worry item"—the high cost of probate, in this case.

A letter inviting me to attend the annual Direct Marketing Day in New

York opens with "The news couldn't be much better!" It goes on to tell me of all the benefits of attending this event. That is the more traditional and more popular approach—promising me gains, rather than appealing to fears.

A one-page sales letter from the publisher of an annual directory, *The National Directory of Addresses and Telephone Numbers,* solicits my purchase of the new edition but does not try to motivate me until the middle of the letter. It opens with what appears to be a totally irrelevant observation about a delivery of the new edition from the printer and how many are being shipped out. ("As I sat down at my desk to write this letter to you, I heard a truck rumble up to the loading dock . . . unload our printer's latest delivery of *The National Directory* . . . ").

I am offered the alleged special price of "only $44.95" for a publication that has gone to this price from the $19.95 I paid for the first edition only a few years ago. Since the author of the letter recognizes that I am a buyer of earlier editions, he or she ought to know that I am well aware of how much the price has escalated each year and how thin is the argument that I am being offered a special discounted price. Had I not been studying this sales letter expressly to discuss it in this book, I would not have read as far as the middle of the page. Nothing in the opening sentences gives me a reason to read further, and my awareness of the success of this publication makes me also aware that there is no good reason other than greed to go from $19.95 to $44.95 for a cheaply produced newsprint publication that has grown far less in size than in price.

Leads and Headlines

The headline of a print advertisement should be designed to capture attention and arouse enough interest to persuade the reader to read further. Some writers of sales letters use headlines too, an acceptable practice. However, most do not, but rely on the "lead"—the opening sentences—of the letter to arouse interest. The opener of the "Direct Marketing Day in New York" letter ("The news couldn't be much better!") does that, and the letter goes on to explain that optimistic, upbeat opening, with the promise of exciting benefits to be gained at the event.

That approach is obligatory for all advertising and sales materials. Those materials can't do their jobs if they are not being read, and they won't be read if the readers' interest is not aroused by the opening statements—by promises made early with evidence supplied. We have become so inured to our daily "junk mail" that we require only seconds to decide whether to even open the envelope, much less read what is inside.

Study all the DM packages you receive with these principles in mind. Remember that the basic principles are the same for all sales and advertising materials, whether they are sales letters, brochures, print ads, magazine articles, press releases, or other appeals. Persuading editors to give you some publicity by using your release or to buy and publish your article is no different from persuading an individual to send you an order for what you are advertising: People act in what they perceive to be their own best interest; selling is simply persuading a prospect that it is in his or her best interest to do what you suggest.

One other area worthy of special mention is that of public relations. It, too, offers many opportunities for freelance writers. Let's take a brief look at this special market for freelance writing.

PUBLIC RELATIONS

The activity known as public relations covers different kinds of activities in different organizations. The nominal objective of PR is the creation and maintenance of a favorable public image. Thus the PR function may include speechwriting, responding to letters, responsibility for advertising copy and programs sponsored, and a variety of related functions, most of them involving writing. In many cases, the real objective is to gain free advertising, which is what favorable PR amounts to. That links PR to marketing, and indeed, anyone who has a marketing responsibility of any kind is well advised to understand PR. Since PR depends heavily on writing, the freelance writer will find many opportunities for business if he or she is able to turn out effective PR copy that impresses editors and results in publicity.

The Press Release

The most basic PR tool is the press release, known also as a news release, publicity release, product release, or just release. Anyone conducting PR on even the most modest scale generates releases and sends them out to newspapers, magazines and trade journals, newsletters, and newsrooms of radio and TV stations. Many marketers even include releases in direct-mail packages.

Many thousands of releases are written and mailed every day, and every busy editorial office finds a bundle of releases in the mail every morning. Since competition for media space is intense, poorly written and poorly executed releases have little chance of being published. The vast majority of releases are discarded by editors with hardly more than a glance, and usually deservedly so.

The Sins of Release Writing

The sins of writers of releases fall into two categories. One is the matter of failing to use acceptable formats, which are designed for the convenience of the editor in using the release. (You can hardly expect an editor to be well disposed toward publishing a release that will be a problem for him or her to use.) The other, greater sin is that so many releases are completely lacking in newsworthiness: They simply do not merit publication. That requires some discussion, but first let's discuss the more mechanical aspects of the format, elements, and organization of a proper release.

Elements and Format

Following is a list of the elements and characteristics generally considered to be obligatory for a properly constructed release. Figure 7–4 is an example of how they are used.

1. Identify the release by such words as RELEASE, NEWS, NEWS RELEASE, or PRESS RELEASE. A news release announcing and introducing a product may be referred to as a "product release." (In that case, it is often appropriate to include a drawing or photo of the item.)

2. Identify the issuing organization. The release may be on a special form or on the regular letterhead of the organization. That is a perfectly acceptable practice.

3. Include a dateline identifying the city and date of origin.

4. Double- or triple-space the copy.

5. Type the copy on one side of the paper only.

6. Use a headline. This is arbitrary: Some advocate against it, some for it. I am for it, to capture the editor's interest and help him or her grasp the essence of the story immediately. The argument against it holds that editors prefer to write their own headlines, which is true enough, but irrelevant. The editor is always free to change the original headline and very likely will.

7. Include a contact—a name and number to help the editor follow up. The editor may wish to ask for photos, verify or validate the story, or otherwise pursue more information and perhaps even get "the story behind the story."

Herman Holtz
HRH COMMUNICATIONS,. INC.
P.O. Box 1731   Wheaton, MD 20915
Fax: (301) 649-5745   Voice: (301) 649-2499Z

NEWS

6/28/88

For Immediate Release

Contact:
Jane Eager
301 460-0000

HOW TO SELL TO THE $200 BILLION GOVERNMENT MARKET

Information Now Available in Audiocassettes

Wheaton, Maryland, 6/28/88 - For years business people have complained about the difficulty of getting information and guidance in selling to the U.S. Government, despite the literature on the subject, much of it published by the government. Written literature, unfortunately, has not proved very helpful to the newcomer to this market.

Now, for the first time, a complete information and instruction package on selling to the government is available in a convenient audiocassette form. The set includes four 1-hour cassettes and a 65-page directory of government purchasing offices, with a summary of the Federal Acquisition Regulations (FAR). The package was developed over the past year by a team of government-marketing experts, who interviewed dozens of government purchasing officials and reviewed over 12,000 pages of official documents to distill this 4-hour program.

The program incorporates the latest information available, as of October 1, 1987. It is available from HRH Communications, Inc. at $98.50 (discounted for quantity purchases).

# # #

Figure 7–4.   Model of a one-page release.

8. Provide guidance: If the release is more than one page long, write "more" at the bottom of each page to let the editor know that there is more copy following, and write "End," "###," or "-30-" at the bottom of the last page.

9. Write either "For immediate release" or "Embargoed until [some date]" when the release covers a future event such as a speech, convention, or other yet-to-happen event.

Achieving Newsworthiness

News releases rarely carry "hard news" like the front page of a daily newspaper carries. It is more likely that a release will announce a new product, changes of personnel, mergers and acquisitions, business failures, new contracts worthy of note, election of officers in an organization, and other such items of news within the given industry. People want to know about such happenings *in their own sphere of interest*. That last phrase is an important qualification. What is newsworthy information to one is of no interest to another (e.g., a General Motors executive is interested in just about everything in the automotive industry but probably is completely indifferent to what is happening in the garment industry.)

One of the common mistakes made apropos of this is misjudging where to send releases and, more specifically, how to address them. It is generally a mistake to address a release to a large publication or other medium without specifying an individual by functional title (e.g., Financial Editor) at least, if not by personal name. (An exception to this is the case of a small newsletter or other publication where the release could not possibly get lost or misdirected.) Remember that in large organizations mail addressed just to the organization is usually opened in the mailroom, where someone attempts to judge its proper destination within the organization. On a large newspaper, your release is likely to wind up on a managing editor's or city editor's desk, but it could wind up on the circulation-manager's desk if you have not specified otherwise. That individual may or may not spend the time to read your release and decide that it ought to go to the business editor, food editor, or state desk. He or she may simply be too busy to bother and drop it casually into the "circular file" without further thought. Even if the individual decides to pass it on to someone else, it still stands a good chance of winding up in the wrong place.

On the other hand, even if you do manage to get your release to the individual you intend it to reach, it is still necessary that the release be right for, be of true interest to that person. In other words, instead of writing a release and then deciding where you ought to send it, you should follow the reverse pattern, along the lines of the following procedure:

1. Decide what readers/viewers/prospects you want to reach.

2. Decide what kinds of media—which periodicals, what columnists, what radio or TV programs—are most suitable for reaching those prospects. (What do they read, watch, listen to?) Bear in mind that every editor, columnist, news reader, talk show host, and other prospective respondent is not interested in material of special interest to him or her personally, but is seeking material that is of special interest to readers, viewers, and listeners. You need to understand who those readers, viewers, and listeners are.

3. Decide what angles would be most likely to interest the editor/columnist/producer; that is, how to slant your release.

Slanting Copy

Slanting copy is a simple concept. It means writing the release in such a way as to address the direct interests of a given audience. Suppose, for example, that you are selling computer software programs and are preparing a release to help make your establishment more widely known. You wish to offer a free demonstration and how-to-do-it seminar as a means of attracting prospects to your place of business.

There are several possibilities open to you. Your release will have to suggest a particular program or kind of program you will be demonstrating. Suppose you have a choice among a new inventory control and management program, a new word processing program, or the latest and most popular computer game. Which one is most likely to attract the prospects you want?

That depends on the kind of prospects you want. An inventory program is going to attract only businesspeople for whom inventory control and management are important. It certainly is not likely to appeal to the owner of a small luncheonette or a high school youngster, just as the game program will not appeal to the businessperson. That's a rather obvious case, but it points up something: You can create more than one version of a release so that you can attract many people.

You must also think in terms of the periodicals and other media to which you slant your material. Even that can vary from one publication to another. What one newspaper calls the "Financial Editor," another may title the "Business Editor." This is even more critical when you want to send releases to columnists. Each columnist must normally be addressed by name, and since many are syndicated and are not on the staff of the periodical carrying the column, you must either determine what the columnist's mailing address is or send your release in care of the periodical.

Not everything can be slanted effectively. It would be difficult to slant to a male audience a release explaining how crocheting is making a strong comeback. On the other hand, relatively few women are enthusiastic about fly fishing. So an article or release on fly fishing might be slanted to fly fishermen with different interests (some like to tie their own flies, while others prefer to buy them ready made and will try every new one they can find). It is possible that you might be able to slant material on fly fishing even to women who have no direct interest in fishing if you address them as the wives and sweethearts of fly fishermen and present an appeal to buy fly-fishing gear or accessories as gifts. With a little imagination, basic material can be developed with a wide variety of slants.

Many products lend themselves to multiple uses and users, and each of these suggests the key to a slant. When I wrote releases to publicize my own newsletters, books, and reports on marketing to government agencies I found many ways to slant them to different audiences. The most obvious and basic slanting opportunities were the following:

1. To companies already doing business with the government. The theme was how to do *more* business with the government.

2. To companies who had done little or no business with the government. The theme was how to break into the government market most effectively.

3. To professionals; that is, consultants, educators, architects, engineers, and writers who ought to become acquainted with the government markets for their services.

These were basic markets, but there were many other possibilities: I could slant releases to small businesses generally, to minority-owned businesses, to very small businesses such as freelancing individuals, to businesses by the nature of what they sold, to businesses by the nature of the kinds of customers they would be going after, and so forth. I could even slant material to be used as training material for marketing department personnel! With an active imagination and a bit of introspection on possible uses and users, slanting is usually not difficult.

This idea has wider application than releases. It is equally useful in writing advertising copy, sales letters, newsletters, brochures, magazine articles, and just about everything else that might be addressed to the public generally or to any specific group of people. The key is simply finding the link between the reader's interest and what you wish to publicize.

Caution

Be careful. If you make a mistake that causes an editor to commit a *faux pas* and be embarrassed thereby, you will probably kill your chances of ever having that editor consider your releases seriously again. It is therefore especially important to be careful about accuracy. Your relationships with editors are at stake, and that is an important factor in conducting PR successfully.

Newsletters

Much—perhaps even most—of what has been said regarding releases is equally applicable to newsletters. Probably the second most frequently used and most effective device for PR is the newsletter. There are many thousands of newsletters produced in the United States; estimates range from 30,000 to 100,000. Many are produced as purely commercial enterprises as profit-making ventures in and of themselves, but many are PR devices, produced to be mailed out to customers and prospective customers as a promotional device. (There are also newsletters produced for employees in the interest of enlightened employer-employee relations.)

The content of a newsletter depends on the objective sought in publishing it. If it is strictly a commercial enterprise, the content is entirely editorial copy. (Few newsletters find it practicable to rely on paid advertising.) If it is a PR effort, up to about one-third of it may be devoted to advertising of the publisher's products or services. The remainder ought to be useful editorial content, if the reader's interest is to be held.

The format problem is a simple one. The classic newsletter has what is referred to in the trade as a *nameplate*. Figure 7–5 illustrates this. Generally, the nameplate carries an identification of the issue, most commonly the month and year, but sometimes a simple issue number, as the one in Figure 7–5 does. Usually, the copy is set up in two columns, since computers make it so easy to do so, but we will look more

---

WRITING FOR MONEY

"No man but a blockhead ever wrote except for money."
--*Samuel Johnson, 1776*

No. 101   Editor/Publisher Herman Holtz $60/year
P.O. Box 1731 Wheaton, MD 20915 301 649-2499 Fax: 301 649-5745

Figure 7–5.   A typical newsletter nameplate.

closely at this later when we discuss the use of the personal or desktop computer in this work.

Brochures

Brochures are such a basic element in marketing and promotion of all kinds that it has led to the coining of a term, *brochuremanship*—the art of molding opinions and persuading others through brochures. In principle, brochure writing is not markedly different from any other kind of writing to persuade. The difference between the brochure and the sales letter lies principally in the fact that you have much greater freedom of form, format, and content in creating a brochure. It can be of almost any size, as many pages as desired, using illustrations and a variety of typefaces, and with a number of other special devices such as page dividers, tabs, card stock, and bindings.

Dr. Jeffrey Lant is something of a phenomenon. A graduate of Harvard, he became a consultant, wrote and published his own book on consulting, and has gone on to write and publish many other books since. He also finds time to lecture, sell his and others' books in a mail-order bookstore enterprise, write columns for periodicals, and run a successful direct-marketing venture, which is illustrated by Figures 7–6 and 7–7. They show one of his marketing brochures, printed on 8 ½- × 11-inch stock so that it can be folded to fit into a regular business envelope. Note the use of graphics to lend eye appeal and variety. The right-hand panel of Figure 7–6 is the outside of the folded brochure—the panel the reader first sees—so it is designed for eye appeal. Note the promise stated on the cover page, backed up by a clear (quantified) statement of cost: "less than 1.2 cents each!"

Note, too, the middle panel. That is the back panel, one that the average reader is likely to look at before unfolding the brochure, so it ought

Figure 7–6. First side of small brochure.

1991 Schedule

Mail Dates	Closing Dates
April 15	March 15
July 5	June 3
October 1	September 2
January 2, 1992	November 28, 1991

Rates

100,000 cards per deck	Cash Price
1 card	$1199
subsequent cards same deck	$1100
Second color	FREE
Four-color process	$151
C/1/S enamel paper stock	upon request
Advertiser-supplied inserts	upon request

Production Requirements

Binding method	Loose deck
Trim size	5 1/2" x 3 1/2"
Maximum copy area	5 1/16" x 3 1/8"
Stock	.007 Hi-bulk

Art Specifications: Screened film negatives, right reading, emulsion side down, 120-line screen. Camera-ready art and veloxes are also acceptable. No bleeds. If camera-ready art is not submitted, we bill you for any charges. These charges are due upon receipt.

See for yourself just how our prices compare with other companies targeting business decision makers

Company	Basic Rate	Second Color	Cost Per 2-Color Card	Add'l For 4-Color
Marketing Bulletin Board (120,000 circ)	$3,390	$175	3.0 cents	$250
Marketing Manager (150,000 circ)	$5,700	$400	4.1 cents	$1000
President's Exec Deck (200,000 circ)	$3,995	$200	2.1 cents	$400
Venture Advertising Sales & Marketing (100,000 circ)	$3,000	$300	3.3 cents	$450

...and *all* other decks in the industry are comparably priced!!!

(source: Standard Rate & Data December, 1990 Edition)

Now look at us:

Jeffrey Lant's
Sales & Marketing SuccessDek
100,000 circulation

Basic Rate	Second Color	Cost Per 2-Color Card	Add'l For 4-Color
$1199	You get 2nd color FREE!	1.2 cents!	$151

Five Reasons Why You Should Advertise In Our Sales & Marketing SuccessDek

1) *You're paying too much If you advertise anywhere else.* Why pay 2 to 3 times as much for leads when you can get what you need from us? That's just stupid. (If you can't think of any other way to spend your money except buying overpriced cards in other people's decks, send it our way. We'll know what to do with it!)

2) *You get high quality deck-responsive names.* We pay top dollar for our names and the names we use are recent (not older than 120 days), often "hot line" names. We know you want to get access to the best names. We've got 'em. The best names ensure you access to the best leads and most likely buyers. We mail to a minimum of 10 and usually more lists, merged and purged so the same people aren't getting your offer. The final list is zip code corrected to improve list quality even more!

3) *Free second color.* You pay extra for color with other decks. You get it free from us. And if you want four-color, you pay virtually cost price. You're paying a premium for four-color processing everywhere else.

4) *Fewer competitors.* Ever noticed how in most decks there may be three, four or even 8 competing offers? We know this irritates you. While we can't promise that every offer will be unique, we do our best to cut down the competition in the deck. Our goal is to get you maximum response not just sell cards. We know our success is predicated on your success... and we run our business accordingly.

5) *Friendly service.* We really do try harder. Lots of people in the advertising world are difficult, condescending, and rude. We're not perfect either, but we do aim to help you. Frankly, we don't just want your business once. We want you to profit from our lead-generating system for years to come, and we're willing to work hard to make you happy. We don't just want customers. We want friends.

Figure 7-7. Second side of small brochure.

115

to back up the front panel. In this case it does; it reinforces the promise of reaching "100,000 business decision makers" made on the front panel.

Finally, the left-hand panel provides the evidence, explaining how and why Jeffrey Lant can promise the lowest prices in the industry.

The reverse side (Figure 7–7) then provides the details, further substantiating the earlier messages and providing ordering information. It is an integrated package of information, as a brochure ought to be.

Chapter 8

MARKETING YOUR SERVICES

No matter how good your new mousetrap is, the world does *not* beat
a path to your door. You must still go out and sell it.

NOW COMES THE HARD PART

Norman Bauman, the hard-working, New-York-City-based writer introduced in Chapter 2, remarks, "I have always observed that marketing skill
seems to be as important to the success of a working writer as the writing
skill itself." The versatile Canadian writer Sidney Allinson (advertising
copy, public relations, commercials, scripts, fiction, and novels, among
other things), who will also appear later in these pages, has something to
say on that subject too:

> *Selling, Marketing, Prospecting.* Those are the most important aspects
> of any freelance editorial service or writing enterprise. No matter how
> proficient a writer is, if he or she does not market services aggressively,
> the chances of success are slim.

They are quite right, of course. Every freelance writer soon learns, as
does everyone in business, large or small, that business starts with sales
and without sales the business simply does not exist. The sad truth is that

most of us are far better writers than we are marketers. And ironically, as in the case of the proverbial shoemaker's children who go barefoot, even those of us who specialize in writing effective advertising and sales copy for our clients are less effective at marketing for ourselves.

There are many reasons for this delinquency, and one is simple reluctance. Many, perhaps most, of us simply do not like to knock on doors, even when it is only figurative door-knocking. Mailing out sales literature and getting no response or only a sparse response is still rejection of a sort, not quite as traumatic as having doors literally slammed in your face, but still unpleasant.

Another cause for reluctance is cost. Advertising—whether it is via print media or by other means—is expensive, and most of us find money to be a rather scarce commodity, at least in the early years. However, it is possible to do quite a lot of advertising and other sales promotion on a modest budget, with the chief expenditure being your own time and energy. Following are many ideas for marketing that, in most cases, require very little cash or no cash at all. But before we get down to the specific ideas, we had better get a good handle on what marketing means for us and learn about a common problem for anyone writing his or her own copy.

MODESTY: A LUXURY YOU CAN'T AFFORD

We have no trouble lauding our clients when we prepare their marketing literature, but many of us have a problem doing the same thing for ourselves. We fear the appearance of bragging and displaying bad taste. If you have that problem, start getting rid of it right now. You can't afford that modesty, whether it is false or real.

The key to overcoming the problem easily, I found, was to get one thing straight about writing in general, whether for marketing or for other purposes: Hyperbole is rarely good writing. The appearance of bragging most often results from larding language with elaborate adjectives, adverbs, and other superlatives. Bad writing produces far too many "best," "biggest," "most experienced," and other such extreme terms. Here are just a few examples. Shun them and all others of a similar nature:

Greatest	Biggest producer of	Unsurpassed
Latest	World leader in	Astonishing
Least expensive	Inspiring	Fantastic
Lowest cost	Awesome	Fabulous
Oldest firm	Magnificent	Breath-taking
Industry leader		

What is wrong with all these terms is not just that they are self-congratulatory, but, even worse, they reflect claims or opinions and not facts. That makes them suspect immediately. Let's take a for-instance. Compare the following two statements:

I have many years of experience with a highly successful background as a marketer, having won millions of dollars' worth of contracts for past employers and clients.

In the 12 years since 1960 I have won over $360 million in government contracts for past employers and clients.

You will note that the first statement attempts to describe and characterize the writer through adjectives and inexact claims. Who can say what such terms as "many years," "highly successful," and "millions of dollars" really mean? How *many* years? *How* successful? How *many* millions of dollars? Such inexact, sweeping terms always smack of hype, and hype is what they will be taken for by most people.

The second statement is reportorial, simply stating flat facts without making observations. I would agree with anyone that the first statement sounds immodest, and I would be reluctant to use it in marketing my services. The second statement bothers me not at all because it simply reports facts objectively without commenting on them.

It's that simple, I have found, although I have also found it useful to offer an apology for any immodesty, preceding a recital of credentials (even a factual, reportorial one) with a declaration along the following lines:

Please forgive me if I seem to brag, but you have the right to know my credentials before entrusting your important work to me.

Note one other thing about the factual or reportorial presentation: It bases its impact on *quantified* information—number of years, dates, number of dollars. Because quantified information, by its nature, appears to be factual, most people tend to accept it without challenge.

Another hazard to credibility is the too-convenient rounding off of numbers: "Millions" is far less persuasive than "3.87 million." When I negotiated a contract for which the proposal listed "150 percent" as our overhead figure, the contracting official was properly skeptical and insisted on negotiating a 125-percent overhead. (He goodnaturedly admitted that had our proposal listed 149.3 percent as the overhead, he would not have questioned it.) Even if you are providing an estimate, use a formula and report the exact figure the formula provides, without rounding it off. This not only overcomes the false modesty problem, but also lends a great deal more credibility to any statements you make in your literature.

Sidney Allinson has been kind enough to allow me to use his little brochure (see Figure 8–1) as an example. It appears on one side of a standard 8 1/2- × 11-inch sheet, which enables him to fold it fit easily into a standard business envelope. Notice the quiet, dignified tone of the copy, and a few key points he has made:

- 25 years' experience in the various jobs he lists.
- Experience on staff with a number of major firms.
- Lists of the kinds of end products he has written.
- Recognition that many needs are "rush," and willingness to handle rush jobs.
- Honest, sober presentation of fee structure, with flexibility clearly indicated.

It is an example calculated to inspire confidence—a model worth emulating.

THE MARKETING PROCESS

Selling professional services—and I strongly urge that you consider yourself a professional and defend that position vigorously—is not the same marketing proposition as selling canned soup or shoes. Clients do not ordinarily buy such services as casually as they buy canned soup or shoes. Much more is at stake for the client who engages you to write a report, a proposal, or a manual. Thus, you will normally have to market in at least two phases—possibly even three—to wit:

1. Prospecting
2. Following up
3. Closing

Let's explore this a bit and see just what these two or three phases mean in practice.

Get your sales, technical, financial, corporate copy written faster, easier, by a thorough-going professional.

Business Writing Services for industry, finance, & government.

Assign those tough "rush" copywriting chores to a skilled, reliable, business writer. My name is Sidney Allinson, and I'm a pro at helping people to produce communications material: —

advertisements	brochures
sales promotion	annual reports
films, videotapes	speeches
catalogues	Ministry programmes
direct mail	technical bulletins
proposals	case histories
sales letters	newsletters
press releases	publicity campaigns

Your Communications Needs

When you or your clients need clear, fresh, copy that thoughtfully interprets and persuasively explains products and services of industry, business or government . . . when you need extra help with writing and creative direction in print or broadcast advertising . . . when there's a "crunch" on getting a batch of material out in a hurry . . . when you could use honest straightforward counsel — that's when you can benefit from my skill as a communicator who simply gets things done. Fast, accurately, and on time.

SIDNEY ALLINSON
Communications Consultant
Advertising • Public Relations • Documentation
24 Ravencliff Crescent,
Scarborough, Ontario M1T 1R8
Tel: (416) 493-9627

Sensible fees:

Quoted up front; no surprises. My fees are based on a rate of $50.00 an hour; $400 per day. Or you can hire me by the job, with a firm estimate. Reasonable charges, indeed.

Experience you can use:

You could gain from my 25 years' experience as an ad agency creative director, copywriter, account executive, promotion manager, film producer, editor, journalist, and senior governmental communications advisor. I've been on staff at Ogilvy & Mather, Baker Lovick, MacLean Hunter, Avro Aircraft, The Guardian, and the Ontario Government. I've successfully freelanced for three years.

My assignments range from major advertising and public relations campaigns, to TV commercials and public service announcements, and full-length documentary films. Others are for direct mail that pulls orders: technical literature; sales-promotion programmes; presenting ministerial initiatives; public safety programmes; collateral material; banks; credit cards; mutual funds; mining prospectus'; capability brochures, industrial plants, machine tools, travel; market surveys; association material; and dealer presentations.

Special attention:

Low-budget videotaped field reports and presentations; financial fund introductions; direct mail requiring innovative techniques; governmental programmes; TV commercials; newsletter start-ups; annual reports; communications counsel.

For reliable help with your copywriting workload and communications projects, call the professional. Today.

(416) 493-9627
Sidney Allinson
Communications Consultant

Figure 8–1.   Sidney Allinson's brochure.

121

Prospecting

Prospecting means exploring for sales leads—that is, identifying potential clients. You may do that in a variety of ways. One is "knocking on doors"— making cold calls to see who throws you out of the office and who is willing to listen for a few minutes (i.e., shows an interest in or need for the kind of services you offer). Another is mailing out brochures, sales letters, and other literature to see who responds with at least mild interest. Another is to talk to people at association meetings, conventions, and elsewhere, exchanging cards, handing out your brochures, and collecting names and telephone numbers. Still another is telephoning all your friends and acquaintances, trying to induce them to recommend you to others. Give free lectures and seminars. If you do these well, you will often be con- fronted with listeners who want to know more, and many will want to retain you professionally. At the least, you should be able to judge which are serious prospects, the ones you should follow up.

Key Idea: Do keep in touch with and solicit business from your former employers. They are always excellent prospects, since they know what you can do and you know the people there. Many freelancers get their start with assignments from former employers.

Following Up

Don't waste your time and money trying to follow up prospects who did not respond to your initiative. In this phase you are trying to convert prospects into sales leads, and they do not become leads unless and until they show a distinct interest in retaining you to provide your services. However, some of those who responded in some manner are not true leads, because they were being kind and courteous and were not really interested or because they do not have the money or the authority to retain you.

Finding out whether a prospect is truly interested and has or can get money and/or authority to retain you is known as *qualifying* the prospect or conferring on the prospect the title of *sales lead*. Investing time in prospects you cannot qualify is a waste; abandon them. Press on with those who *do* qualify. They are the ones that call for follow-up action and closing efforts.

Closing

Many people use the term *closing* to mean "getting the order." In true marketing parlance, it does not mean *getting* the order, but *asking for* the order. It's a strange phenomenon, but even those prospects who have decided they wish to use your services will often hold back from saying "Sign here," or whatever other term means "I want your service." You must press them into actually ordering by saying something like "When do you want me to start?" or "Do you need me to write a brief statement of work for your purchase order?" Often you can close when you qualify a prospect as a true sales lead, but you may have to make additional calls and presentations in many cases. The prospect may need to have you come in and present yourself to his or her superiors, for example. It is essential that you understand how such things work in many different types of companies, especially large corporations, and perhaps help your potential clients sell you and/or their need for your services to their own management!

The three phases presented here are not necessarily single, separate steps. You may be able to accomplish all three in one or two steps, but you may also need to have more than one step in each phase—especially the final one—to get the signed purchase order or contract in your hands.

MARKETING STRATEGIES

Your marketing strategy may be to be the cheapest writer in town. It may be to *appear* to be the cheapest writer in town—bait and switch. It may be to simply *claim* to be the cheapest writer in town. Or it may be all three. Of course, it can get a great deal more sophisticated than that. You can play many themes, such as fast service, reliability, integrity, lengthy experience, impressive references, impressive achievements, or other such persuasive ploys. You can (and probably will) combine several of these sterling attributes in your claims. That is all right, if done intelligently. But, as General Alexander Haig is fond of saying, here are a few caveats:

- Don't claim mutually exclusive attributes, such as alleging yourself to be the cheapest, fastest, most reliable, and best. Aside from the logical inconsistency of such a combination of claims, it is protesting too much and is more likely to be taken as overblown hyperbole than as serious assertion.

- In general, don't huff and puff. State your case with quiet dignity. Bear in mind that clients typically hire you for good, mature judgment, as well as technical skills. You are essentially a consultant, whether you claim to be or not. It is important to keep that dignity and so inspire some respect.

- Don't go to the other extreme out of some excessive sense of modesty and do yourself an injustice by failing to do yourself justice.

A FEW SPECIAL MARKETING IDEAS

As a freelance writer, you are running your own business. Never lose sight of that: It confers on you the freedom to do whatever you want in conducting your business. You can do all those things you tried to recommend to your former employer that he then brushed aside. You can try out your own marketing ideas. One freelance advertising copywriter revealed to me recently that when he gets a literature package in the mail that he finds pretty badly done, he prepares a brief and partial critique, with an idea or two for improvement, which he sends to the mailer with his offer of services. He says it has produced some excellent assignments for him. Even help-wanted advertisements are such fodder: I have found that many employers have trouble recruiting suitable people because they do not know how to make their recruiting ads attractive to the right kinds of prospective employees!

Many executives get themselves into schedule problems (e.g., they discover on Thursday that a report or proposal promised to an important client or required absolutely for Monday morning will not be ready for some reason). Panic sets in. This is the time for what some in the trade call "quick reaction" or "quick response" services. A great deal of business awaits the writer who is willing to sacrifice his or her evenings and week-ends to satisfy the emergency needs of customers. In most cases, the customer will gladly pay suitable premiums, such as double-time rates, to get the job done and will be grateful to you for the rescue. If you are willing to offer such services, at least in the early months while you are building a clientele, by all means make it clearly known by featuring it in your literature. Try also to get a line or two about it in local newspapers and on radio and TV.

If you have the equipment to help customers who are having difficulties, make that capability known. For example, if a customer needs 25 copies of a report or proposal on Monday and can't get a local print shop to work on the weekend, the job can be done by laser printer, even if that is not the most efficient way to do it. This is where the lettershop function can help you succeed as a freelance writer: If you have a laser printer, you can run the job, but even if you don't have a laser printer of your own, you can probably find someone who does and make arrangements for access to it! (A writer I know in Oakland, California, does just that for his clients.)

Be ready to do favors for prospective clients, such as composing a handful of pages in a pinch, even if there is not enough profit in it to make it worth your while. You can trade on this later to make the prospect a client worth having.

Be easy to talk to—quiet, calm, laid back, pleasant, and forthcoming—so that prospects are not reluctant to ask questions. Some people are suspicious of everyone, suspecting that they are being used, which is a definite turn-off for others. Perhaps some of those who approach you with questions are trying to use you, to pick your brains free of charge. So what? Every business finds it necessary to give out samples in some form or other.

THE NEED TO MARKET CONTINUOUSLY

Whether you have been freelancing for some time or are just about to start working independently—even if you have a well-established clientele and all the business from those clients you can handle—it is risky to discontinue all marketing. You really cannot afford to be too busy to market. Every business has its ups and downs, and you can lose even your most faithful clients for any of many possible reasons. (There are lots of able competitors out there trying to woo your clients away from you, as you wooed them away from somebody else!) In fact, most of us find it necessary to market continuously and to make a continuous effort to improve our marketing and the results it brings. For that reason, I urge you to study the ideas offered here to implement your marketing, although admittedly they are offered as reminders, pointing you in the right direction, not as a full-blown discussion of marketing.

If You Are a Beginner . . .

If you happen to be new at freelance writing or are only now planning to launch a career as a freelance business writer, it would not be surprising if you read some of the previous paragraphs mumbling to yourself, perhaps resentfully, "Yeah, easy for *you* to say; you have the background. But what do *I* do? I don't have all that experience and track record." That is a great concern when you are starting a new practice, and to the extent that it is true, perhaps the injunctions you just read are not entirely fair. Nevertheless, there are several things you can do to help yourself get started, even if you have never before sold one cent's worth of your writing services.

First of all, you probably have more experience than you realize. As Bob Bly says in his invaluable report, *Tips for Beginners: How to Get Started in High-Profit Writing*™ (self-published), "*Everyone* has done some writing." It is unlikely that you have no writing experience at all. We all started somewhere, perhaps on the high school or college newspaper, an organization's newsletter, helping others with résumés, preparing reports for an employer, or writing something while in military service or doing volunteer work. Dig deep into your memory. It is almost impossible to have survived growing up in the recent decades of this century without doing some kind of writing.

Work up a checklist of everything you have written—what, where, when, how much, and, if at all possible, with what results. Be as specific as possible and quantify as much as possible. Gather up samples. (Always collect and save samples of your work in the early years. Later you will have less need for them, but in the early years they are a must.) Get letters of commendation for your writing whenever you can. And do some volunteer work, too, if you need more or better samples. Recent writing usually provides better and more persuasive samples than does writing of earlier years.

Make up a brochure and a portfolio of some sort, using your best samples. However, remember that all too often salespeople blow their sales by saying too much, by being too eager to offer information not asked for and not required to make the sale. Why even raise the question of your experience and competence if you do not have to? Many people will not ask to see your credentials or even demand a recital of them. You will find a surprisingly large number of people ready and willing to accept you at face value: If you say you are a writer, they see no reason to doubt it. So don't be too hasty in using the portfolio. Have it ready, but don't trot it out unless and until you are asked to show samples. Don't offer descriptions of earlier projects if they are not asked for.

Where Best to Start

Normally, it is far easier to market your services to private citizens than to executives of organizations. Individuals are usually less critical and demanding and are far less likely to demand to see samples and other credentials. Therefore it is easier to begin by soliciting writing assignments from individuals.

Individuals are easier to get orders from than are organizations. You can get started by offering to write résumés and letters or offer editorial assistance with reports, term papers, theses, and dissertations. You can advertise these services using several avenues:

1. Small classified advertisements in local newspapers.

2. Notices posted on bulletin boards in supermarkets.

3. Brochures and small signs posted on bulletin boards elsewhere, such as local recreation centers and public libraries.

4. Notices on electronic bulletin boards (if you have a computer and modem, as explained later).

5. Small signs posted in other public places; for example, tacked or taped to telephone poles.

Using Mail Order/Direct Mail

A great deal of writing work can be handled via mail and telephone, and quite a few freelance writers operate in this manner. In fact, many operate exclusively by mail and telephone, often from offices in their homes, as witness the advertisements shown in Chapter 5. When I wrote résumés, I ran small classified advertisements in the *The Wall Street Journal* and did a fair amount of résumé business by mail as a result. I have done and still do business with many clients I have never met face to face or even talked to on the telephone. That is more and more the case now, with the fax machine in such widespread use, including one in my own office. In fact, the fax machine is itself a marketing asset. Here is an example of one experience in which my fax machine played a key role, handling a small and profitable assignment that I could not have handled in any other way.

Not long ago, I had a call from a small advertising agency in Jacksonville, Florida. They were seeking help in responding to a federal government solicitation and were too close to their proposal deadline to trust the mail for the necessary exchanges of information. After some conversation, I suggested a means to help them: If they would fax me a copy of the RFP (government's request for proposals), I would study it and respond with suggestions. I quoted them a price for this, and we proceeded on the basis described. I did what I promised, the client then called back with some questions, and we concluded the task. I invoiced them and was paid the next month.

After more than one such experience, I think the fax machine is a must for the freelance writer who is going to work with clients via mail and telephone, and it is useful in general for anyone in business. You can market only the service you can deliver; the fax enlarges on the service you can deliver.

In the case just cited, the fax machine acted as a special high-speed mail service. It has many uses in that respect, and it can be used to follow up leads and furnish estimates and quotations. However, not only can free-lance writers do business by mail, we can also market by mail. It should come as no surprise that those who write copy for the direct-mail industry use both media advertising and direct mail to solicit business. But here we must turn to the U.S. Postal Service as a practical matter in marketing via direct mail.

You Need Mailing Lists

Using direct mail to solicit business means mailing out envelopes of sales literature seeking orders. To do that successfully, you must have a mailing list, or perhaps several mailing lists—names and addresses of people who are reasonable prospects for the services you offer. Even when the list is a good one, in terms of suitability of prospects for what you offer, a good return on the mailing is likely to be 2 to 4 percent, or even less for some offers. Obviously, a list that is not well suited to your offer is not going to produce even that percentage of response and is probably not worth a mass mailing.

You can rent mailing lists from dozens of list brokers. The secret of success, however, lies largely in selecting the right lists. That is, you must select lists of people who are most likely to need or want what you are selling, and those lists are not always easy to find. Despite the great number and diversity of lists offered by the industry, sometimes it is difficult to find lists that are truly suitable to your needs. I found this when I solicited customers whom I could offer information and other help on proposal writing. I found it necessary to compile my own mailing lists. This may or may not be a practicable alternative for you. I was able to find sources that would provide me with what I wanted, but you may not be able to do the same. There is another way to build your own lists, however.

Inquiry Advertising

If you have never heard of inquiry advertising, it is time to do so. It is the link, or crossover, between mail order and direct mail. (The two are closely related, but not identical.) The objective of inquiry advertising is to build a list of sales leads, a mailing list in this case. You run media (print, usually) advertisements designed to elicit inquiries from people who would be suitable prospects for what you wish to sell. Suppose, for example, that you wish to sell a résumé-writing service by mail, as I did. I don't know where you could find a mailing list of people who are likely to be in need of résumés. However, there is a way to go in search of such people: You can run a classified advertisement in some nationally circulated periodical offering an inducement that would attract responses from individuals who are interested in getting a better résumé. For example, suppose you advertise as follows:

WHAT'S WRONG WITH YOUR RÉSUMÉ? FREE report.
Write Résumés, P.O. Box 7777, Tysons, TX.

The free report you advertise can be a single page, but play fair with respondents: Do include a report with some useful information, but devote the rest of your package to explaining and selling your service.

There are other ways to use this same general idea, and you have probably seen them in use without thinking about it. If you have some means of distributing inquiry literature to a large number of the right prospects, that also produces names for your mailing list. You might, for example, make up a simple piece of literature offering an inducement to inquire, such as the hypothetical small advertisement just described, and distribute it. Of course, you can be much more persuasive when you can use several hundred words to appeal to prospects. You might leave bundles of such notices in public libraries on their free-literature shelves, give them out at conventions and seminars, and send them out as press releases to publishers of newsletters and other periodicals. (I have used that method with great success.) Or you may leave your information as a form to be filled out and mailed to you or left for you to collect later. (This is done often at trade fairs and similar conclaves.)

In doing some of these things, I found, to my surprise at first, that if your language is persuasive enough many people will pass your name and literature on to their friends and neighbors. That becomes tantamount to an endorsement, despite the fact that it is made by someone who has not used your services.

Other Sources of Names and Addresses

Inquiry advertising is not the only way to build your own mailing list, although it is an excellent way. I built my own mailing list of companies who were habitual government contractors from the help-wanted advertising (I could recognize most of the prospects from their names or from the kinds of people they were seeking); from lists of government contractors in *Commerce Business Daily*, a daily periodical for government contractors; and from a few other sources including the membership directories of many associations whose members were "right" for me. Many of those directories are available to anyone who asks, although a small payment is required in some cases.

Using PR

Public relations is a flexible marketing tool that offers a variety of approaches. As one approach to getting publicity that will generate a few orders, you can send out releases announcing your service. However, there are other ways to put PR to work effectively. Moreover, there are special rewards in using PR: The more you use PR successfully in your own behalf, the more able you become to use it in behalf of your clients. Not only do you become more and more experienced in using PR effectively, but you add new and fresh samples to your portfolio. For that alone it is in your interest to use PR in your own behalf. Among the most potent and powerful weapons are press releases, articles in magazines and trade journals, and your own newsletter.

Bylined Articles

Most periodicals, whether they are sold on newsstands or are available only via individual subscription, are not entirely staff written. In fact, almost all articles are written by "contributors," individuals who work in the industry served by the journal or who are regular freelance writers. Regular freelancers expect to be paid for their articles, of course, and if they are full-time freelancers they depend on such payments. Industry executives and workers who contribute articles to trade journals are usually paid some small sum, although what they seek is PR, not payment. (In fact, some corporations will reward employees who manage to get an article printed that mentions the corporation.) In any case, if you can plant a few articles that identify you as a professional freelance writer whose services are available for hire, that alone will bring in inquiries that will result in some business. However, that is not the sole benefit; enterprising writers turn those articles to advantage in other ways, one of which is to order reprints in quantity. Most periodicals will furnish reprints at modest prices. Each reprint then becomes a valuable marketing tool, enclosed with the writer's DM package as evidence of capabilities.

Articles About You by Others

In many respects, articles *about* you, written by others, are far more valuable than articles *by* you. They are by their nature presumably more objective; thus they generate more and better word-of-mouth promotion. The question is, of course, how to get other writers to write about you.

There is no easy answer to this, although I did manage, on occasion, to stir a writer's interest in me and what I was doing enough to promote an interview and an eventual story. Letters to established editors, journalists, and freelance writers can produce such a result if they are intriguing enough. Most often, such stories grow out of your work and your own PR generally. In my own experience, it was often my public speaking that produced this result.

Press Releases

Having written a proper press release, you must use it well to gain benefits from it. Aside from simply mailing it to list of publications and newsrooms, there are a few other things you can do with it. One is to include it as an element of your direct-mail packages, if you use direct mail. Another is to enclose a copy in all your business correspondence, including quotations, proposals, invoices, and statements you mail out. Still another, a most efficient way to get circulation of a release, is to send 400 copies of your release to the Washington News Service, 908 National Press Building, Washington, DC 20045, telephone (202) 737-4434. That organization will distribute your release to 400 periodicals and news services for a small fee (currently $65), less than the postage and related cost of mailing out the 400 copies yourself.

Your Own Newsletter

A newsletter of your own is a special marketing tool of great power. Instead of *depending on* the media, you *are* the media, at least to the extent that you can gain publicity through your newsletter. And you can do a great deal with it if you employ it artfully, for there is more to using a newsletter well than simply mailing it to prospective clients. You should, of course, do that, but you should also send it out to other publishers of periodicals in whose pages you would like some publicity, with permission to use any of your material as long as they identify the source (i.e., with attribution). If you want circulation beyond your local area, you can send it to periodicals that are circulated nationally. Folded down to a convenient 8 1/2- × 3 1/3-inch size, you can carry a supply with you to use as a handout brochure.

A *word of caution:* Do not create an unabashed, 100-percent advertising brochure disguised as a newsletter. That will earn only a swift discard of the newsletter and a loss of face and reputation for yourself. You are entitled to have both direct and indirect (subtle) advertising of your services in your newsletter, but you must play fair with the reader and provide a reasonable degree of objective coverage of news and other useful information. My own estimate of reasonableness in this is not more than one-third open and candid advertising, plus a maximum of one-third more useful information that serves an additional function as a relatively subtle promotion.

Public Speaking

Unfortunately, many—perhaps even most—of us shrink in near-panic from public speaking. Somehow, standing before an audience and speaking to them is a frightening prospect. That is a serious handicap for anyone seeking to turn PR to his or her advantage, for public speaking is one of the essentials of PR. It may even be the most powerful element. Proficiency in speaking from the dais can be a key element in freelance success. Try to cultivate mastery of public speaking. You will find this to be rewarding in many ways. It is the key to making speeches, presenting seminars, and guesting on radio and TV shows. From those appearances stem business opportunities in abundance. For example, after one TV appearance in the Washington, DC, area, I was so swamped with telephone inquiries that I set up a series of miniseminars to handle the questions of the callers. That enabled me to handle all the inquiries in a manner that satisfied the callers and was profitable for me at the same time.

Public speaking can be turned to advantage in a number of ways. It can lead directly to clients and contracts. I produced and staged a series of all-day seminars on proposal writing, for example, charging each attendee a suitable fee. It was a profitable activity itself. Even in the dollars of that era, each seminar produced a gross profit ranging from about $1,200 to about $3,000, and many of those presentations resulted in clients engaging my services as a consultant and contract proposal writer for substantial fees. Later, being pressed for the time necessary to advertise and promote the seminars, I resorted to presenting them for a fixed fee, under contract to companies, universities, and associations. A seminar of this type can be done on many subjects—writing résumés, starting a small business, programming computers, business writing, and hosts of other subjects.

Many colleges and universities, especially community colleges, run special adult education courses of short duration—some as short as one evening, others a couple of hours a week for several weeks. They also offer seminars and other special programs, and they are almost always in the market for speakers. Usually, they will respond to your suggestion for a subject. The pay is rather modest, but you should consider this to be a marketing activity, and the modest income means it is self-supporting!

In my own county, and I suppose in many other counties, a person can offer a free miniseminar or lecture in one of the library's free meeting rooms. The library will post the announcement to let people know about it. Again, many of the people who attend such events become clients, and the advertising is free. (You can amplify the advertising by sending out releases to local periodicals announcing these seminars.)

NETWORKING

Networking is practiced by many consultants and independent professional practitioners of various kinds. Of itself, it is probably too limited to constitute your main marketing program, but it is an appropriate adjunct to other marketing efforts, and it can be used in mutual support with many of those other efforts.

The principle of networking lies in establishing a web of contacts with others who can be of help to you, such as other writers who may need to call on associates to help with large projects and other professionals who may turn into clients or provide an opening to clients. For example, engineers are good contacts if you are a technical writer, and medical specialists if you are a medical writer. Thus, networking means belonging to as many relevant associations as you can manage and being as active as possible in these organizations. Attend and participate in meetings, conventions, and other programs. Meet people and maintain the contacts. Out of these come opportunities to speak to groups, exchange ideas, and become more and more visible yourself.

Because of such contacts, I was invited to be one of several speakers at a series of seminars. I had the opportunity to meet people attending the seminars, while I practiced my public speaking skills, distributed my business cards and other literature, and became a bit better known myself. (In many cases I even received a modest honorarium for speaking.) Out of these experiences came my own seminars as a profitable independent venture, and ultimately many consulting assignments also resulted.

MARKETING TO GOVERNMENTS

Although I discussed marketing to governments in Chapter 4, a few remarks are in order here to reinforce some important points made in that chapter. One of them is that selling to the government is not greatly different from selling to a corporation. There is a certain amount of bureaucratic red tape in both situations, but the government has made a greater (and more successful) effort to reduce and simplify that red tape than have most corporations. For small purchases—under $25,000, in the case of the federal government—it can be simpler to contract with a federal agency than with even a medium-size corporation. The government does not pay more slowly than do most corporations, and it pays more promptly than many.

By far the biggest and most important difference is that private businesses and individuals can do business with anyone they choose on just about any terms they wish to, whereas government agencies must do business as prescribed by law, and that is to your advantage. Work at learning not only how the system works but what the law requires of the various government agencies. (I have found it very much to my advantage, at times, to be more familiar with the law and the practices than even the contracting officer was.)

In most cases, even for small purchases, you will be asked to submit a proposal, since what is required is almost invariably custom work. (It can be a brief letter proposal, in the case of small jobs.) Since you are in pursuit of writing or editorial work, it is important that your proposal be a good example of your professional skill and ability. (The client will almost surely study it with that in mind!) Be extra careful about all matters of grammar, punctuation, spelling, rhetoric, and related matters. Keep your style simple and straightforward. Purple prose can cost you the contract. (A suggested proposal format/outline is given in Appendix 4.)

PART II

EVERY WRITER A PUBLISHER
Selling the Products of Writing

The role of the freelance writer of yore was to labor and create a story or article and then try to find a publisher for it. It was because of that modus operandi that we have inherited an image of the freelance writer as a starving wretch stubbornly scribbling away in an unheated garret. Whatever the validity of that romantic tradition (it was probably true to a large degree as recently as 40 to 50 years ago and may even be true of an isolated case or two today), I will make no further reference to it in these pages. The modern freelance writer need not suffer so unless he or she is determined to write the great play or novel and believes (as some apparently do) that personal suffering is a necessary ingredient for literary eminence. The average modern freelance writer works in a comfortably heated or air-conditioned room, is reasonably well fed, and struggles with the complexities and blessings of modern computers and word processors in creating the literature of our times.

Therefore, instead of commiserating with you on the sad state of freelance writing and freelance writers in a traditionally cruel and competitive world, Part II discusses the more modern, more practicable, and more achievable world of specialty publishing as one of the means by which the freelance writer can pursue a successful writing career while enduring no physical discomforts.

Part I was devoted to methods for selling your services as a writer and/or editor. Part II is devoted to another means for survival as an independent freelance writer: methods of creating certain kinds of written products on your own initiative and out of your own imagination and selling them directly to the end users of such information. In fact, that describes publishing itself.

In this Part I am going to talk about how to become an independent publisher on a very small scale. Some call this "self-publishing," but they are generally referring to publishing books. Relatively large sums of money—at least four or five figures—must generally be invested to produce your own professionally typeset and bound volume in quantity, especially if you want the so-called "library edition," with cloth covers and sewn bindings. Then you must invest most of your energies in getting the book distributed—marketed, that is.

That process is not what is meant here by the term *specialty publishing*, although publishing small books on a modest budget is not unheard of, and you will read of such cases here. However, exceptions aside, the term better describes special kinds of publications that will be considered in this Part, and it involves little of the risk associated with self-publishing a commercially manufactured book. It requires little capital for investment or operating funds and calls for only limited distribution. It is an entirely different world, and you may find it as attractive as many other freelance writers do.

Chapter 9

Specialty Publishing

Publishing is a rather broad term today, and it includes the creation and sale of many products other than those printed on paper. *Specialty*, however, is a qualifier used with full consciousness that most freelance writers have limited resources.

REPORTS: THEY CAN BEGIN WITH GOPHERS

Figure 9–1 is a page from a typical catalog describing some of the kinds of specialty publications referred to in this chapter. (I confess, unblushingly, that it is my own, focusing primarily on how-to-write instructions.) These are generally monographs, dealing entirely with a single subject. They are usually referred to as *reports*, and most of them are rather brief, ranging from a few hundred to a few thousand words. They can be on any subject. Jerry Buchanan, of Vancouver, Washington, is a writer who publishes a monthly newsletter, *TOWERS Club USA*, targeted especially for writers engaged in specialty publishing of some kind. He explains that he started a number of years ago by researching methods for ridding a property of gophers. When he found a reliable method for doing so, he wrote a little how-to-get-rid-of-gophers report, which he sold by mail for $2 a copy. He managed to sell 14,000 copies of this report, which inspired him to write and self-publish a small book for writers—which he also sold by mail—and to start his monthly newsletter.

105: Make Money Writing About Your Troubles

A great way to find sure-fire ideas for your writing projects. You will be surprised at the enormous potential of the simple idea expressed in the title of this report. It has been the basis of a great many successful articles and books because it addresses the primary concerns of many prospective readers......................................$4 [ ]

106: Make it Big with Your Own Newsletter

An almost ideal approach for the talented freelance writer. Addresses critical questions: What does it take to get started? Insight into newsletter business. Economics of newsletter publishing. Strategy to cut those high costs. A few other spinoff benefits. Pricing your NL. Where to get information. Where and how to get subscriptions..................$4 [ ]

107: The Truth About Copyright Law

Explodes the myths and explains the current law: What is copyright? What can and can't be protected by copyright. How and where to register a copyright and many other important details........................$3 [ ]

111: $50,000 a Year Thru Self-Syndication

Content: What syndication is. General topic ideas. Specialization versus generalization. Ideas and tips. Length. Getting started. What to charge. How to expand................$5 [ ]

125: Sell Your Book Before You Write it!

Content: The beginning of a full-time freelance career. In quest of an agent. A few lessons learned. What should be in a book proposal? About contracts, royalties, and related details...........................$4 [ ]

131: Government Markets for Writers

This is valuable, hard-to-find information provided by a seasoned expert. Content: How the government buys. Small-purchase opportunities. Best government markets. Editorial services. Training. How to learn of opportunities............................$4 [ ]

133: Anyone Can Make Money Writing or as a Writing Consultant

Approaches to writing for money. Creating and selling your writings. Typical prices paid. The freelance writer as a writing consultant. How to get clients. What to charge. A few useful books..............$4 [ ]

108: 15 E-Z Ways to Make Money at Home

This brief report is an overview of many home-based businesses--freelance writing and publishing, resume service, typing, singles club, and others...........................$3 [ ]

113: Double Your Business Rapidly, How to

Content: Merchandising. Copy that sells. Charges and credit. Tie-ins and follow-up sales. Increasing the average-sale size. When price counts...............................$4 [ ]

109: Consulting: Today's Opportunity

Content: What consulting is. Examples. Getting started. Should you have a trade name? Incorporate? Services, rates, fees..$4 [ ]

110: How to Make Money as a Consultant

A window into the wonderful world of consulting: Problems of consulting. Giving advice away free, how to avoid. Contracts. Invoicing and getting paid. Other income sources. Getting started.................$4 [ ]

Figure 9–1. A typical catalog sheet describing reports.

Some reports catch on better than others with the public, and that is usually quite unpredictable. Probably the most popular of my own reports was one I wrote on minimizing financial problems in business by various methods, including several methods that enable you to get paid in advance for orders, thus having customers finance part of your business operations. Bob Bly's reports are on subjects for freelance writers, with heavy emphasis on copywriting, a subject in which he is especially expert. At least part of the explanation of why some reports do better than others in the marketplace is the result of how well the writers choose their markets and how effectively they attack them. Not everyone has a gopher problem; obviously, Buchanan's success with his gopher report was due as much to his success in reaching prospects who were experiencing the problem as it was to the intrinsic value of his report.

These reports tend to deal with self-help and other how-to subjects primarily: how to solve some problem, be successful, make money, find love, or even bake a cake. Here are a few typical subjects:

22 Tips for Beginners in Mail Order

Sell Books by Mail

17 Ways to Get FREE Advertising

15 Ways to Cut High Printing Costs

How to Get FREE Typesetting

How to Remember Names

37 New Ways to Prepare Hamburger

14 Often-Overlooked Tax Deductions

How to Incorporate Yourself

How to File Your Own Divorce Suit

Why People Buy Reports

Prior to the last decade, computers were all large mainframes or minis (smaller mainframes) and numbered in the thousands. Along came desktop computers—soon numbering in the millions—and new industries were born, among them the *information industry*. There had been a trend toward something called by that name, but now it truly took root and spawned a swift-growing web of public databases. There were now customers paying for information, pure and simple. A customer now dials up the host computer of a public database—whether it is a general one such as CompuServe®, GEnie, or Prodigy®, or a specialized one such as LEXIS or CBD Online—and pays for the time on line, the information items downloaded (transferred from the host computer), or both. The world of commerce now recognizes that information itself is a commodity worth money.

That is what specialty publishing is about: the sale of information. One can buy a handsomely bound book hundreds of pages long today for perhaps $20 to $25, more or less. Yet, people uncomplainingly pay $5 to $10 and even more for a dozen or more typed pages bound together with a corner staple or a small booklet with a paper back and a glued binding. Why do they do so? The reason is simple: They are aware that they are not buying paper, ink, and bindings that will grace a bookshelf; they are buying information: sharply focused, practical, how-to guidance in some well-defined subject.

Until recently, most publishers of such items composed them on a typewriter and then had them printed or duplicated by mimeograph or some other inexpensive means. Today, with computers, word processors, laser printers, and office copiers, it is no longer necessary to invest in keeping a stock of printed copies or in the storage space necessary to house stocks of perhaps several dozen such reports. With modern equipment, you can keep all these reports stored in your computer to print out on demand or keep master copies that you can duplicate with an ordinary office copier. Or you can compromise, probably achieving greater efficiency, and have a quantity of your most popular reports printed and kept in stock while you turn out the slower-moving reports as needed.

FORMATS

The typical format for such reports is a sheaf of 8 1/2- × 11-inch sheets, bound with a corner staple. Figure 9–2 shows the first-page/cover sheet of one such report as originally created in 1977. The composition is via ordinary typewriter, with a ragged right margin. The title was pasted up by hand, laboriously using individual letters.

The same report is shown in Figure 9–3 in its most modern version, typeset by computer and printed on a laser printer. The copy is now right-justified, and is set in the Times Roman typeface. (It is possible to get almost any typeface you wish.)

Bob Bly, who was introduced earlier in this book, markets his own reports as one of his several freelancing activities. He uses a simple, clean

Closeout–Surplus Directory

by Herman Holtz

If you like to trade, and enjoy dynamic, fast-moving
business situations where you must keep your wits
about you, you will probably love this field.

AN INTRODUCTION TO CLOSEOUTS

America is a land of plenty. We have enormous surpluses of many things, especially manufactured goods. When a new product appears--transistor radios, pocket calculators, videocassette recorders, and many other items--it is often an immediate sellout at high prices. (Small, transistor calculators sold for $300 and more when they first appeared, and many people paid up to $2,000 for the first videocassette recorders.) Mass production and subsequent market saturation, plus competition from cheaper models--somebody will always find a way to make it cheaper--drives the prices down, and suddenly manufacturers and dealers are holding huge, slow-moving inventories. Or it may be style changes, bankruptcies, miscalculations, "dumping" by foreign manufacturers, or other misfortunes and chance occurrences that result in such great surpluses of inventory. Whatever the cause, the result is usually the same: The goods become *closeouts*, items offered far below their normal prices, even below their actual cost frequently.

These are all opportunities for dealers, brokers, agents, finders (who don't even have to buy and sell or even see the merchandise to make thousands of dollars as a special kind of middleperson or broker) and other alert and astute individuals.

Some of these entrepreneurs buy the items for resale--in bulk, individually, at wholesale, at retail, by mail, to foreign countries, and perhaps even in other places and by other means. Sometimes these entrepreneurs buy closeout and surplus goods for their scrap or salvage value. (Some products contain valuable metals, such as copper, iron, and gold, for example.)

Some finders work entirely in closeouts, tracking down both buyers with needs for sources and sellers with needs for buyers, matching them up and collecting a finder's fee from one party or the other. Or, as a variant of this, the

Figure 9–2.   Typical precomputer specialty report.

HERMAN HOLTZ
P.O. Box 1731   Wheaton, MD 20915
301 649-2499   Fax 301 649-5745

CLOSEOUT/SURPLUS DIRECTORY

WHAT IT IS, HOW IT WORKS

by Herman Holtz

*If you like to trade, and enjoy dynamic, fast-moving
business situations where you must keep your wits
about you, you will probably love this field.*

AN INTRODUCTION TO CLOSEOUTS

America is a land of plenty. We have enormous surpluses of many things,
especially manufactured goods. When a new product appears--transistor radios,
pocket calculators, videocassette recorders, and many other items--it is often an
immediate sellout at high prices. (Small, transistor calculators sold for $300 and
more when they first appeared, and many people paid up to $2,000 for the first
videocassette recorders.) Mass production and subsequent market saturation, plus
competition from cheaper models--somebody will always find a way to make it
cheaper--drives the prices down, and suddenly manufacturers and dealers are
holding huge, slow-moving inventories. Or it may be style changes,
bankruptcies, miscalculations, "dumping" by foreign manufacturers, or other
misfortunes and chance occurrences that result in such great surpluses of
inventory. Whatever the cause, the result is usually the same: The goods become
closeouts, items offered far below their normal prices, even below their actual
cost frequently.

These are all opportunities for dealers, brokers, agents, finders (who don't even
have to buy and sell or even see the merchandise to make thousands of dollars as
a special kind of middleperson or broker) and other alert and astute individuals.

Some of these entrepreneurs buy the items for resale--in bulk, individually, at
wholesale, at retail, by mail, to foreign countries, and perhaps even in other
places and by other means. Sometimes these entrepreneurs buy closeout and
surplus goods for their scrap or salvage value. (Some products contain valuable
metals, such as copper, iron, and gold, for example.)

Figure 9–3.   Same report turned out by modern
computer system.

typescript, as shown in Figure 9–4, page 1 of his report on moonlighting. However, Bly adds the refinement of a cover sheet in a tinted paper, rather than using the self-cover as I do. The cover sheet of his moonlighting report is shown in Figure 9–5.

Of course, many other formats are possible. Some freelancers write small books on the order of 25,000 to 40,000 words (about 60 to 100 pages) and have them printed and bound via saddle stitching (folded with staples in the center) or perfect binding (single sheets and cover glued on the spine), as mass-market paperbacks are usually bound. Such books are usually offered at from $10 to $20. Two representative titles are *The Lazy Man's Way to Riches* by the late Joe Karbo and *Out of the Rat Race and Into the Chips* by Hubert Simon. Both books provide accounts of the authors' personal misfortunes, subsequent travails, and eventual victories as a guide to helping the reader go and do likewise.

Sidney Allinson, of Ontario, Canada, (also introduced earlier), is a freelance writer who calls himself a "communications consultant," probably mandated by the wide array of writing assignments he handles. He says that military history is a personal interest that led him to the development of a book and many magazine articles on the subject. His research for those also led to his own publication, the *Military Archives: Military Publications International Directory*, which he updates each year (see Figure 9–6). On the subject of specialty publishing in general, he says he has ventured into that market several times and observes that

> this is probably one of the most neglected areas for writers. It has the great advantage of letting each writer follow [his or her] own particular interest, while making some money, too. Whatever interest or field writers are in professionally, or whatever their personal interest is, specialty publishing can offer real opportunities.

Because you are selling information, and not paper and binding, format is of relatively little importance. The important considerations are convenience of use for the reader, understandability of instructions, and efficiency of presentation. Keep the readability factor in mind when writing— or, probably more to the point, when re writing. For many of us, especially when working with a computer and word processor, it is most efficient and effective to write out a first draft without worrying too much about organization and language, and then rework it in successive drafts, reorganizing and simplifying the structure and the language. As a sage on the subject once observed, all good writing is rewriting. The best style here is one of straightforward explanation with an economy of language.

Special Report #608

SUCCESSFUL MOONLIGHTING: HOW TO EARN AN EXTRA $2,000 A MONTH
FREELANCING PART-TIME
                                           TM
by Robert W. Bly, Your High-Profit Writer

      Full-time freelancing is a great life. A wonderful life. And a lucrative
business. But it is not for everyone. At least not at first.

      Because everyone is different:

      * Some people are risk-takers. Some are not.

      * Some people can live with uncertainty and a degree of insecurity. Others
need the regularity of a steady paycheck, the security of having a corporate
employer take care of their health insurance, dental plan, retirement benefits,
etc.

      * Some people do not have significant financial responsibilities and are
able to live inexpensively while they test the waters in the freelancing
business. Others have a family, mortgage, car payments, college tuition, and
cannot risk jeopardizing their present income.

      * Some people have the financial reserves to see them through 6 or 12 lean
start-up months as they get their practice established. Others do not have this
type of financial reserve.

      * Some people are not dependent on their working income because they have
money from other sources: spouse's income, investments, real estate, pension,
social security, etc. Others have no other source of income and are completely
dependent on salary or self-employed income for survival.

      Whatever your situation, you need to determine what is the best course of
action for you at this moment:

      * Should you quit your job, take the plunge, and go out on your own today?
in a month? six months from now? a year?

      * Should you put aside your dream of freelancing and continue working at
your present employment until the time is right for you to make a change?

      There is a third alternative:

      * You can MOONLIGHT. You continue working at your regular job full-time
while taking on commercial freelance writing projects done on evenings,
weekends, and vacation days.

Figure 9–4.   First page of one of Bob Bly's reports.

Special Report #608   *$7*

Successful Moonlighting

How to Earn an Extra $2,000 a Month
Freelancing Part-Time

---

by

Robert W. Bly

The High-Profit Writer™

Figure 9–5.   Cover sheet of Bly report.

ISSN 0821-5537

MILITARY ARCHIVES

Military Publications
International Directory

Libraries, advertisers, military historians, militaria collectors, and researchers can benefit from the unique, respected, International Directory of Military Publications. This compendium of worldwide information, rarely available elsewhere, helps you contact military buffs who share your interests or are potential customers. IDMP lists 600 military and defence magazines, newsletters, and periodicals on a wealth of topics:-

Armaments	Defense policy
Military history	Battlefields
Regimental activities	Military Science
War campaigns	Revolution
Aircraft archeology	Colonial wars
Warships, naval affairs	Nostalgia
Militaria	War Museums
Disarmament movements	Armour, Tanks
Servicewomen	British army
Weaponry	Veterans Assocs.,
Espionage	US Civil War
Badges, insignia	Viet Nam.
Zeppelins	Soviet forces
Two World Wars	Napoleonic era
Air forces	Korea

Plus a hundred more categories, in over 600 hard-to-find military publications from over 20 countries, including: Australia, Belgium, Canada, England, France, Germany, India, Israel, Japan, NATO, Pakistan, Roumania, Saudi Arabia, Soviet Union, Switzerland, United States.

$12.00 (U.S)   Order your copy today!

Published by Sidney Allinson
242 Mary St, Suite 1118, Victoria, BC, V9A 3V9, Canada

Figure 9–6.   Circular for Allinson's self-published book.

MARKETING REPORTS

These specialty publications are generally sold by mail order and direct mail. Both approaches involve taking and filling orders by mail, although in recent years prospects are also invited to order by telephone. Mail order presumes advertising in the print and broadcast media, whereas direct mail presumes advertising by mailing literature to lists of names and addresses. The distinction is not very important, and it is perhaps not recognized by everyone. There is a tendency to refer to both approaches collectively as "mail order." Those who work in direct mail are probably the most eager to make the distinction, which is understandable, for the preparation of and mailing out of direct-mail literature is an important industry. A writer can easily make a full-time, long-term career in this field alone.

There are a number of periodicals that are especially appropriate for advertising specialty publications. Many publishers of such items, even of recipes, advertise in the classified advertising columns of the weekly tabloids sold in supermarkets (e.g., *The National Enquirer* and *The Star*). These periodicals have relatively high advertising rates, even for classified advertisements, because they have such wide circulation—millions of readers. There is another class of periodical, a much less expensive one, that is widely used to sell specialty publications. These are also tabloids frequently, although some are in a magazine format. They generally have a circulation of a few thousand readers (probably 5,000 is a fair average), but there is a large number of these periodicals, and their advertising rates are relatively low. They represent a good way to get started on a modest scale. (A starter list of such publications is offered in Appendix 2.)

NEWSLETTERING

Depending on whose figures you choose to accept, there are between 30,000 and 100,000 newsletters produced in the United States. They are produced daily, weekly, biweekly, semimonthly, monthly, bimonthly, quarterly, semiannually, and possibly even annually, but the most popular publishing schedule for newsletters is clearly monthly. They are one page, two pages, four pages, and larger, but the most popular size is four pages, usually an 11- × 17-inch sheet printed on both sides and folded to make a four-page presentation.

The majority of those newsletters are published for some special purpose: as the information medium of some organization, as a marketing tool, or as a publicity device. Many, but by no means the majority, are published as for-profit ventures. They can be highly profitable, and if a certain degree of caution is exercised, they can be launched on a small budget with minimal risk.

Here I am likely to encounter some difference of opinion from newsletter mavens. There are many so-called "experts" who will assure you that a newsletter venture requires a startup capital of many thousands of dollars. These dollars are deemed necessary to launch a large-scale promotional advertising campaign to obtain enough initial subscriptions to gain the economies of scale in printing, fulfillment, postage, and other costs that will all but ensure success. Alas, these megadollar newsletter launches fail as often as the minidollar launches do. Dollars spent on promotions are not guarantees of success. Moreover, beneficial and desirable as it is to minimize costs, the printing and fulfillment costs are not the major critical factors.

The number of small newsletter startups is a large figure, but it does not exceed the number of newsletter failures by a great deal: The casualty rate in newsletters is formidable. As Sidney Allinson observes, many writers are tempted by what appears to them to be an easy and profitable field. (I might add that many nonwriters make the same mistake.) It's a "monkey on your back," as Allinson puts it, which you soon discover. The time between issue deadlines, even on a monthly schedule, seems to be almost zero. Perhaps it is a good idea to start with a more leisurely schedule— bimonthly or even quarterly. You can always change to a more frequent schedule later. There is also the constant research, seeking interesting and fresh material for the next issue, and sometimes a frantic last-minute drive to plug holes in the issue.

Still, newsletter publishing is attractive, and a successful one can be a pot of gold: There are many multimillion-dollar newsletter-publishing companies. One publisher of a number of newsletters located in the Washington, DC, area sold out a few years ago for about $15 million.

A Few Tips and Guidelines

Figure 9–7 shows page 1 of a typical simple newsletter format. The area set off by lines at the top of the page is known as the *nameplate*. If you publish on a regular schedule, you include here an identification of the issue (e.g., June 1993) and whatever else you wish to include, such as volume number and issue number. In this case, the number 101 identifies the issue, since it is on an "occasional" schedule, published when I see fit. Generally, a subscription price is printed here too, even if you use the newsletter for marketing purposes and never actually charge anyone for a subscription.

WRITING FOR MONEY

"No man but a blockhead ever wrote except for money."
--*Samuel Johnson, 1776*

No. 101   Editor/Publisher Herman Holtz

HOW DO YOU BECOME A WRITER?

The complaint of a fellow worker at RCA many years ago has stayed in my memory ever since: He complained that an individual graduates from college with a degree in dentistry or engineering and is then a dentist or an engineer, but he graduated with a degree in literature and still wasn't a writer. He thought it most unfair.

He was referring to a career as a freelance writer, which is the real challenge for a writer and the kind of writing career to which most "wannabe" writers aspire. It is also the writing career we are discussing here.

One does not--can not--become a writer by going to college. One *need* not go to college to become a writer. A college education is always useful, but it has little to do directly with one's success as a writer. Most writers are self-taught, reading, studying, and practicing, often for many years, in quest of success.

THE QUEST FOR WRITING SUCCESS

Unfortunately, many seek the fruits of writing success in the wrong orchards. Probably most beginning writers have the notion that they will write short stories, great novels, or even plays. But we are not all novelists or playwrights. There is equally great need for writers of non-fiction. In fact, more than half the books produced commercially (and on best-seller lists) are works of non-fiction.

There is more to it than that, however. There is the basic definition of freelance writing: Just what is it?

THE MODERN MEANING OF FREELANCING

The classic freelance writer of old conceived and wrote his or her stories, articles and books, at his/her own expense and on his/her own timetable, and then tried to sell them to commercial publishers. In the beginning, at least, most wrote these things "on spec," in the hopes of selling them. Many literally starved and shivered in unheated garrets, a la Edgar Allen Poe and many others whose works are classics today.

That is where the years of disappointment--rejection slips--came in and still do for many who choose to freelance in this manner. One day, when and if the freelance writer becomes well established and well known as a dependable writer, editors may offer assignments, with guaranteed payment and even with guaranteed expenses paid. But that day is far off for most struggling beginners. In the beginning, the writer wants only to see his or her first acceptance. That is freelancing the hard way for most of us. It means working on spec and praying to find buyers, and the failure to sell the manuscripts we write in those early years may have nothing to do with the quality of our writing. There are lots of reasons for even excellent manuscripts to earn rejection slips instead of acceptance checks. But there is another way, another meaning to that word *freelance*. Instead of working

Figure 9–7.   A simple newsletter format.

"News" in a newsletter is not news of the day, of course, since your newsletter is likely to be a monthly, or so I shall presume. In fact, your newsletter may not attempt to present news of *any* kind, but if it does, it might include such features as the following, pertaining to whatever industry, profession, or other field it covers:

- Personnel notes: New hires, promotions, moves, obituaries

- Industry events: Startups, mergers, shutdowns, closings, bankruptcies

- Special events: Meetings, conventions, trade fairs, association news

- New products, new programs, offers (yours and others)

There are many other kinds of items you can use. You may wish to include letters, brief abstracts, comments, or questions from readers. You may wish also to answer readers' questions in an "Ask the Expert" kind of column. You may write editorials or invite guest editorials from others. You may discuss issues of interest in your field or have guest writers do so. There are really no limits to the coverage but your own imagination and the resources to which you have access.

Marketing Newsletters

Newsletters are ordinarily marketed by mail, usually by direct mail. In most cases, alternative marketing methods prove less successful and far more expensive. There are many ways to promote your newsletter via releases, giving away free issues at conventions, and offering complimentary subscriptions to other newsletter publishers, with offers to permit free use of your material as long as attribution is given.

One requirements for newsletter success is an adequate rate of subscription renewals. Some experts believe that a 65-percent renewal rate is necessary for success. That is why you get so many frantic efforts to renew your subscriptions as expiration dates loom. Getting new subscriptions is an expensive proposition; it is much less costly to keep the ones you have. Jerry Buchanan, who was mentioned earlier, reported once that he tried getting early renewals from subscribers by offering a two-year subscription for one cent more than a one-year subscription. He got a great response, with many of his subscribers signing up for two additional years. However, this cost him in later renewals, since so many of his subscribers were now signed up for two years instead of one.

Defining Newsletter Success

If your newsletter sells well and brings you a large income, there is no need to talk about defining success, it is well enough defined by itself. But newsletter success does not necessarily mean a large net profit on the newsletter itself, desirable although that is. Many newsletters operate marginally or even at a loss in those terms, and yet are well worth the time and money invested because they are profitable in another way. They are marketing tools, and their publishers turn an adequate profit on reports, books, tapes, computer disks, and other products sold using the newsletters as a marketing medium.

Jerry Buchanan is one newsletter publisher who runs a mail-order bookstore. James Kennedy, who publishes a newsletter for consultants, is another, and there are many others who sell books relevant to the subjects of their newsletters. Jim Straw, publisher of the well-known *Business Opportunities Digest*, sells his own library of reports and books.

This suggests that your newsletter has a far better chance of succeeding if you have other things to sell and can use your newsletter as the medium by which you reach customers. Those other "things" need not necessarily be reports, books, tapes, or computer disks, however; they may be writing/editorial services or seminars. Tied together in this manner, the newsletter; the books, reports, computer disks, and tapes; the writing/editorial services; and the seminars support each other. Together, they comprise an interesting business venture. You may judge for yourself which aspect interests you the most and then concentrate on that aspect. Like many others, you will probably find that your writing/editorial services venture has turned out to be considerably different from the one you had anticipated. Never mind; you are not the first, nor will you be the last, to discover that you don't often end up where you thought you were going when you started!

Chapter 10

The Tools for the Job

There are three kinds of tools needed to turn out specialty publications: hardware, software, and personal skills. But with the right kind of modern hardware and software, the need for many specialized personal skills is greatly diminished, replaced largely by the 'skills" and "knowledge" embedded in the computer software.

THE COMPUTER REVOLUTION
HAS ITS HOLDOUTS

Columnist Robert J. Samuelson composes his column with a computer, rewriting, reorganizing, and revising his copy until it is ready to ship off to his publisher. He marvels about the efficiency and convenience of working his copy in the computer this way—of *composing* it there, that is. But he has a problem: He says that he can't "actually *write* [emphasis mine] on a computer." He writes his drafts with an old Royal manual typewriter and then inputs the copy on a computer for his refinements and embellishments. But he must have paper copy on his desk in front of him, he says, to create the drafts he will eventually key in to the computer.

He is evidently not alone in this peculiar mental set. (It seems to me an aberration of some sort.) I have heard similar ideas from writers who *do* write at the computer keyboard, but are able to create only the roughest of drafts there. They say that they must have hard copy—words on paper in $8^{1}/_{2} \times 11$-inch sheets—to do their self-editing, reorganizing, revising, and rewriting. They feel unable to do this on screen.

I have frequently witnessed this problem in many offices where bright—even brilliant—professionals shrink in near panic from the desktop computer, many still writing their drafts in longhand on yellow legal pads before entrusting them to word processor operators.

I suppose it is the classic problem of old dogs and new tricks. In fact, you do not have to be that old to have trouble writing at a keyboard attached to a screen that displays only 11 or 12 lines at a time, if you use double spacing. I experienced some initial difficulty in working with this mere fragment of a page myself. I soon discovered that it is easy to use single spacing on screen, displaying 24 or 25 lines, while still printing out double-spaced hard copy from the single-spaced display. However, I found it difficult to work with single-spaced copy before me and so opted for keeping the familiar double-spacing on screen. I was determined to adjust my mental set appropriately to the situation.

It is also possible to get a full-page monitor and work with a full-page screen, although this setup has not become very popular, probably because of its expense and the clumsily large size of the monitor. Most writers have learned to work with the smaller screen display.

I sympathize with Samuelson, not because I share his difficulty but because I am saddened by his loss, his inability to enjoy the fruits of what is to me a marvelous writing machine. He complains that the Computer Age has not produced noticeable improvements in efficiency or productivity over all, while he freely confesses to lumbering along with an old manual typewriter! (Yes, I am an old dog who is a computer enthusiast; there are quite a lot of scribblers of my era who are writing with these machines as enthusiastically as the young. That old saw about old dogs and new tricks is not as true as some pundits would have you believe.)

The modern machines are an enormous asset, no matter what kind of writing you do. They are especially advantageous to the writer who is also a specialty publisher. In fact, they are all but tailor-made for specialty publishing.

THE RIGHT HARDWARE
AND SOFTWARE

Specialty publishing has become especially attractive and viable in recent years. This is the direct result of the development of modern desktop computers and related technological achievements, especially the spectacular advance of computer software and laser printers. Less than a decade ago, when I first published my own special reports and newsletters, it meant composing or "setting type" laboriously, via an IBM® Selectric typewriter, which had become an almost universal choice as a technological advance in itself—probably the most successful and most popular typewriter of all time. If I wanted a distinctive headline or title, however, I had to resort to such laborious means as "rub-down" or "transfer type," which were really decals, as shown in Figure 9–2. I then trotted out to a local copy shop to have xerographic or offset copies of my manuscript made, according to how many I needed. In fact, one of the few compensations for being in an expensive downtown office suite was the ready availability of copy shops and other necessary services within easy walking distance.

It is entirely possible to continue this practice today. The Selectric is still an efficient tool for composing, transfer type is still available, although not absolutely necessary, and you can either go out to a local copy shop to make a few copies of your report or newsletter or buy your own copier. A copier can be had for as little as about $375 today, and even the least expensive copiers do an excellent job. (If you need a few hundred copies, it is probably less costly to use the offset printing available in most local copy shops.)

However, desktop computers have become so popular and are priced so modestly that it is possible to own a complete computer system, with adequate software and a serviceable printer, for well under $1,000. Thus, it is reasonable to assume that you will be working with a computer and word processor eventually, if not initially. Preferably, that will be a modern desktop computer, rather than one of those dedicated word processors that are a compromise between a computer and a typewriter. They look like typewriters, with small liquid crystal display screens (although some have computer-type cathode ray tube monitors), and they have some computer features, such as a small memory and replaceable disks for longer-term storage. But the cost differential between these machines and full-blown general-purpose computers is not a great one, while the difference in capabilities is enormous.

Although you can do the job without this modern hardware and software, you will have enormously improved flexibility with such equipment. In fact, you will need far less personal expertise when you are properly equipped: The special knowledge needed for many functions resides in the software. If it happens that you are not a very good speller, for example, the spell-checking and dictionary programs are there to help. If you are searching for synonyms or a more appropriate word, you may consult the thesaurus that accompanies most major word processors. In addition to these items, you are likely to get an outliner program that facilitates planning your writing for content and format. WordStar® and other modern programs offer a columnar mode and right justification also, if you want these features. A "find" feature will help you find every occurrence of some word or term that you have used, and if you want it changed (e.g., from "Brown" to "Braun"), you can have the program make the change automatically each time it encounters the word in its search.

Additional software can provide you with help in correcting grammatical errors, laying out your copy, creating art and inserting it in the text passages, and performing many other tasks. (Some word processors may include several of these functions also.)

Initially, in the Stone Age of personal computers (circa 1981–1982), there were editors and formatters. These were combined in what became known as *word processors*. Then "dtp"—desktop publishing—programs came along, as the hardware became more capable, with more memory and greater storage capacity. Dtp programs were designed to facilitate the creation of newsletters, brochures, catalogs, and other publications, including those combining text and illustrations. They took most of the pain out of creating layouts and otherwise designing products.

Not to be denied, the makers of word processing programs added many dtp functions to their own products, and so today simple dtp needs can be satisfied by the more sophisticated word processing programs, although dtp software is used extensively by many with more sophisticated and complex dtp needs.

Thus, most of the expertise needed for many tasks resides in software programs, and the expertise you need is often merely knowing which programs and features to use and how to run the programs. (For example, when I was working on this manuscript, I wanted several of my lists to appear in two columns. I typed them as a single column and had WordStar convert my keyboard input to a two-column format. WordStar did all the calculations for formatting the printed-out hard copy. WordStar also did the two-column, right-justified formatting of Figure 9–7.)

Perhaps even more important than the skills provided by the many specialized software programs is the great flexibility that any word processing software provides you as a writer. Before I became the proud owner of a desktop computer, I did much of my rewriting by literally cutting and pasting, to minimize the amount of retyping I had to do. I filled my wastebasket with clippings and discards every day. With computers and word processing, you no longer need to wage an internal battle to decide whether it is better to cut and paste or retype a passage you want to save; a few keystrokes and you have reorganized the material electronically, while your discards vanish without a trace.

The advantages are at least twofold: It is much easier to create the original material, and it is much simpler to update it when updating or revision becomes necessary. Look at Figure 10–1, which lists two copyright dates of a report I originally wrote in 1977 and decided to revise completely in 1988. I deemed the changes important enough to merit a new copyright date for the report at that time. The original manuscript existed only as ink on paper. Now it is preserved as a computer file, and future revisions will be easy to carry out.

As an alternative to copying on office copiers or at least the local copy shop, you can use a high-speed printer. For a time, I used a 24-pin dot-matrix printer. It is a feasible way to print out copies of your reports if you need only about 200 or 300 pages per day. There are faster dot-matrix printers, but they are so costly that a laser printer is a more practicable idea for a greater volume of perhaps 1,000 or more pages per day. I use a laser printer today and find it almost ideal: It can print large type, easily to 60-point and greater (the original report title of Figure 9–3 is in 24-point type), and it can mix boldface, italic, and other type styles also. With the proper software, you can easily insert illustrations and tables or matrices, integrated with the text in single- or multicolumn formats. You can also use condensed type, right-justify the copy, and stylize copy in several ways. You use cut sheets in these printers, unlike the computer paper that you must "burst" (remove the strips of paper with the tractor holes at the sides and separate the pages). That distasteful job has become a chore of the past.

COMPUTERS AND
OTHER HARDWARE

Although there are a few mavericks in the desktop computer field, there are only two major types to consider, from a practical viewpoint: the Macintosh, of Apple® Computer Inc., and the IBM® PC type and its compatibles, made by several dozen other companies. The "Mac," as Apple's Macintosh® model is generally referred to, is generally conceded to be the leader in computer graphics. If your own involves graphics extensively, you will probably do well to give serious thought to the Mac. Otherwise, think about the IBM or one of its clones, by far the more popular computer type, which easily dominates the field. Compatibility with the equipment of clients and suppliers is a serious issue. (Many shops keep both a Mac and an IBM type to ensure compatibility with all others.) Apple has made efforts to improve compatibility with IBM-type com-

Herman Holtz

P.O. Box 1731   Wheaton, MD 20915
Fax: (301) 649-5745   Voice: (301) 649-2499

THE TRUTH ABOUT COPYRIGHT LAW

by Herman Holtz

Copyright law is one of those things about which a great many myths and misunderstandings have sprung up. Here are the basic facts, some of which will probably surprise you.

POPULAR BELIEF: To get copyright protection you must register your property with the Copyright Office.

WRONG: Copyright protection is far simpler to secure than that. In fact, in the words of the Copyright Office, here are the facts:

Copyright protection subsists from the time the work is created in fixed form; that is, it is an incident of the process of authorship. The copyright in the work of authorship immediately *becomes the property of the author who created it.*

Copyright was always easy to get, but under the newer law (the Copyright Act of 1976, which became effective January 1, 1978) it became even easier. It is not necessary to register a copyright with the Copy right Office to get the protection of copyright. However, there are reasons for registering a copyright in many cases, as you will soon see.

WHAT IS COPYRIGHT?

Copyright means literally the right to copy or the right of ownership of the creation, and it is available for literary works, computer programs, music, drawings and paintings, and similar works of creation. As the author of the work, only you and/or others to whom you grant permission or assign your rights can reproduce, copy, or make other use of your property.

The current law provides copyright protection for the life of the author plus 50 years, with no renewals authorized.

WHAT CAN BE PROTECTED BY COPYRIGHT?

Copyright covers the specific and unique *combination* of words, musical notes, colors, brush strokes, computer commands,etc that constitute the artistic property. It is only that combination of elements that is so covered and protected by the copyright.

Figure 10–1.   First page of a typical report after revision.

puters, so this may well become less of a problem, but it is one to consider. The IBM types, which use DOS as their operating system, have advanced steadily. Currently, the 386 series of AT (advanced technology) computers—those using the 20386 microchip—are highly favored because they are speedy and versatile, although the 486 is now beginning to loom large. There are many variations of the 386, from the 386SX, which is the least speedy of the series (although still speedy), to a model that is a bit more than twice as fast as the SX model.

Aside from that, there is an enormous variety in features included in any given model (known as its *configuration*). Probably most popular at the moment is a 386 model with 1 megabyte (mb) of memory; a 3.5-inch, 1.44-mb floppy disk drive; a 5.25-inch, 1.2-mb floppy drive; and a 40-mb hard disk. I chose to have 2 mb of memory; a 305-inch, 1.44-mb floppy drive; a 5.25-inch, 360-k (kilobyte) floppy drive; and a 65-mb hard drive, although I could have gotten along easily enough with a simpler configuration.

This is a relatively sophisticated computer, one that replaced the 286 series of AT computers rather quickly after the 286 succeeded the XT (extended technology) series. Still, the XT and 286 AT computers are highly serviceable and adequate to do the job most of us need to do, so if you own one of these, you need not change. If you can get one cheaply enough, consider it seriously. You can always trade up later—when it becomes truly obsolescent—to whatever is then the state-of-the-art machine.

Printers

Printers have gone through the same evolutionary changes and developments that other equipment has. Initially, daisywheel printers, using a print technology similar to that of the Selectric typewriter but with a type wheel instead of the Selectric type ball, were the top of the list. They produced the only true letter-quality print, while the output of 9-pin dot-matrix printers was of a barely acceptable second quality. Soon, improved 9-pin printers were offering a "near letter quality" print mode by a technique of double-striking, while they also offered a fair degree of versatility in their ability to switch to italics, boldface, other font sizes, and graphics, all under the control of the software. As those capabilities developed, daisywheel printers began to fade from the scene.

Still later, 24-pin printers, offering something very close to true letter quality and greater speeds became popular. Meanwhile, along came the laser printers with near typeset quality, greater speed, and almost silent operation. Today, 9-pin, 24-pin, and laser printers co-exist. Laser printers, which cost thousands of dollars when they originally came on the market, are now offered in much less expensive versions. You can choose today from a wide variety of laser printers offered at from under $700 to less than $1,000, although there are still a number of more expensive models offered. Once you have a laser printer and proper software (font sets, primarily, with their accompanying software), you will have solved several problems. For one thing, you will be able to set your own type and will never have to buy typesetting services again, unless you have a quite unusual typesetting need. Most laser printers today can produce copy that is satisfactory for all but the most exacting printing needs.

Modems, Public Databases, and Electronic Bulletin Boards

Briefly, a modem is a device that enables one computer to "talk" to another over an ordinary dial-up telephone line. It does this by converting the inaudible electrical signals from within the computer circuits to an audible signal that a telephone line can transmit. It also does the reverse, reconverting the audible signal to electrical pulses that the computer can "hear." In this manner, you can send information to and receive information from any other computer equipped with a modem. The modem is attached to your computer as another "black box" on your desk or as an internal device that is installed within your computer's housing as a "card." Functionally, it makes little difference.

A computer with a modem is an enormous asset to a freelance writer. It is possible to do a great deal of your research via the window on the world that it provides. There are thousands of files available in public databases and electronic bulletin boards that are valuable sources of information you can search without leaving your desk. You can actually transfer ("download") these files—electronic copies of them, that is—to your own computer, where you can store, edit, cite, use the information in them, and even include them in your own manuscript if they are not copyrighted. You can participate in discussions and on-line seminars, ask questions, and even exchange ideas with and get answers and advice from others, all while seated at your own desk. It hardly pays to invest in a computer and other equipment without adding a modem to your system and gaining the wealth of additional benefits bestowed by this device.

Copiers

A copier of your own must not be an absolute necessity because I managed well enough for a long time without having one of my own. However, now that I have my own copier, I find it indispensable. I once wasted a great deal of time running out to find a copy shop and waiting in line there for my turn.

I paid $400 for my copier, and there are now similar copiers available for a bit less than that. So you can see that there isn't much reason to deny yourself the asset of your own copier. If you have or buy a fax, you will find a copier of sorts built into it, but it is a copier of limited capability—not a good substitute for a plain-paper copier.

Fax Machines

Depending on the kind of work and clients you have, a fax machine can be an even more indispensable asset than a copier. Even with the only occasional use my own fax machine gets, I would not care to be without it. When the occasion does arise for its use, the alternatives are all unacceptable.

WORD PROCESSORS

The most indispensable software for a writer is the word processor— software for writing, editing, formatting, and otherwise creating and managing manuscripts. Although it is spurned by many today in favor of the popular WordPerfect® and Microsoft Word®, the granddaddy of word processors is WordStar®. It was the predecessor of what have become the standards for word processing and other software. Once, it was without peers, the leader in the field. However, although it still exists as a major player, WordStar has lost its position of eminence to WordPerfect, a rival word processor that is acknowledged as the leader in the field in terms of popularity and sales. Word is the Microsoft entry into the field of word processing, and it is also highly regarded as a major contestant in the field, with its own retinue of supporters and champions.

XyWrite is a kind of maverick word processor, quite different in many ways from its competitors, much revered by many writers and apparently a favorite in many newspapers and other periodicals.

Whatever word processor you choose, bear in mind that you will probably want a spelling checker, thesaurus, and outliner as main features. You may also want to consider capabilities for indexing, footnoting, collecting a table of contents, and producing running heads or feet. These are all useful features that modern word processors can furnish, but you must check in advance to be sure that the word processor you choose offers them.

ELECTRONIC COMMUNICATIONS AND RESEARCH

With a modem connected to your computer, you can be in touch with the world from your own office, as suggested earlier. However, there is a great deal more to be said about the subject of electronic communications and research.

Communications Software

Your modem is a piece of hardware, and it needs communications software to run properly. Your word processor may include its own communications program, as mine does. There are many available; some excellent ones are offered as "shareware." These are programs written by individuals who will permit you to try them without charge, placing you on the honor system to pay for them if you like them and continue to use them. They are available without charge on many electronic bulletin boards, but there are also many small companies offering such programs on disks for a small fee to cover shipping and handling. WordStar's communications software is called TelMerge. Some of the better known communications programs are ProComm, QModem, and Telix, and there are many others.

Special Application Software

There are many programs that are highly specific to writers' needs. If you write résumés, for example, you can get special résumé software. One excellent one that I have used, mentioned in Chapter 6, is named Spinnaker™ Better Working™ Résumé Kit, written and marketed by the Spinnaker™ Software Corp.

There are programs available for a broad array of applications. Most of them can be modified and adapted to your own preferences, and they save you a great deal of time and effort. There are programs of form letters, some of them highly specialized (e.g., collection letters). There are programs of items useful for publishing your newsletters, brochures, and specialty reports (e.g., clip art, quizzes, humorous stories, fillers). There are forms generators and programs offering outlines and models for such things as proposals, annual reports, and catalog sheets.

Many of these programs are available as shareware. This is one of the instances in which a modem can be especially useful to you: It enables you to examine the shareware files available on bulletin board systems, which you can download to your own computer and try out.

Bulletin Board Systems

The majority of electronic bulletin board systems (BBSs) are available at no cost, run by individuals as a hobby. Others are run or sponsored by computer clubs, business firms (e.g., computer manufacturers), government agencies, and other nonprofit organizations. A few charge a modest annual fee, as much to discourage mere curiosity seekers and children as to help defray the costs of operation. However, there are also BBSs that are dedicated to and encourage calls from teenagers; some experienced users refer to these as "kiddy boards."

The typical fare on a bulletin board is centered on one or more "conferences," which are the areas where callers post messages on any topic, addressing the message to another individual or to "all." Some BBSs have many conferences; some have only one. However, most have a files area where software files of all descriptions are stored. Usually, there is a listing with a brief description of what is contained in the file. BBSs with extensive files in storage also subdivide the files into separate lists, including such categories as the following (a partial list):

> File utilities
> Disk utilities
> Word processing
> Text files
> Graphics
> Database management
> Business
> Games

Public Databases

Public databases are designed as research and information resources for specialists such as lawyers, physicians, investment advisors, physicists, and engineers. With the aid of such systems, a lawyer need not spend many hours researching in dusty libraries for precedents, for example; a few minutes on line with LEXIS or one of the other public databases for the legal profession will probably supply all the precedents necessary for any given need. Physicians and lawyers often access the MEDLARS system, the electronic medical library of the Public Health Service on the campus of the National Institutes of Health in Bethesda, Maryland. But not all public databases are so specialized; there are many of a more general nature that may interest almost anyone on either a business or personal basis.

Hybrids

There are commercial systems that are something of a hybrid, combining the features typical of the BBS with those of the public database. They tend to resemble the BBS more than the public database, although they are of a more sophisticated nature and charge "connect-time" fees (e.g., $12.50/hour) and bill per minute of usage. In addition to the basic fee, some have special areas to which access entails paying an additional fee. CompuServe, mentioned in Chapter 9, is probably the best known of the commercial systems designed for the general public. Genie and Prodigy, two other well-known systems, were also mentioned in Chapter 9.

For the writer, these systems represent a priceless research capability. For example, in searching for a given book, a list of books on a given subject, or even for journal articles on some subject, I have examined the catalogs of public libraries and universities throughout the United States while seated comfortably at my desk. A great many standard reference sources are available via this medium. A client once asked me to determine the potential government market for shelters made of steel. I used my computer and modem to access the *CBD Online* database and searched the columns of the *Commerce Business Daily* for government procurements of such products. Within an hour I had downloaded all the relevant information and was then armed to write my report. I included the downloaded data directly, entering it into my word processor. After removing extraneous information that was not germane to the listings and information the client wanted, I edited the material and incorporated it as the focus of my report.

A Few Special Tips

Other uses I have made of my modem include the following:

- *Soliciting Information for Research*
  I have often left messages on various bulletin boards—including CompuServe—soliciting information, opinions, and ideas from others. This usually produces substantial results, often even directing me to other sources, whose existence had been unknown to me.

- *Surveying Opinions*
  I have used this same method to gather a mailing list of qualified

sources to help me with opinion polls either through mailing questionnaires or asking questions and getting responses electronically.

- *Informal Promotion*
  Although using bulletin boards for direct advertising is generally
  taboo, there are acceptable ways of using them indirectly for promotional purposes (e.g., planting a simple announcement of your prod-
  uct/service while querying others on a related subject or simply
  making comments). For example, if someone asks a question regarding copyright, it is legitimate for me to respond with a brief answer
  and mention of my report on the copyright and related subjects.

- *Informal Marketing Testing*
  It is acceptable to ask opinions of others to get some idea of the
  market for a product you are contemplating producing or to use
  indirect means for getting a few orders or inquiries as an alternate
  method for market testing.

These ideas are hardly exhaustive. With a bit of imagination and experience, you will almost surely come up with many more.

PART III

THE SECRET OF
SUCCESS IN WRITING

It is not news that the average person has an aversion to (or is it fear of?) writing. I suppose that is why our letters so often go unanswered or bring only a hastily scribbled note at the bottom of the initial letter, a brochure, or a form letter (often completely irrelevant) as a reaction. Anything to avoid being forced to actually *write* a response. Even the executives of major corporations are reluctant to respond to letters from customers. Twice, my letters to Hewlett-Packard (in reference to a printer I bought from them) went unanswered until I wrote a second time. Even that produced a telephone call, after several weeks, rather than the letter I expected,

Why is that? What makes writing such a difficult and distasteful task for so many? Why is it that schools at all levels find that courses in writing have only limited success?

One reason, I am sure, is the confusion in the minds of many over what writing is. Writing courses are loaded with rules and guidelines in grammar, spelling, punctuation, rhetoric, imagery, and other mechanics of the art. That is, they teach the use of the *tools* of writing. But a person can become expert in using tools and still be woefully inadequate in creating a finished product. The ability to use a hammer and saw does not translate directly into the ability to create a beautiful cabinet, or even to build a shed or a set of shelves. A person can have a beautifully modulated voice and flawless delivery and yet be a complete flop on the speaker's platform if he or she has nothing to say that is worth hearing. And a person can be the perfect grammarian and rhetorician and still write something that says nothing worth the time required to read it. It is necessary to discriminate between the tools of the trade and the arts of conceptualization and design. And it is necessary to recognize the validity of and the necessity for that discrimination.

As an even more important ingredient than excellence in using the tools, the art of writing includes having something to say. That involves several other considerations, one of which—the art of thinking—I have yet to see featured in lessons on writing. This notion was born as a result of some years of experience as a writer, editor, and manager of publications and related editorial functions. For many, if not most, of those who write badly and fiercely resist writing even a simple letter, the real problem is not a difficulty in understanding and using the mechanics of the written language; it is a reluctance to think, perhaps even a fear of thinking.

The kind of thinking I mean—considering available information, analyzing it, and drawing conclusions from it—is hard work. It also requires courage, because it requires you to exercise intellectual independence, thinking for yourself and quite possibly disagreeing with conventional wisdom or what "everyone knows." But that is what writing is all about. Thinking is an indispensable basis for writing. We can write only what is in our heads, no matter how it got there.

Many of us start a piece of work with stream-of-consciousness writing, simply jotting down ideas as they occur. Perhaps that constitutes a rough first draft for some, but for many of us it is little more than making notes. I have heard it called "thinking on paper" by some writers for whom it is a means of sorting out their notions. For others, it is a means for developing a lead. It is a special way of outlining for many of us who prefer not to draw up a formal, detailed outline. As such, it is almost certain to be vague, disorganized, pompous, and half-baked. That does not mean that it is not useful, however. The danger lies in forgetting what it is and treating it as an actual draft, which it is not.

The professional writer is a disciplined writer who never doubts the truth of the old writer's cliché that all good writing is rewriting. Those of us who subscribe to that doctrine don't believe that we are geniuses who are so inspired as to write well in a single draft. Whether you have a detailed formal outline or start with a general outline that exists only in your mind, expect to rewrite at least once. Yes, rewriting is usually tedious, often boring, hard work. As the *Reader's Digest* once pointed out, the secret of success is hard work, which is why it remains a secret. Any experienced writer could have told you that.

Chapter 11

Good and Bad
Writing Habits

It is almost as easy to develop good habits as it is to develop bad ones, and it makes life a great deal easier. That is as true for writing as it is for other things.

BAD HABIT NUMBER 1: SELF-DECEIT

At one point a number of years ago (circa 1960), I was the editor of one of several groups of technical writers at an RCA plant in Riverton, New Jersey. We were developing technical manuals for the Ballistic Missile Early Warning System being installed in Greenland, England, and Alaska. Among the drafts I was handed to review and perform my own ministrations on was a slender manuscript purporting to explain the priority system of the on-site telephone systems.

I found it difficult to follow the explanations. Fortunately, as the beneficiary of an education in electronics engineering, I was able to read and understand the wiring diagrams for the telephone system. I therefore searched these out and used them as a reference to help me follow the explanations in the manuscript.

I soon found that this was of limited help. I could understand the system well enough from my brief study of the wiring diagrams because it was simple enough, but the text did not furnish the needed information to explain how the design invoked priorities. I had to interject most of it mentally, deriving it from my own study of the drawings.

I was perplexed. I knew the young technician who had written the manuscript. He was an articulate, bright graduate of Air Force technical training, and I did not doubt his ability to express himself well. I invited him to confer with me about his manuscript.

I asked the author if he were having difficulty in understanding the system. He assured me that he had no such difficulties: He understood the system well enough and thought that he had explained it well enough. I then asked him a few pointed, technical questions to test that alleged understanding. His answers did not satisfy me that he did, in fact, have an adequate technical understanding of the system.

I decided to experiment. I told him that I would hang onto his manuscript, but I asked him to spend the entire day studying the drawings and then try once again to write the manual, starting over from scratch. He agreed, albeit reluctantly. A few days later, however, he submitted a perfectly lucid, totally acceptable manuscript.

I don't think that young technical writer had consciously lied to me. I think he had convinced himself that he knew the system. Self-deceit is not that hard to fall into. What we call "bad" writing is all too often "bad" in that the writer does not know what he or she is talking about. He or she has not thought the subject out and formulated firm ideas. That may be due to sheer laziness, but more often stems from inadequate research, although that also may be due to laziness. In other words, it is not bad writing as much as it is bad thinking or lack of knowledge of the subject. Even when the writing itself *is* bad, it is often the writer's compensation for bad thinking—an unconscious effort to cover up and conceal, even from himself or herself, the inadequacy of the information presented.

DISGUISING BAD THINKING WITH DOUBLETALK

Bad thinking shows up in different places and in different ways. It shows up often in technical manuals when an author gives highly detailed explanations of a part of the system that he or she understands thoroughly while skipping hastily through subjects about which he or she knows next to nothing. It often shows up as purple prose, by which the writer is trying to conceal ignorance and lack of preparation behind a smokescreen of pompous doubletalk. That kind of writing is not always the author's attempt to appear erudite and eloquent, as many of us are inclined to think; often, it is an unconscious effort by the author to conceal from himself or herself the lack of something to say. Why else would anyone write something as meaningless as the following passage from a federal report?

> The ratio (or amplification factor) of private sector activity to federal activity can be characterized by the ratio of privately financed to federally financed solar heating and cooling systems installed annually.

If the writer had taken the trouble to get some actual figures or even a gross estimate of the ratio referred to, he or she would have provided some information and had no need for this kind of doubletalk. Moreover, the use of the term *amplification factor* in apposition to the word *ratio* implies that private-sector activity is amplified by federal activity in the installation of solar heating systems. Or is the amplification in the opposite direction? There is no way to know which is the case or whether either is the case.

SYMPTOMS VERSUS DIAGNOSTICS

The preceding example of bad writing is a symptom of something. Because it is meaningless phrase-making, further aggravated by a vague hint of one factor inspiring a rise in the other, the passage is not only noninformative, but confusing. Why raise the matter of ratios at all if you have nothing concrete to say about them?

Were I to write something as deplorable as this—and I am quite capable of doing so in a first cut, as many writers are—no harm would be done. No harm would be done because the passage, as written, would never survive my own editing. I would, almost by reflex, grin and say to myself, "What in the world could I have meant by that?" I would have had to decide, first, whether it was important to present the information at all. If so, I would have done more research to get the information that should have been included in the passage. If the information was not available, I would have been forced to either drop the passage or, if I thought it necessary to express that vague idea, I would have stated clearly that this information was not available at present. Even then, the writing could be vastly improved through simplification:

The ratio of private-sector activity to federal activity is indicated by comparing the number of solar heating and cooling systems installed by each.

There are two points to be made here. The first is that self-editing, especially of your early drafts, is absolutely necessary. You must assume that there is always a need to review what you have written, and you must learn how to do this objectively, a skill that you can acquire with practice and discipline.

The second point is that symptoms of problems such as the one this example illustrates should be used as diagnostic tools for the conscientious writer. When I edit my work and find such symptoms, I am able to recognize them for what they are so that I can correct the problem. I have learned to recognize the vague and rambling writing that reveals that I either have not done enough research or have not studied and thought out the materials I gathered. If you make it a habit to use such symptoms as these to guide you in your self-editing, your writing will improve steadily.

HOW MUCH SELF-EDITING?

Self-editing is difficult because it requires you to try to be objective about and critical of your own work. It requires discipline to do so, but the reward is a better product. The question is, How much self-editing should a writer do?

There is no easy answer. In my case the number of self-edits I need is as many times as it takes until I am satisfied, and even that is not totally accurate. I am no Henry James, endlessly polishing my work and weighing every word. Yet, like most writers, I am never completely satisfied with what I have written, no matter how many times I have rewritten, revised, reorganized, and polished. I compromise between what I want and what is practicable before I reluctantly go on to my next writing task. I must be reasonably well satisfied, but my schedule is a factor in how many times I will go through my copy. I know that my first draft is never good enough and my second draft is rarely good enough. I usually go through several drafts, and I may rewrite, revise, reorganize, and polish some portions of my manuscript—especially my lead—almost endlessly. Even then I may finally despair and discard it all in favor of a fresh start. I believe that the willingness to do this is indicative of one's integrity as a writer.

OBJECTIVES OF SELF-EDITING

A common mistake many writers make is to misunderstand the specific objectives that should be pursued in self-editing. Many writers settle for a mere subjective judgment of their eloquence. In fact, there are a number of objectives in self-editing that require logical analysis a great deal more than they require artistic appreciation. Following are a few common problem areas:

Grammatical Errors

Most common errors are well known. Unfortunately, many reflect everyday colloquial expression. Thus, we unconsciously come to accept split infinitives, sentences that begin with conjunctions and end with prepositions, and dangling participles. The same thing applies to punctuation, as we fail to distinguish between dependent and independent clauses, misuse colons and semicolons, or use too many or two few commas.

These are not cardinal sins. Today it is generally considered better to split an infinitive than to create an awkward construction. In some cases a writer will commit a grammatical error deliberately, as in simulating conversation, for example. However, it is important to be alert to problems and correct them when they are not justifiable.

Poor Transitions

Bridges must be provided to proceed smoothly from one topic, paragraph, or sentence to the next. The lack of a bridge jars and confuses the reader. This is especially the case when you are finishing with one subject and proceeding to a new one. Here, you must alert the reader to what you are doing. Sometimes the transition is self-evident from the nature of the material. Sometimes a simple word or phrase such as "however," "on the other hand," or "in addition to" is sufficient to introduce the new element. In other cases, especially where the change is quite abrupt and to a subject unrelated to the one you have just been discussing, you may have to be quite specific and write an introductory sentence or paragraph to keep the reader informed.

Ambiguity

This is a particularly tricky area because it is a common problem in writing and often not easy for the writer to detect. Ambiguity usually results from a lack of precision in writing. It is most important to develop a sensitivity to it. When you encounter a suspect sentence or paragraph, ask yourself, "Is it possible to interpret this reasonably in more than one way?" If you train yourself to do this conscientiously and objectively, you may be surprised at how often you will find yourself rewriting passages that could easily be misinterpreted by the typical reader.

Right and Wrong Words

We all have more than one vocabulary. We have at least three: vocabularies for reading, speaking, and writing. The popular notion that a large vocabulary is important for writing is mistaken. It is helpful to have a large vocabulary because that helps you think out ideas, whereas a limited vocabulary limits your range. But if you want to be understood easily by your readers, you should keep your vocabulary simple. Try for a level about that of *Reader's Digest* unless you are writing for some highly specialized readership.

One of the problems is finding and using exactly the right word for your purpose. The word *stubbornness* can be used to laud or to criticize, according to its context, for example. But some words bear their own implications, no matter how you use them. *Rascal* may be used as a term of affection, but *scoundrel* is always an epithet, and *gay* will never again mean what it once did. I once abandoned the use of *epitome*, although it was exactly right for my purposes, because I learned that few readers know *precisely* what it means, and precise understanding was necessary for the context in which I had used it.

One of my pet peeves is the frequent misuse of the word *convince*. It should always be used to indicate an act of persuading someone to *believe* something, and never as persuasion to *do* or *not* do something. "He convinced her that he was right" is correct. "He convinced her to leave her husband" is not correct. The latter sentence ought to be "He *persuaded* her to leave her husband."

The dictionary is of no help in this. It furnishes definitions but is not entirely clear on connotations. Only being sensitive to usage and the fine shades of meaning that distinguish synonyms from each other can help you understand why it is jarring to discriminating readers to read something such as "He convinced her to go to work with him." Following is how my on-line dictionary (*American Heritage*) defines the word *convince*:

convince
verb. -vinced, -vincing.
To bring to belief by argument and evidence;
persuade.
convincer noun.

convincing adjective.
convincingly adverb.

You must also consider what words are "right" and "wrong" in terms of how they will be received or interpreted by the reader. This changes with the times. In these times of heightened sensitivity to inequalities, for example, you must use even the term *ladies* with great care. I received several letters of bitter denunciation as a result of using that word in a newspaper column. A few female readers found the word patronizing and condescending, almost as bad as *girls*, and they did not hesitate to let me know their feelings. Nor should you refer to an African-American male as "boy," even if the person to whom you refer is a mere boy. African-American men have been sensitized by society and history to regard that word as degrading.

The Overall Goal of Self-Editing

Someone has pointed out that a main goal in all editing is the reduction of the number of words. That idea is based on the notion that the typical writer overwrites badly and is far too verbose, repetitious, and redundant. Speaking as a writer who has published millions of words, I plead guilty to that charge. Even after I have endured the pain of discarding thousands of my own words as repetitious, boring, and generally unnecessary, my editors discard many more, and I generally suffer in silence, acknowledging my unnecessary verbosity.

An overall goal in self-editing is to reduce your verbosity. It is all but certain that you can eliminate many of those adjectives and adverbs, parenthetical remarks, asides, and other extraneous observations. Using the active voice will itself tend to reduce verbosity, since it is usually more economical of words than is the passive voice. The result is tightened copy, a much more vigorous and brisk style, and greatly improved readability.

STYLE

Your style is as individual and personal as your working habits. Take Ernest Hemingway, for example. His style resulted primarily from an early experience with an editor who convinced him of the beauty of a terse, simple style. He learned to use the active voice and to keep his sentences simple and declarative as much as possible. Academicians will probably urge you to avoid sentence fragments and to follow many other rules that acclaimed writers frequently ignore to achieve certain effects such as a representation of how people really talk. (Most of us do speak in sentence fragments and otherwise ignore rules of usage in our conversations.)

Of course, there is more to a writing style than this. If you write enough, you will in time develop your own style without conscious effort. (Hemingway was so unconscious of his distinctive style that he would insist that he had none in particular!) It is a mistake to try to develop one consciously or to imitate someone else's. You simply need to have a clear idea of what you are trying to say, always focus on your reader, and make your meanings as clear as you can. Your style will evolve spontaneously. However, do try to avoid the trap of using the heavy-handed, pompous, and often jargon-ridden language that is referred to derisively as "purple prose." Also try to minimize your use of adjectives and adverbs if you want to develop an efficient and energetic style. That alone will tend to steer you away from "purple prose."

AUTOMATING YOUR WRITING

The computer and word processor automate your writing. That does not mean that your writing is made mechanical. What it *does* mean is that certain functions are mechanized or made automatic, principally the functions that are tedious, laborious, time consuming, and wasteful of your time. The essential benefits of the word processor are that it electronically cuts and pastes for major reorganizations, copies material that requires repetition, checks your spelling errors and typos and corrects them, searches out items, and otherwise saves you time and energy. For me, two-finger typist that I am, the spelling checker is among the most valuable software features. Two-finger typing, even after many years of practice, requires at least a casual visual surveillance of the keyboard. As the years have taken their toll on my eyesight, the incidence of typos in my writing has risen rapidly. I am sure my editors are grateful for my conscientious use of spelling checkers to weed them out!

NEW WRITING HABITS

If you are new enough to the world of writing that you have never worked with a manual or electric typewriter, you don't have old habits to unlearn. Writers of my generation started before electric typewriters, many of us on the classic old Underwoods (so slow that typing with only two fingers did not exact a great penalty in productivity) and Corona portables. We thought we were in heaven when we acquired Selectric typewriters, and we were ecstatic when the desktop computers and word processors appeared. Unlike poor old Samuelson (Chapter 10), many of us were eager to embrace this new blessing and learn how to use it. Still, we had to develop new writing habits, and many writers, like Samuelson, had trouble doing so.

A major benefit of using a word processor is that it encourages revision and rewriting by making it so easy to do. Having written for many years with a manual typewriter, later an electric typewriter, and a now a word processor, I have become an enthusiast. Rewriting with a typewriter meant discarding and retyping many pages—often the entire manuscript. Even changing a few words on a page usually meant retyping the page. It is agonizing enough for even a proficient typist to throw 10 or 20 neatly typed pages of a draft into the trash basket once, but almost intolerable to force oneself to do it several times over. Even with a computer and word processor, I used to find it painful to discard hard (printed) copy. But I learned to cope with that and other problems by developing new habits.

Those bits and bytes in the computer are copy. The computer will translate them into characters on the screen or, via your printer, to characters on pages of paper. Somehow, however, it is not genuine copy to me until it is on paper. Because of this, I don't have as much trouble trashing copy that is still on a disk as I do trashing copy that is on paper. Therefore, I never print out my copy until I have finished revising, rewriting, reorganizing, and otherwise editing and making changes to it. That is, until I *think* I have finished with it. Even so, occasionally I am wrong and must dump the paper and go back to the computer anyway, but the new habits I have acquired have reduced the amount of wasted paper considerably. I find it much easier and less painful to delete words on a screen and move things around this way. My practice is to print out one chapter at a time, but not until I have been over that chapter again and again, even a dozen times, polishing it. Only then do I print out the completed chapter.

It was not easy to teach myself to do this. At first, I insisted on printing out my copy every few pages. Somehow, I didn't feel as if I had accomplished any work unless I could see it as a growing stack of manuscript on my desk. However, my modus operandi has finally become this: I start my day's writing by reviewing the current chapter from the beginning, editing it and making any changes I believe necessary. Normally, I then go on to add as many pages to the chapter as I can manage. This approach allows me to warm up for the day, and I rarely experience the phenomenon known as "writer's block." If I am underwhelmed by my own copy, I begin to consider whether my entire approach to the chapter has been all wrong. That may lead to my discarding everything I have done so far and starting over. (I have sometimes found it necessary to trash as many as 50 pages in these circumstances. That can be painful, but it is necessary if I care about the product. In one case, when I started over after getting rather deep into the writing, the final product turned out to be the most successful book I had written to date.)

These are habits that allow me to take advantage of the capabilities of these marvelous new machines. Something like them will work for you too, but your own needs, reactions, quirks, and work habits are surely much different from mine, so you must develop your own variations. You must learn to work differently from the way you may have worked in the past if you are to get the fullest benefits of the new hardware and software.

Chapter 12

The Preliminaries to Good Writing

Now that we have spent some time together talking about how to write, let's put the cart before the horse and talk about *preparing* to write.

ADVANCE PLANNING VERSUS EXCESSIVE REWRITING

Bringing up the subject of preparation for writing after the discussion of how to write is not as illogical as it may seem. Having had a look at some of the problems that arise as a result of inadequate planning and preparation ought to have been a good, sobering preview for this chapter. If you are anything like most other writers, you will find a direct relationship (albeit an inverse one) between the amount of preparation you do and the amount of rewriting that will be necessary. Even with careful planning, a certain amount of rewriting cannot be avoided. However, the ratio of preparation to rewriting is not one to one: Each hour invested in advance planning and preparation is likely to save you considerably more than an hour's worth of rewriting. That's the first and probably best reason for taking the time to think out your objectives and your material. Even writing a brief note requires that you think about what you want to say before you set pen to paper. You need to know to whom you are writing and what the objective of your writing is—what you want the reader to do as a result of reading what you have written.

Of course, the planning required for a simple note or memo is substantially less than that for a book or other lengthy piece of work, but the difference is in degree and not in kind. You don't need to think hard or long before writing a note to the super to check on the hot water supply in your apartment while you are at work, but you *do* when you have accepted a contract to write a user's guide to a computer software program or a book on sightseeing in Europe.

FIRST THINGS FIRST

The essence of planning and preparation is the outline, preferably a well-detailed one, unless you happen to be the kind of writer who works by "thinking on paper" with rough first drafts. Even if you are that kind of writer, as I am, a book-length writing project will usually require at least a general outline before you are ready to begin serious writing. But there are beginning steps to take even before you address the subject of how to develop your detailed outline. Consider the following three items as basic objectives to address as you are planning:

1. Identify the reader.

2. Decide what you want the reader to be able to do as a result of reading what you have written.

3. Decide how your material must be organized and presented to meet the second objective.

Identifying the Reader

I hope that even without a great deal of thought you will agree that you need to know who your intended reader is. You are unlikely to address a housewife as you would a bank president, if you hope to appeal to their interests, nor would you use the same language in writing to immigrants who are barely literate in our language as you would to professors of English. If you are working for a client, you must expect the client to furnish the identification of readers, but if it does not occur to the client to do so, it is still your responsibility to ask.

What Do You Want the Reader to Do?

I want you to be a successful freelance writer, selling whatever editorial services you choose to sell. That is my objective in writing this book. To the extent that you succeed as a result of what you read here, I will have succeeded.

I have written other works, pursuing other objectives. I have helped some engineers learn how to take some of the pain out of technical writing. I have persuaded many executives to award contracts to me, my clients, or my employers. I have helped some professional specialists add public speaking to their career activities.

Deciding what you want the reader to do is your reason and justification for writing. Without this objective, your writing would have no purpose. It would be like sailing a ship without a rudder or compass: How would you set a course without having a destination?

Deciding How to Organize Your Material

With this third objective, we get down to the real meat of preparing to write: the outline or master plan. Just how should the material be organized to satisfy the first two objectives? The objectives are interdependent, and their interdependence depends on how compatible they are. Here is a case in point.

Some years ago, the Environmental Protection Agency (EPA) issued a Request for Proposals (RFP) for a written program to train janitorial workers in New York City in methods of firing coal-burning systems to minimize air pollution. The trainees-to-be were described as "functionally illiterate," although some might be literate in another language.

The incompatibility of the identified readers of the proposed training program with the program's objective was apparent to everyone but those who wrote the RFP. Respondents all pointed out that a written program was not likely to be effective with trainees who could not read. EPA, clearly embarrassed, thereupon quietly dropped the idea and canceled the RFP.

Assuming that identity of the readers is compatible with what you want to accomplish, however, it is necessary to plan a presentation that is both compatible with and likely to achieve your objective.

METHODS OF ORGANIZATION

There are many ways to organize material, and in many cases there is more than one "right" way. Here are some of the most frequently used methods:

Chronological, from earliest to latest.

Chronological in reverse, from latest to earliest (retrospective).

Cause and effect, from cause to effect.

Cause and effect reversed, from effect to cause.

In order of importance, from least to most important.

In order of importance reversed, from most to least important.

Deductive, from established principle and analysis of evidence to conclusions.

Inductive, from observation and analysis of evidence to formulation of principles.

Of course, it is always possible to mix or combine these methods. That approach is most likely in lengthy pieces such as manuals and books in which certain sections or chapters require special treatment. You may use one approach over all for the book, but another for certain chapters.

You will probably not be able to decide on variations from the main approach and theme up front in your overall planning, but you must establish your overall approach, and that approach much be consistent with your objectives. If you are writing a user manual for a computer operator, for example, you have no need to go into the history of computers. You need only explain what the operator needs to know. If you are writing something you intend to sell or publish independently, you must define your audience and your overall approach by yourself. If you are writing something for a client, you should ask the client to help you decide just who your audience is and what it is that your reader ought to do as a result of reading what you have written. The client may expect you to have an opinion and make recommendations (as a freelance business writer it is difficult to avoid being forced to be a consultant), but the final decision must be the client's, not yours.

The same principle applies to the organization of the material and, for that matter, its coverage. On some occasions a client may offer you a general or detailed outline and a package of resource materials including all necessary data. Alternatively, a client may offer you a list of sources you can research to get the necessary information. Whatever the case, you are likely to regret it if you do not get the client's specific approval of your outline, which ought to specify the coverage as well as the mode of presentation.

PRESENTATION STRATEGY

Choices of approach and organization are not made at random. They are made to support and implement a perceived strategy of presentation. Having defined your reader, and identified your objective in terms of what you wish the reader to do as a result of reading what you have written, you now need to decide on a strategy to achieve that objective.

There are many ways to explain the purpose of a written product. It may be said that the purpose is to argue, refute, inform, persuade, teach, explain, reveal, or otherwise influence the reader. However, all of these are covered by the simple verb *persuade*. Everything that is written has persuasiveness as a purpose, even when its ostensible purpose is simply to inform, as in the case of a news story told as objectively as the writer can tell it. At the least, the writer wishes the reader to believe that the events in the story are true and took place as described. That is an act of persuasion. The real difference that distinguishes one piece of writing from another, as far as purpose or objective is concerned, lies in what the writer wishes to persuade the reader to do. Here is a small sampling of things you might wish a reader to do as a result of reading what you have written:

- Send in an order with payment.
- Vote for a given candidate.
- Come to a meeting.
- Come and visit a showroom.
- Send in a form asking for more information.
- Subscribe.
- Sign up for a course.
- Turn out for a rally.
- Come out for spring practice.
- Learn what CPR is.
- Learn the news of a great sale.
- Remit payment of an overdue bill.
- Come in and see the new models.
- Request a free demonstration.

The basic strategy is always to demonstrate to the reader why and how it is to his or her advantage to do as you suggest, but there are many ways to do this. There are also many possible obstacles to overcome, and that consideration will certainly affect your thinking in devising a strategy. If, for example, you are preparing a brochure that will be sent out only to those who have specifically requested it, you need not go to special pains to persuade the recipient to read it, although it is often a good strategy to remind the reader that he or she did ask for the brochure. Perhaps you have received envelopes that said, on the outside, "Here is the information you requested." If you can anticipate that the reader may not be interested in reading it, you must offer motivation. A teaser such as "Here is information that may enable you to save someone's life" is likely to induce the reader to be curious enough to read the brochure.

Motivation, the factor that ought to persuade someone to do as you suggest or read what you have written, is not always apparent to a reader. You must furnish the motivation. Here is an example.

On one occasion, when the editor of an engineering journal rejected my article on technical writing, I pondered for a while and then sent the manuscript back to that same editor with the addition of one brief paragraph as a new introduction. The paragraph said, "Most engineers hate to write, but your job requires that you do so occasionally. Here are a few tips to make the job easier." The editor bought it immediately. I had told the reader why he should read it, and that told the editor why he should buy it.

This consideration alone may affect your plan of organization. If you are trying to sell someone a new device, it may be more persuasive to tell how the device was developed chronologically, starting with the difficult problem the device was intended to solve. Charles Kettering invented the automobile self-starter for Ransome Olds, builder of the Oldsmobile, because Olds knew that he would never sell many automobiles to women as long as the automobiles had to be hand cranked to start them. Kettering took on the job that every astute engineer "knew" was impossible technically. The story of Kettering's success in doing the impossible can be told in either forward or reverse chronology, but it is the kind of story that is far more interesting if you first hook the reader by explaining why and how the self-starter was a foolish idea in the opinion of most engineers of the day. Then, with that scene set, the story of Kettering's struggles and eventual success unfolds. We all know that he succeeded, but once we have learned why it was considered to be an impossible task, we are drawn into the story, curious to discover the secret of his success.

If you are preparing straight sales literature for a $19.95 device of some sort, you are going to try to inspire direct orders from your readers.

However, if you are trying to sell a $999.95 item, you know that you are unlikely to get a single direct order. What you must do to pursue sales of that big-tag item is to build leads by persuading readers to do something that will identify them as being interested in the product. You may ask them to call, send for something, return a postage-paid card, or come in for a visit and demonstration.

Of course, you do not make an arbitrary decision on strategy. You work with the client, offering your ideas and reaching agreement. That is a most important element in custom writing. Effective liaison and coordination are essential.

THE HAZARDS OF LAX LIAISON AND COORDINATION

It is always hazardous to make assumptions, and especially hazardous when you are doing custom work for a client. When a dispute arises between contractor and client, who do you suppose is the loser? The contractor, of course. The way for you to win such disputes is to prevent them. No matter what the client has furnished or how you came by your final outline, you are on thin ice if you do not get the client's specific approval of your plan as represented by your detailed outline. A vague or too freely generalized outline offers a tempting opportunity to the client to decide that the product has not turned out as it was envisioned and approved. Therefore, the more detailed and specific the outline you develop and have your client approve, the greater your protection from disputes.

RESEARCH AND DATA-GATHERING METHODS

When undertaking a custom writing job for a client, it makes sense to look to the client as a first source of information. The client can usually supply at least some material and suggestions regarding sources for additional material. There are many other sources available as well:

- Knowledgeable individuals. (Interview and quote when possible.)
- Libraries and librarians.
- Public databases.

- Your own knowledge.

- Government agencies and their records.

- Associations and other nonprofit organizations.

- Manufacturers and other for-profit organizations.

When using libraries, be sure to ask the librarians for help. They are well acquainted with what is in their stacks, and they are usually delighted to help you find what you want. Also use the computers and microfiche readers found in modern public libraries to read old newspaper files and look up references. See whether you can get access from your own computer to CARL (Colorado Alliance of Research Libraries) via some local number. That will enable you to search the stacks of many public and university libraries throughout the United States. Check also on whether your own public library catalogs are available by computer. It is a growing trend that may well be established in your locality.

Electronic bulletin boards and public databases were mentioned in Chapter 10. These are valuable sources of data too, and they can be accessed without leaving your office. Learn where they are and how to make best use of their offerings.

Don't overlook the many public sources: government offices, associations, business owners' clubs, your local Chamber of Commerce and Better Business Bureau. Through such organizations you can not only find a wealth of printed materials that will aid your research, but also meet those knowledgeable individuals referred to earlier, many of whom will be only too happy to aid you in any way they can. Don't be hesitant to ask people for help. You will often be surprised at their willing and enthusiastic response.

Associations are often excellent sources of information, both quantitative and qualitative. There are several thousand associations representing virtually every industry, profession, career field, hobby, business, and other interest. For example, seeking information on the temporary-employment industry recently, I found an association of companies in that industry only a few miles from my office. A single telephone call, and I soon had an envelope stuffed with all the information I needed and much more. Your public library probably has more than one directory of associations.

There are also other types of nonprofit organizations that can help you, such as Chambers of Commerce, Rotary and Lions Clubs, and labor unions. Sometimes local universities and community colleges can furnish needed information and direct you to individuals who are willing to be interviewed and quoted. Make it your business to compile information on all such resources: They are valuable assets.

It does not occur to many writers that for-profit corporations can be a great asset to a writer. Many large for-profit corporations have public-information and public relations officers, and all have marketing departments. It is in their interest to cooperate with you in every way possible, as long as you do not represent an activity that is in conflict with their

XI. FINANCIAL CONSIDERATIONS

```
* Profit and loss statement
  - units sold
  - reserves
  - costs of goods sold
  - operating expenses
  - net income (loss)
* Cash budgets
  - beginning cash
  - cash from operations
          ● sales
          ● interest
  - cash from other sources
          ● investors
          ● lenders
  - cash uses
          ● capital expenditures
          ● cash operating expenses
          ● cash interest expense
  - ending cash
* Balance sheet
  - current assets
          ● cash, investments
          ● receivables
          ● inventory
          ● other
  - fixed assets
          ● machinery and equipment
          ● accumulated depreciation
  - total assets
  - current liabilities
          ● accounts payable
          ● notes payable
          ● other
  - long-term liabilities
          ● notes to officers
          ● term debt
          ● other
  - equity
          ● paid in capital
          ● retained earnings (loss)
  - total liabilities and equity
```

Figure 12–1.   Example of a detailed outline.

interests. I have used this resource frequently to get information, photographs, drawings, and other materials, usually with permission to reproduce, cite, or quote from them freely.

OUTLINE FORMATS

There are many ways to structure an outline, varying according to purpose and degree of specific detail. Some outlines merely describe what topics will be discussed, while others specify what will be said. When reaching agreement with a client on a custom-writing assignment, it helps to be as specific as possible, for the reasons already given.

Figure 12–1 presents a portion of a rather lengthy outline of a business plan. Note first of all the several levels of presentation provided by this format, four levels shown here in the figure, but six in the full presentation. This is the most difficult outline to prepare, but it is helpful in solving both your writing problems and your business problems to have such an outline.

Note next the specificity of the individual items: The "financial considerations" involve three major areas, the profit and loss statement, cash budgets, and balance sheet. Each area is detailed in the outline, which specifies what items will be presented in each case. In some cases, an additional level of detail is presented. Sources of cash ("cash from operations" and "cash from other sources") are listed, among other items at the same level, leaving little doubt as to what will be in the document described by the outline.

Not only does such detail head off disputes and give you an advantageous road map for your writing, but reviewing this kind of outline stimulates the client's thinking and encourages his or her active participation in offering criticisms and contributions that are often helpful. At the least, reviewing your outlines tends to involve the client in the planning process, a major factor in getting maximum client cooperation and minimum probability of subsequent disputes.

Chapter 13

Production Lore

Whether you wish to be or not, you are often compelled to be a consultant. Clients will look to you to be an expert in all phases of the process from original concept to printed product. Knowhow in these matters, including the the ability to counsel clients with great aplomb, helps to solidify the relationship.

WHAT HATH TECHNOLOGY WROUGHT?

Galloping technology has changed a great many things, and the production of typical business publications is one of the things most affected by technology. Before the desktop computer introduced electronic correction, my editors expressed the suspicion that I bought correction fluid by the gallon and correction tape by the case. Certainly, I kept my scissors and paste pot busy, trying to salvage what I could to minimize retyping as I revised early drafts. I was also one of the most familiar figures hunched over the machines in our neighborhood self-service copy shop, making new "originals" of shabby paste-ups, heavy with white correction fluid. The proprietor and I got to know each other quite well.

With my initiation into the world of the desktop computer and printer, a few changes took place. When I bumped into the copy shop owner in the supermarket some time later, he expressed relief in finding that I was still vertical and inquired as to where I had been the past few months. I stammered something about having become much less dependent on copiers.

Important as those changes are, they have not been the only ones; they merely ushered in an era of rapid and almost continuous change. Recently, I helped a client in Puerto Rico prepare a proposal to be presented to a county government in Maryland. As usual in proposal work, the finale was a frantic last-minute effort to do what should have been done a week earlier. My client and I kept the voice and fax lines between our two offices busy enough to keep the telephone company happy. Fortunately, the fax quality was good enough to be reproduced legibly on an office copier. This was an indispensable element of production: The schedule would not have allowed time to retype all that material. (Remember that in proposal work, unless there is a last-minute extension of the due date, delivery on time is essential. No proposal is worth less than one delivered after the deadline: Being late even by minutes means being rejected.)

WHO HANDLES PRODUCTION?

Ordinarily in proposal work, the client handles all matters of production, although he or she may seek your counsel. But it is not an ideal world, and you may very well find yourself caught up in an unanticipated situation, as I did in the case of one proposal. The client, unfamiliar with government proposals, would not have been prepared to print and bind the required number of copies of the proposal even with my guidance, given the problems of distance and schedule pressures. The ability to handle this kind of emergency situation successfully is more than an asset; it is an absolute necessity to your reputation as an expert in your field. But it involves both knowledge and equipment. I do not use my fax machine every day nor even every week necessarily, and I can say the same thing about my copier and some other equipment I use to support my activities as a writer/editor/consultant. But just one project, such as that proposal, can justify and pay for all this equipment, even leaving a profit. These are the tools of the trade, and acquiring a complete complement of the tools you need should be a priority, to be accomplished as rapidly as circumstances make it possible.

In the case of proposals, only a limited number of copies is normally required—not more than a half dozen, usually, for any but the largest projects. It therefore isn't practical to go to formal printing; in most cases the reproduction of copies can be handled adequately by an office copier. You can go out to a local copy shop to do this if the client does not have a copier that is accessible to you. However, there are many cases when this is not a good solution, and it is far more efficient to have your own copier. Small, inexpensive models are easily available today, and they produce copies of the same quality that the most expensive machines do.

UNDERSTANDING PRINTING AND PRINTERS

Clients will often look to you for guidance in getting their printing done, and they may even ask you to handle the printing. (Even some rather large companies have asked me to have substantial amounts of printing done for them.) Thus, an understanding of commercial printing, at least its basics, is a necessity.

You must understand first what printing is today. Traditional printing from raised type, à la Gutenberg, has long since been phased out of modern industrial processes except for special cases. After World War II, the transition was rapid: Virtually all commercial printing today is via photo offset lithography, also known as *photo offset, photolith,* and simply *offset.* (All those terms mean the same thing.) Whereas *lithography* literally refers to printing from a flat stone by the offset process, modern lithography uses photographic methods for creating metal, plastic, and paper plates that substitute for the flat stone. Modern printing is based on the simple fact that oil and water do not mix. The inks used are oil-based. The text or graphic to be printed appears on the print plate as an image that will accept oil or grease, but reject water. The plate is therefore first coated with water and then with ink. The areas to be printed reject the water and accept the ink, and the rest of the plate accepts the water and rejects the ink. The plate transfers the inked image (a mirror image of the original) to a soft roller called a "blanket," and the blanket then transfers that image to a sheet of paper, again reversing the image so that it comes out right side up.

Despite automation and other changes in many of the processes and methods of production, the old terms are still in use: *camera-ready, layout, makeup, roughs, mechanicals, halftones, make ready, masks, rubylith, windows,* and *negatives,* among others. We are still in a transitional stage, with technological advances not yet spent and the process still changing rather swiftly. Therefore it may be more important to understand computer technology and its term than to recall the older terms and methods. However, since there are still many old-timers with whom you must be able to communicate, it is useful to recognize the most common older terms and know what they mean.

Camera-ready copy is copy that has been composed (typeset) or is otherwise in final form, ready to be photographed and printed. This was traditionally done by photographing each page and then "burning" a metal plate from the negative(s). (Large presses use plates bearing the images of many pages.) Photographs and other *continuous tone* material are first photographed through a screen that breaks the material into many dots, thus creating a *halftone* negative, from which a halftone plate is made.

Over the years, new kinds of platemaking processes have been invented that are xerographic in principle (i.e., based on the same technology as office copiers are based on), making it possible to make and print from much less costly paper or plastic plates (although halftones are still best printed from metal plates, in the opinion of many). These less expensive plates are made without the negative, saving that cost immediately, as well as the cost of metal plates.

Layouts, the sketches that show how copy will be arranged on the page, were once done by specialists, usually illustrators, who first sketched rough layouts, planning the positioning of all the material to be printed, and then pasted up the *mechanicals* when all the camera-ready copy was available. The mechanical was the finished page, with all typeset and other camera-ready material pasted up to form a complete page from which plates could be made. The terms *camera-ready* and *mechanical*, are not exactly synonymous, however. A mechanical is ready to be photographed as one or more pages and is itself camera ready, but *camera-ready* may simply describe copy that is only a portion of what is to become a mechanical.

If a metal plate is to be used to print a page containing a photograph, the makeup may include a *mask*, which is a rectangle of black or deep red paper (*rubylith*), which the camera sees as blacker than black. When the page is photographed, the negative includes a transparent area or window through which the halftone negative may be seen when the plate is made.

This involves combining two kinds of negatives, *line negatives* and *halftone negatives*. Line negatives are those having only type and/or line drawings, with no screened or halftone negatives. Combining the two is known as *stripping*. Even a full-page photograph usually requires stripping because it normally includes a line or two of text.

Today there are alternatives to the classic halftone process. With modern platemaking equipment, a printed copy of a halftone may be pasted up and used as part of the camera-ready copy for platemaking. The final product will not be quite up to the quality standard of the conventional process of making a halftone, but it is acceptable for many uses. It is also possible to produce a reasonably good halftone via computer processes today.

Sizing applies to illustrations used in page makeup. It refers to determining the actual size of illustrations that will appear in the final product. Typically, original art is larger than the final paste-up chart or other illustration. Illustrators tend to prefer working "oversize" or creating a piece of artwork that is many times the size it will be in the final printed product. For example, I have had illustrators prepare charts in 4- × 5-foot poster size when each was to be printed as a single 8½ × 11-inch page, Slight irregularities in the original drawings disappear in the reduction, thereby greatly improving final quality. This is still a valid approach today, but if the art is done by computer (i.e., by desktop publishing hardware and software), the computer will do whatever sizing is necessary.

Modern computer equipment has taken over many of the makeup chores, especially for smaller publications, and most layout and the cutting and pasteup necessary to make up mechanicals can be done on screen and printed out as assembled camera-ready pages—mechanicals ready for the platemaker. Modern laser printers can produce copy of very good quality, although many traditionalists may still insist on using older methods. It takes a discerning eye to distinguish high-resolution laser-produced copy from copy produced by more traditional methods.

Changes have taken place in many areas, but not as extensively in printing. Operators of print shops usually calculate such items as the following in determining their prices:

- Camera work, negatives, and plates (already discussed).

- Make ready. This is the labor of setting a press up to print, making all the necessary adjustments to mount the plates, align the paper stock, and other such preliminaries.

- Color washes. This is the cost of washing down the press and switching to ink of another color if you order printing in colors other than black. (Every color requires another run of the pages through the press, plus careful *registration* (a more complex and exacting make ready) to ensure that the colors do not overlap each other.)

- Color separations. Printing line work (text and line illustrations) is relatively easy, with a color separation for each color. (Each part of the copy that is to print in a particular color must have its own mechanical and plate made. Such separate mechanicals are called *color separations*.) When continuous tone copy is involved, such as a color photograph, the separations are done by camera processes, and the separations are quite expensive. Two processes for color separations and printing are normally used, the three-color process and the four-color process. The latter is superior in quality and costs more. The inks used in such work are transparent; they blend in the printing, as in color TV, to reproduce the tints and tones of the original faithfully.

- Impressions. This is relevant for long runs (i.e., many copies) and is calculated in cost per 1,000 impressions.

- Paper. Standard costs are based on white sulphite bond, usually. Colored paper and stocks other than white sulphite bond are extra and are usually quoted individually. Very smooth (e.g., *calendared* and *coated*) papers add another level of difficulty because the ink dries slowly on them and special processes are needed to speed up the drying and prevent wet ink from transferring from a just-printed sheet to the back of the next sheet.

- Bleed. Printing that runs over the edge of the sheet, usually when it is a solid color.

- Collating.

- Folding.

- Binding.

- Trimming.

- Miscellaneous (e.g., storing).

SHORT-RUN VERSUS LONG-RUN PRINTING

There are short-run printers and there are long-run printers. The two are quite dissimilar, although occasionally a long-run printer will also have a short-run shop for special orders. Neither of these two types of printers can do efficiently what the other does. Long-run printing is equipment intensive: It uses large presses and is highly automated. Short-run printing is labor intensive: It uses small presses, is lightly automated, and does much of the work manually. The rationale is easy enough to grasp: To turn out 1,000 copies of a four-page newsletter on a large press would be highly impractical. The product would cost several dollars per copy! On the other hand, it would be hardly more practical to print 75,000 copies of a 200-page magazine on a small press.

There is no sharp line distinguishing between the two, but it is usually easy enough to make a sensible judgment as to which category is the right one for your own printing requirement. In any case, the manager of a print shop will normally redirect you to the right kind of shop if you have made a bad choice. It is not in his or her interest to take on printing jobs that are all wrong for that plant.

ULTRA-SHORT-RUN PRINTING

Since xerographic printing, originally introduced to industry and business by the company now known as Xerox®, first appeared, the original patents have expired and many improvements in the process have been made. Today, even the most inexpensive office copiers, such as my own Ricoh LR-1, produce copy as good as and often better than the originals. Competition, along with federal antimonopoly pressure, has forced prices down, so that xerographic copying is today competitive with short-run printing prices. That accounts for the neighborhood copy shop that advertises "Printing" but actually provides xerographic copying, collating and simple binding.

Again, the line between short-run printing via printing press and that done by office copier is primarily one of judgment. If you do not require more than 25 to 50 copies—or even 100, in many cases—copying may be a better and is almost certainly a faster solution.

THE TIME FACTOR

It is not unusual for schedule pressures to make time more important than cost. Submitting material to be printed by offset presses in conventional printing usually involves the wait of at least a day or two, whereas duplication via xerographic copying methods can almost always be on a while-you-wait basis and can even be done in house under your direct control. In cases in which the schedule requirement is absolutely firm, cost becomes a secondary consideration and schedule a primary one. This is another situation in which the use of copying equipment is the most practical solution.

CONTROL AND PLANNING
FOR CONTINGENCIES

Ideally, you ought to be in total control of every aspect of every project you undertake. I have spent many paragraphs preaching this doctrine so that you can minimize your dependence on others. Yet I know that the goal cannot always be realized: In many situations not all can be under your direct control. Many printing jobs can only be done by a commercial printer, for example, and many other support jobs also depend on outside services.

It does not take more than one race with disaster to demonstrate the need for contingency planning—alternative ways of achieving that which you cannot control. In my own approach to this problem, I prepare a primary and a secondary plan for each function for which I can foresee a tight schedule or other threatening possibility. For a large or difficult requirement for typesetting, printing, illustrating, or other production need, I will usually have a second source lined up and ready to take over the job should my primary source let me down. I study the production and delivery steps to detect the areas most likely to be problematical and plan accordingly. Such planning has prevented me from failing to meet my goals on more than one project.

Every case is different, of course, but there are certain commonalities. In some cases, part of the job is to be done by another department in the client's company. It is therefore not your problem if the other department fails to make good on its commitment to support the project. Yet, you feel morally responsible for getting the job done. Where this is the case, I recommend discussing with your client the alternatives available (i.e., contingency plans) should the support department fail to do what it is supposed to do. Your client may well have the authority to go to an outside commercial source if his or her own company cannot provide the necessary support service. Although you are not legally or morally obligated to point out the need to develop contingency plans, it is in your own best interest to do so.

QUICK-RESPONSE SUPPORT

In Chapter 8 I mentioned the advantages of supplying what the trade calls "quick-response" or "quick-reaction" services by being ready, willing, and able to work evenings, weekends, and holidays to bail out clients in trouble. Knowing suppliers and support services (typists, word processor

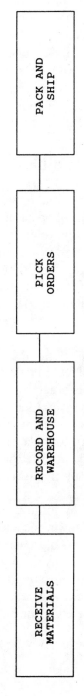

Figure 13-1. Top-level drawing of a series.

operators, compositors, editors, illustrators, artists, photographers, blue-print shops, etc.) who are ready, willing, and able to provide such services is an important asset for you. These are the resources that often save your skin by working on absolutely impossible schedules—doing what no one else can or is willing to do. There is no surer way to build your business than to develop a reputation for doing what no one else can do. You can and should charge appropriately for such super service, of course. Most clients will pay your bill gratefully and regard you as a savior.

SOLVING A SPECIAL PROBLEM

One common special problem that may arise is the need to present something graphically that cannot be easily presented in a single page or even in a pair of facing pages. There are two ways to solve this problem: One is to present a series of illustrations, from the high-level view to a series of lower level breakout drawings. Figure 13-1, for example, is a high-level chart presenting the chief functions of a process. A separate drawing might then be developed to elaborate on the functions referred to by each block. If necessary, the process might be repeated to create a third level of detail.

Sometimes this is a practicable method, but sometimes pullout draw-ings, which may run to several feet in length, are more suitable to satisfy such needs. This, however, may create another problem: Where and how can you reproduce a drawing several feet long?

One way some have addressed the problem, at least when only a few copies were required, has been to make copies of the several pages that make up the drawing and tape or glue them together. That is a rather clumsy solution and does not make a professional-appearing final product.

Another approach followed by some companies has been to go to the great expense of having such drawings copied by printing them on a large press, although they may require only a handful of copies. That is not only costly but slow, and ought to be used only as a desperate last resort.

There is another solution: Most blueprint shops can make a negative and ozalid copies of such a drawing at a reasonable cost, often while you wait. This is probably the best compromise solution for such problems.

Chapter 14

Word Processing Is Not Automatic Typing

Few people gain the full benefits of word processing. For some, that is because they do not understand everything that a word processor is and can be. For others, it is because they are "unable" (read "unwilling") to learn the new habits, perceptions, and orientations that word processors require if they are to deliver their full benefits.

OLD DOGS AND NEW TRICKS

The case of columnist Robert Samuelson (Chapter 10) is something of an aberration. Samuelson says he can *compose* his copy at the keyboard but can't *write* it there. He says he still pounds out his drafts on an old manual typewriter. Unlike Samuelson, most writers today write at the keyboards of their computers. Still, there are a significant number of writers who insist that they can't do their editing and proofreading on screen—that they can perform those functions only on hard copy (paper). They therefore print out what they have drafted and go over it laboriously with pen or pencil, then return to the keyboard to correct their files accordingly. That presumably includes rewriting and reiteration of the process an indeterminate number of times, which is hardly an efficient use of the medium.

It seems to me that writers who function in this manner are not much better off than those who still scrawl penciled manuscript in longhand on yellow legal pads and have a word processor operator keyboard their copy and return printouts to them for review, editing, and other editorial processing. They are getting little benefit from the use of computers and word processors. They might as well be using typewriters accompanied by scissors, paste pots, and correction tape.

Admittedly, it does take a little adjustment to learn to work with only a fraction of a page on display at any time, although there are compensating advantages. It is possible to have a full-page monitor. Because they are more expensive, they have never really caught on with the average writer. In any case, it is not the limitation of what can be presented at one time that is the real problem. The real problem is the unwillingness of many to unlearn old habits and overcome old self-conditioning, a reluctance to turn away from the familiar and comfortable old habits and accept the temporary discomfort of learning new and better ones.

It is my belief that everyone (even Samuelson) can learn new tricks, especially those as rewarding as learning to write with a computer and word processing software. There are enough computer-using individuals of my own age or near it to bear this out. Certainly, I can assure you that my own experience proves that it is possible for even old-timers to learn to write with this new technological miracle. (I freely confess to having been on the cusp of conventional retirement age when I confronted my first computer keyboard.)

THE COMPLEMENT OF TOOLS CALLED A "WORD PROCESSOR"

One of my aims in this chapter is to clarify what word processing means. Far too many writers perceive it only as a superior, labor-saving way of preparing final text. It is that, of course, but it is much more than that. In the early years of the era of personal computers, word processors did not, in fact, do a great deal more than prepare copy, with electronic cut-and-paste and limited search capabilities. Today's word processor, however, is quite another story. It is a research tool, a planning tool, and a complete copy- and office-management system. Modern word processing software has built into it or accompanying it an almost bewildering array of companion programs and special features to carry out a wide variety of tasks that save time in many ways only indirectly related to writing itself. Here, for example, is a summary of the programs and features my own WordStar 6.0 offers, in addition to the word processor per se. It is typical of most modern word processing packages.

- Maillist,™ a mailing list manager.
- Telmerge,® a communications program, driving the modem.
- ProFinder,™ a shell and utility program for dozens of file- and directory-handling tasks.
- PC-Outline,™ a program for developing formal outlines and planning your writing.
- Star Exchange,™ a program that converts (translates) word processor files from one word processor to another.
- Inset,® a program for generating graphics and inserting them into text.

Among the many applications possible are, in addition to general word processing functions, indexing, preparing a table of contents, creating footnotes and bibliographic references, addressing letters and envelopes, formatting newsletters, preparing charts, searching files and directories, sorting lists, moving files, and dozens of other useful tasks. It will run ragged-right or right-justified copy, run multiple columns, mix fonts and type sizes, insert graphics, and prepare camera-ready layouts, among other things. These capabilities are typical of modern word processors, and you should have such features available in your own word processor.

The principle method I am using in this chapter to get this information across is to describe and explain my own working habits, methods, software, and hardware, which have helped me exploit this new medium to become a more effective writer. Most of these ideas are common knowledge, well-known tricks of the trade. A few are ideas of my own devising, developed over years of working at the keyboard all day, every day, solving problems and seeking greater convenience and efficiency.

I hope that some of these ideas will rub off and help you, as they have helped me, become a more productive and even a *better* writer. I am a better writer now in that I now do far more editing, revision, rewriting, and polishing than I did before I had my own computer system. It has become almost fun to rewrite now. I believe that Ernest Hemingway, who claimed to *hate* rewriting with all the passion of which he was capable, would not mind doing so today were he equipped with this tool.

Before getting into the technical aspects of word processing, it is only fair to discuss its down side, for there is a down side in the ever-present hazard of a disk crash (the failure of your main storage device) and with it the instantaneous vanishing of your manuscript and every other bit of data stored on the disk. It can be a nightmarish disaster if you are unprepared for it, but it is a problem easily solved by preventive measures.

CRASHES AND BACKUPS

In the earliest days of the desktop computer revolution—the early 1980s—few of us could afford hard disks, which were most costly at the time. Most of us had computers with one or two floppy disks of 360 kilobytes (360,000 bytes or about 175 double-spaced pages) each. Generally, if we had two such disk drives we used one for programs and the other for copy. If we had only one, we had greater limitations, but we still managed to make do and turn out our copy. Little did we even suspect what great changes were coming or how soon they would arrive.

Floppy disks don't often crash, but things can still go wrong with them, so it was always a good policy to make a backup copy of manuscripts on a second floppy. My first machine had two floppy disk drives of 384 kb each, and so I kept a backup disk in my second ("B") drive and copied my drafts to the second disk every few pages.

Today, it is a rare machine that does not have a hard drive, usually at least 20 mb (megabytes) and often much larger than that today. Hard drives offer many advantages: They have much greater capacity (my 65 mb drive can hold thousands of pages of copy); their great capacity permits you to store many software programs that help you in writing; and they are much faster than floppy drives. They have one great disadvantage: They can crash, causing the instantaneous loss of all data on them. Sometimes most of the data on a crashed disk can be recovered, but that requires computer expertise most writers do not have, and it is by no means assured, in any case. We must assume the possibility of total loss of data. The use of hard disks makes *backing up*—continually creating copies of what is on the hard disk—a practical necessity.

Today, there are several ways to do this. One is a second hard disk in your machine, with a copy of everything that is on the first hard disk. Another is the Bernoulli Box,™ a special kind of hard disk drive that has a removable disk. Another is the floppy disk, and still another is data tape, using a special tape drive.

Using floppies for backup is by far the most common and least costly method, but it is also the most tedious. The largest floppy drives today are the 5.25-inch drive with floppies of either 360 kb to 1.2 mb capacity and the 3.5-inch drive with capacities of either 720 kb or 1.44 mb. That means that you must use at least 17 floppies to back up 25 mb of data. Or you can use alternatives that require fewer floppies, but are tedious in another way, such as trying to keep track each day of every file you have worked on.

As a compromise among the several possibilities, I have chosen the data tape. Tape drives are relatively inexpensive, and I use a miniature tape that will hold 60 mb. However, I keep the problem simplified by not keeping on my hard disk anything that I have only infrequent need for. For example, the only book manuscripts on my hard disk normally are the one that I am currently working on and source material for others for which I have already contracted.

As I write, I copy the day's work to two floppies. I copy an original WordStar-composed version of my manuscript (I still prefer the venerable but modernized WordStar to the more popular WordPerfect and other word processors) to a 1.44 mb disk and an ASCII version to a 260 kb disk. The ASCII version, which can be read by any word processor, will go to my publisher, along with my hard copy. The other disk will be a permanent archive, backing up my tape archive.

I am thus backing up my most important files, my book manuscripts, as I go. At the end of the day I will run my data tape and back up everything on the hard disk, but I am also ensuring that I can never lose the entire day's work, should disaster strike.

Once a book is in print, I not only remove the manuscript files from the hard disk and archive the floppy disk on which the copy resides, but also store a copy on another tape, a 40 mb tape that stores all the books I have written with a computer. (With 22 book manuscripts archived there, I still have room for as many more. Even the 40 mb data tape I use for this archive allows an incredible amount of text storage.) The point is to avoid cluttering up the disk with unused and therefore irrelevant material. Doing so minimizes problems related to disk storage.

ORGANIZING DISKS AND FILES

Computer operations and directory organization stem originally from what the manual calls a *root directory*. Figure 14–1 is a printout of what is in my own root directory at present. All subdirectories are listed here, along with special files that remain in the root directory. The directories labeled WFM and DBM are, respectively, the directory for this book and

ANSI	SYS	1709	09-16-87	12.00P	RAD		<DIR>	05-18-89	8:33P
AUTOEXEC	BAT	128	06-19-91	5:45p	RAMUTIL		<DIR>	05-18-89	8:33p
BAT		<DIR>	05-18-89	5:24p	RPTS		<DIR>	05-22-89	6:26p
CNSLT		<DIR>	06-06-89	2:45p	SA		<DIR>	05-24-91	8:24p
COL		<DIR>	05-23-89	5:29p	SD	INI	2497	06-16-91	6:56p
COMMAND	COM	47845	04-09-91	5:00a	SKD	DTX	1840	06-19-91	3:38p
CONFIG	SYS	256	06-19-91	7:09p	SPR		<DIR>	06-14-91	11:26a
DBM		<DIR>	01-03-91	12:13p	SUPERTXT		<DIR>	06-14-91	8:35p
DCT		<DIR>	03-26-91	5:37p	TAPE		<DIR>	08-13-90	10:33a
DEFSWAP	TMP	196608	06-21-91	11:51a	TD		<DIR>	10-31-90	9:39a
DOS		<DIR>	05-18-89	4:33p	TEL		<DIR>	05-18-89	3:58p
GOMOUSE	BAT	179	06-09-91	10:40a	TITLES	PF	43	06-11-90	5:51p
IBMBIO	COM	23591	09-16-87	12:00p	TOOLS		<DIR>	05-25-91	10:05a
IBMDOS	COM	30632	09-16-87	12:00p	TREEINFO	NCD	715	05-25-91	1:15p
LOGS		<DIR>	05-18-89	5:09p	UTIL		<DIR>	05-18-89	2:54p
MOUSE		<DIR>	06-09-91	10:38a	WFM		<DIR>	02-02-90	10:22p
NEW		<DIR>	02-19-91	10:19a	WIN		<DIR>	06-08-91	5:23p
NU		<DIR>	08-12-89	6:03p	WINA20	386	9349	04-09-91	5:00a
WS6		<DIR>	10-28-90	7:35p					

Figure 14–1. A typical root directory.

one for another book for which I am currently installing resource data as files. Other directories listed are for my tape drive, for an on-disk dictionary I use frequently, for my DOS commands, for my word processor, and for sundry other uses.

There are no hard and fast rules for organizing your disk. You must use your own best judgment and organize your disk to suit your needs. Usually, when you install a new program, the software will come with its own installation program that will, if you permit it to, set up a directory for itself. Other than that, it's up to you. I present seminars occasionally for clients, so I keep my seminar manuals and other related materials in separate directories. One of the subject matter fields in which I do this is consulting, so there is a directory named CNSLT where those materials are stored semipermanently. When I worked on a proposal recently, all data were stored in a directory of its own, now archived on a disk. Directories make life easier for you, especially when you are looking for something and can't remember where you stored it or what you called it. If I were searching for a file that concerns consulting, I would have a look at the files in my consulting directory (see Figure 14–2).

Even that does not always help. Sometimes a file is somewhat ambiguous with respect to its main subject matter, and it might be in any of several directories. Hence, something more in the way of aid is needed, something that helps you search out files when you don't even know exactly what it is you are looking for! There is software of several kinds to help you in this. First of all, there is the search function you will find in every good word processor. It will search out any term you want to find and

ATL	CTY	8576	04-21-90	9:24a	PEPP	MAN	43392	12-14-90	1:26p
BKS		3840	01-09-91	10:28a	PEPP	SEM	9984	09-05-89	6:53p
BOOKS		3712	01-09-91	10:26a	PRP	SEM	12032	09-18-89	1:33p
CIS		2688	03-30-90	4:10p	PRP	SHP	8448	10-08-89	1:19p
CNC	LTR	2176	12-09-89	12:05p	SABER	FAX	2432	02-08-90	9:36a
CNC	OL	8576	12-09-89	12:20p	SABER	SEM	7936	02-14-90	2:33p
CNSLT	MAN	4608	12-14-90	1:08p	SEM	FRT	10880	05-15-89	10:49a
CNSLT	MKT	74368	09-25-90	4:30p	SEM	I	24320	04-07-87	9:35a
CNSLTG	SEM	4992	12-14-90	1:09p	SEM	II	22400	04-07-87	9:34a
NAC	OUT	6400	01-18-88	5:11p	SEM	III	40576	09-11-90	6:04p
FORMAT		1408	09-11-90	7:17p	SEM	X	1280	09-10-90	8:59p
FRT		9088	08-29-89	5:01p	SEM	Y	1408	09-10-90	9:13p
GEN	BIO	6912	05-24-90	4:02p	SEM	Z	6400	09-10-90	9:05p
HRH		8832	06-12-90	4:47p	SMBUS	SEM	2688	10-01-86	5:28p
L	LST	2432	09-12-90	9:50p	SPL	BIO	7808	06-12-89	12:53p
LL		3200	09-12-90	6:15p	TITLES	PF	43	12-09-89	10:16a
METI	0	2048	02-17-87	2:37p	UC	GRP	2304	10-05-87	8:49a
METI	1	2304			Volume Serial Number is 16D2-73F				
MKTG	GOV	3712	03-07-87	11:27a	Volume in drive C is v				

```
40 file(s)      442027 bytes
             25067520 bytes free
```

Figure 14–2.   The consulting (CNSLT) directory.

will also operate on that term if you wish. For example, I can have that function find every mention of "Blank" and display it for me to examine. However, if I wish, I can have each such mention changed automatically to "Blake."

That function works only *within* a given file. But suppose I wish to find every mention of "Blake" within an entire directory. Or suppose I am working on a rather lengthy project—perhaps a large proposal—and can't recall what I said about some subject earlier or even whether I mentioned it at all. Or I may have hundreds of pages of source material in the directory and have to search hundreds of pages for certain items. I need help in this. Fortunately, there is software that does that too. In the case of WordStar 6.0, the software that does this is Profinder. If I want to know whether I mentioned Smartkey™ in any of the chapters that make up this directory, or what I have on file about radar characteristics, I can ask Profinder to search the entire directory for the key words I specify, and it will do so, presenting me with the copy containing the reference.

I have a hard disk that includes some 30 directories plus a number of subdirectories at any given time. (Each directory may have its own sub-directories.) It would be too laborious to plod through each with these programs when I really don't know what directories to search. I need something a bit more sophisticated to search the entire drive. Fortunately, there are many such programs. The one I use was given to me with my subscription to a computer magazine. It is one of many "find it" programs.

It is remarkably efficient in doing its job, and it accepts "wild cards," which are commands that authorize the program to include a range of responses. For example, I might ask the program to find every file I have that uses the term "CNSLT," the abbreviation I normally use for files pertaining to consulting. Figure 14–3 illustrates the results of three different search

```
       Filename      Size    Date      Time    Drive:Path
------------- ------- -------- -------- ----------------------
       CNSLT    .MKT   74368 09/25/90 16:30:04 C:\CNSLT
       CNSLT    .MAN    4608 12/14/90 13:08:12 C:\CNSLT
       CNSLT    .WOM   15581 09/02/90 19:25:18 C:\PRP
       CNSLT    .GVT   22400 02/26/91 08:49:04 C:\PRP
       CNSLT    .ART    9472 12/25/88 16:07:58 C:\ART
       CNSLT    .      19072 04/17/89 14:06:30 C:\ART\MS
       CNSLT    .2     19840 02/09/89 13:21:30 C:\ART\MS
       CNSLT    .ENT   13952 08/23/89 08:10:42 C:\ART\MS
              Search Complete, 8 files found.

       Filename      Size    Date      Time    Drive:Path
------------- ------- -------- -------- ----------------------
       CNSLT    .MKT   74368 09/25/90 16:30:04 C:\CNSLT
       CNSLT    .MAN    4608 12/14/90 13:08:12 C:\CNSLT
       CNSLTG   .SEM    4992 12/14/90 13:09:42 C:\CNSLT
       CNSLTMKT.ZIP   29949 11/05/90 18:02:56 C:\LOGS
       CNSLT    .WOM   15581 09/02/90 19:25:18 C:\PRP
       CNSLTNT  .WM2   19584 10/08/90 01:10:36 C:\PRP
       CNSLTNT  .WOM   16256 07/02/90 14:18:08 C:\PRP
       CNSLTS   .GDE    8576 11/29/90 18:52:18 C:\PRP
       CNSLT    .GVT   22400 02/26/91 08:49:04 C:\PRP
       CNSLT    .ART    9472 12/25/88 16:07:58 C:\ART
       CNSLT    .      19072 04/17/89 14:06:30 C:\ART\MS
       CNSLT    .2     19840 02/09/89 13:21:30 C:\ART\MS
       CNSLT    .ENT   13952 08/23/89 08:10:42 C:\ART\MS
              Search Complete, 13 files found.

       Filename      Size    Date      Time    Drive:Path
------------- ------- -------- -------- ----------------------
       CNSLT    .MKT   74368 09/25/90 16:30:04 C:\CNSLT
       CNSLT    .MAN    4608 12/14/90 13:08:12 C:\CNSLT
       CNSLTG   .SEM    4992 12/14/90 13:09:42 C:\CNSLT
       CNSLTMKT.ZIP   29949 11/05/90 18:02:56 C:\LOGS
       CNSLT    .WOM   15581 09/02/90 19:25:18 C:\PRP
       CNSLTNT  .WM2   19584 10/08/90 01:10:36 C:\PRP
       CNS      .101   31360 03/13/91 10:21:14 C:\PRP
       CNSLTNT  .WOM   16256 07/02/90 14:18:08 C:\PRP
       CNSLTS   .GDE    8576 11/29/90 18:52:18 C:\PRP
       CNS      .SRV   25856 03/04/91 15:05:10 C:\PRP
       CNSLT    .GVT   22400 02/26/91 08:49:04 C:\PRP
       CNSLT    .ART    9472 12/25/88 16:07:58 C:\ART
       CNSLT    .      19072 04/17/89 14:06:30 C:\ART\MS
       CNSLT    .2     19840 02/09/89 13:21:30 C:\ART\MS
       CNSLT    .ENT   13952 08/23/89 08:10:42 C:\ART\MS
              Search Complete, 15 files found.
```

Figure 14–3. Finding all "CNSLT" files.

commands, one for "*CNSLT," another for "CNSLT,*" and a third one for "CNS*." Each of these commands is broader than the one preceding it and thus gathers in a greater number of references to study in the quest for the right one.

Everything I have described here is available in most modern word processors. How you use these various features and capabilities is up to you, of course: Each of us must develop our own working habits. In the next chapter I will offer you a few ideas relevant to the subject of working habits.

Chapter 15

Work Habits

Both the quality and the efficiency of work are affected by work habits. Good work habits must develop around the capabilities of your computer and its software, but you must be familiar with all those capabilities.

YOU'VE GOTTA BE YOU

If you are new to computers and word processing, be prepared to develop work habits appropriate to those tools. If you have been using computers and word processors for some time, it will do no harm to examine the work habits you have developed to see whether there is room for improvement.

Over the years I have developed my own work habits, naturally—habits that suit me and are effective for my purposes. These may or may not be in tune with what many professional writers and editors advocate or what works well for them. However, I am a firm believer in what I was taught many years ago at the U.S. Army's Infantry School at Fort Benning, Georgia: "Whatever works is right." I therefore pass on to you a few ideas, describing some of the habits that work well for me and the rationales behind them. You are welcome to adopt, adapt, or ignore them, of course. If any are helpful to you in any way, my inclusion of them here will not have been in vain. If they are of no use to you, perhaps you can get a chuckle from my foibles.

What is important here is not whether my ideas and work habits are right or wrong, or better than or not as good as others; what is important is only what works for you. It is entirely in that spirit that I pass on here what works for me and helps me earn enough to pay the rent.

THE NEED TO SAVE

Most of us were taught as children the virtue of saving. That word has a special meaning in word processing, and is an even more important idea than that of putting your pennies in a piggy bank. Here is why.

As you write, the copy you create is represented by bytes stored in the random access memory (RAM) of your computer. If you have a modern computer you can store many pages there, probably as many as 100. RAM, however, is only temporary storage, a short-term memory. It is *volatile*, in technical terms, and its contents are erased immediately when you turn the power off. That means that anything in RAM is lost if you have even a brief or intermittent power failure. That is why you have a "save" command in your word processor. That command transfers the copy you have in RAM to a disk, where it is safe from power failures. It is thus wise to save often—every few pages.

Most of the latest word processors will do such saving for you automatically and frequently, if you so order; it is a common option. I do not have my own word processor saving automatically for me; I try to remember to do it myself, and I have rarely lost copy that way. But power failures in my locality, even during thunderstorms, are rather rare, although they have happened and I have lost copy on rare occasions. If you live in an area where there are frequent power interruptions, it is probably wise to exercise the option for frequent, automatic saves if it is available to you. If not, develop the habit of saving frequently. (Actually, power failures are not the only hazard to copy not yet saved: A mistaken move on your part, such as an inadvertent format command, can also cost you copy by dumping copy in RAM. I once managed to wipe out my entire hard disk by making an inadvertent FORMAT command. My many copies on floppies saved the day.)

WRITER'S BLOCK: WHAT
TO DO ABOUT IT

Although I have heard the term *writer's block* used often in discussions of writing, I have never been sure of what it means. Presumably, it refers to a condition in which the writer's brain is in a state of near *rigor mortis*, unable to function above motor levels. The creative juices refuse to flow.

The writer finds himself or herself sharpening pencils, making coffee, staring out the window, staring at the ceiling in some feigned deep thought, and otherwise finding dozens of reasons to avoid the keyboard. Perhaps you have experienced this malady. It seems to come to all of us at times.

This seems to be a problem more commonly associated with writers of fiction than with workaday business writers. Yet, writer's block or something closely resembling it affects most writers of all kinds at one time or another. Perhaps it is ennui, fatigue, or simply laziness. I am not sure that I have ever experienced writer's block, but I have had my bouts with these three afflictions—especially laziness. Happily, I have found a way of overcoming it that works for me and will, I hope, help you banish this obstacle to productive writing.

My way of overcoming block is really a preventive measure rather than a corrective one. I use a method of mental pump priming before beginning each new day's writing session. (This method is especially helpful if I am returning to a writing task that was interrupted several days earlier, in which case I have only a dim recall of what I had drafted prior to the interruption.) The remedy is based on habits I have developed to begin each day by editing, reviewing, rewriting, and/or revising prior copy before drafting new copy. It is a simple enough idea, but to fully understand it requires some background explanation of how I organize my work in general, including how I assign files to my projects.

A short piece of work, usually up to about 50 kb (about 25 double-spaced pages), gets a file all its own. A lengthy piece of work is divided into chapters, sections, or other subdivisions, each assigned its own file running to about 20 to 50 kb. Thus a book, manual, proposal, annual report, or other large work will have its own directory and perhaps as many as 10 to 20 files for chapters or sections, plus miscellaneous files for source data gathered in research, which I store in the same directory.

I start each day's work by reviewing, editing, revising, rewriting, and/or polishing whatever is the current file of work. That ensures that each part of the work will get ample editing and rewriting, although that is not the main point of this discussion. The main point is that this practice prevents writer's block for me. By the time I have finished doing this beginning work on earlier drafts, I am up to speed and rolling merrily along. The very thought of block does not occur!

To ensure that I do this every morning, I never finish a day with a completed file. It is important that I always have unfinished work in progress to address in the morning. If I finish a file or any piece of work, I initiate the next piece/file before I quit for the day, no matter how late it is or how tired I am. I have made it a rule that I must have something to review the next morning so I can get my sleepy brain cells awake and into action.

WHEN TO PRINT HARD COPY

Early in my career at the keyboard, I eagerly printed out my copy every time I had finalized four or five pages. I had not yet adjusted myself psychologically to accepting a growing number of kilobytes reported on screen as evidence of progress. I needed to see the growing stack of paper to believe that I was accomplishing something every day, even if I did have to go back frequently to reprint revised copy and discard what I had printed out earlier. (For some kinds of jobs it is still necessary to print copy for client review every few pages, however.)

I have overcome that need for a psychological crutch to the extent that I now do not usually print out hard copy until I have completed a chapter or section. Despite that, I still have a growing stack of discarded hard copy. I keep it beside me on the desk, blank side up, to use as scratch paper for notes and memos, doodling while on the telephone, and other such uses. Still, the stack gets larger and larger: I am unable to use it up as fast as I generate copy to discard!

TRACKING PROGRESS

In business writing, we usually are paid by the hour or by a flat fee quoted for each job. Still, many of us estimate jobs by number of words or pages, as well as by hours needed to get the job done. I am one who likes to keep track of the number of words, if for no better reason than that it gives me a point of reference or orientation that the number of kilobytes does not always do. (E.g., some illustrations, matrices, and charts require large amounts of bytes and thus can mislead you as to the number of words or pages you have written.) The rule of thumb is that a double-spaced page of 10- and 12-pitch copy runs about 2,000 bytes and has on the order of 300 words. These are rough approximations, but they are accurate enough for general purposes as long as the pages are of text. The rule of thumb is no longer reliable when some of the pages are tables, charts, or illustrations of some sort. The file for the previous chapter is 27,413 bytes, which translates, when divided by 2,000 bytes, to between 13 and 14 manuscript pages and about 4,000 words. In fact, that file is only slightly over 10 manuscript pages long. Figure 15–1 shows the display I get when I invoke the byte and word counter feature of my word processor.

PLANNING AND OUTLINING

A piece of work begins with planning of some sort, usually culminating in an outline. Situations vary, especially when you do custom work. One client may be able to offer you nothing more than a vague idea of what he or she wants. Another may be even less helpful, able only to describe some symptoms of a problem that must be solved by a means you are expected to formulate. (In case you are in doubt, this definitely makes you a consultant!) And still another client may present you with an outline and a rough draft and/or source material. In most cases, the prime responsibility for planning and preparation, including outlining, is yours.

Having worked with writers in a number of organizations, I have seen a fairly diverse set of writeups purporting to be book plans, orientations, analyses, and outlines. In my opinion, however, there are only two basic types of outline—the formal outline (also referred to as a *topical outline*) and the narrative outline—although there are probably numerous variations of each. Certainly there are pros and cons for each of these two approaches.

I rarely use the formal outline, but I cannot say that I never use it. There are occasions when I find the formal outline structure necessary, such as when I am planning a seminar or trying to present a complex idea to a client. Some might say that I am from the old school, or at least that I tend to journalistic styles of writing, because I much prefer the lead to the formal outline as a method for planning in most cases. The difference appears to lie in how much I already know about the subject, or at least in how well I have thought the subject out before attempting to outline an approach. If it is a subject that I have written on extensively before or done enough introspection on to feel completely in command of, I can formulate a well-structured approach mentally. Thus, already knowing the general organization I will use, I can easily develop the formal outline—

```
┌─────────────────────────────────────────────────────────┐
│                                                         │
│    Words: 3379              Bytes: 27413                │
│                                                         │
│    Press Esc to continue                                │
│                                                         │
└─────────────────────────────────────────────────────────┘
```

Figure 15–1.   Byte and word counter display.

main topic, subtopic, sub-subtopic, and so forth. On the other hand, if I am working with the germ of a new idea and plodding to work out details and devise an organization and general structure, I find myself totally unready to begin a formal outline. Instead, I am almost certain to engage my initial planning efforts in what an associate once described as 'thinking on paper." That was before the personal computer, but the concept has not changed. In fact, it's much more appropriate to writing with a computer and works much more effectively (for me, at least) with a keyboard and screen than with a pencil and paper. It's a form of doodling with words, using them to help think about and work out an idea. I then wind up with a lead (introductory material that plots the general course for me) and a narrative outline, which is a set of paragraphs, each describing a section of the work to be written, in the order of their presentation. By this time I can write the formal outline but no longer feel the need for it.

One reason I favor this approach over the detailed formal outline is my own reluctance to lock myself in too rigidly in advance. I find that many ideas I did not have when planning occur to me as I work and, especially, as I edit and review my work. (This very portion of this chapter is a drastic revision of my first draft.) The narrative outline always seems to me to be better suited to and perhaps even to encourage keeping my mind open to new ideas as I work. Another reason I favor it is that each narrative passage is a lead for me, a narrative piece of writing that I will expand into the full draft.

This "Planning and Outlining" subsection of this chapter is an example of writing from a lead. This is the third day I have been working on it. I wrote a brief, general couple of paragraphs on planning and outlining the first day. The second day, as I reviewed what I had written the previous day, I had some more ideas on the subject and expanded the original draft a bit. This third day I have expanded the original writeup significantly as I think more about the subject, recall old experiences, and analyze my own methods. I will know that I am ready for final editing and polishing when I have no new ideas on the subject that I think worthy of passing on to you.

This is *my* way of working. I would not prescribe it for anyone else, but I think it worthwhile for you to consider it and try it if you like. In the end, however, be influenced only by what you are comfortable with and what works best for you.

That said, let us look at a brief example of each outlining approach. Here is an element of a narrative outline for one chapter of a book on government procurement:

THE BASIC PROCUREMENT SYSTEM

Introduction to the Federal Acquisition Regulations and the Uniform Procurement Code; what it means in practical terms. The two basic types of procurement—sealed bids and competitive proposals—and what the terms mean—i.e., low bidder and negotiated procurement. Variants and hybrids of these. Types of contracts—firm fixed price and cost reimbursement, with variants and hybrids of each—cost plus fixed fee, basic ordering agreement, time and material, indefinite quantity, annual supply, and others. A few basic rules of procedure governing each type of procurement and contract. The Small Purchase Act and how it works.

If I were to convert that to a formal outline, it would look something like this:

I: THE BASIC PROCUREMENT SYSTEM
  A. Introduction
      1. Federal Acquisition Regulations
      2. Uniform Procurement Code
  B. Basic Types of Procurement
      1. Sealed bids
          a. Low bids win
      2. Competitive proposals
          b. Technical evaluation and points awarded
  C. Basic Types of Contracts; hybrids and variants
      1. Firm, fixed price
          a. Indefinite quantity, annual supply
              (1) "Laundry lists"
              (2) Time & material, basic ordering agreements

This, you may notice, does not cover everything in the narrative paragraph. The complete formal outline would probably be at least three times as long as this sample. And that is another argument for the narrative outline: It is more efficient in some respects, as well as furnishing a lead or series of leads to the drafting of the piece.

The type of outlining support offered by computer software allows you to have your cake and eat it too; that is, you can have both formal outlining and narrative excursions in the same outline. You can develop outlines with at least a half dozen levels of detail—with the capability of breaking out textual excursions detailing some of the levels—and you can have the software present the outline at various levels of the screen to help you analyze the subject and your approach to presenting it. But that is not all by any means: Outlining programs can do more for you, because by their very nature they are adaptable to other uses. Here, for example, is what the WordStar outliner offers, in addition to its outlining function:

- To-do lists
- Project planning schedule
- Other scheduling
- Daily schedules
- Procedures-writing tool
- Word processing/editing features

Unless you are already firmly committed to some other method for planning and outlining, I urge you to become familiar with and seriously consider using outlining software.

MACROS, BATCH FILES, AND RELATED SHORTCUTS

Keyboard work can become rather tedious when doing unimaginative, routine operations. The software designers are well aware of this and always eager to offer labor-saving ideas. They do save labor, and I have always been grateful to have them available.

Most programs, including word processors, include key-redefinition features: They produce what are called "macros," a slang abreviation for *macrocommands*. In effect, they permit you to code a key or two-key combination to produce a result that would otherwise require a longer series of key presses. For example, among the many macros I use is one that I use to get rid of many "BAK" files generated by WordStar. (They can be eliminated in installing WordStar, but they are a safety feature, and it would be unwise to eliminate them. However, they ultimately become a nuisance and need to be erased.) These are copies of original files saved automatically when I make changes. They are useful in case something makes me wish to return to my original file, but they are excess baggage after I have accepted the revised file. I have a macro that searches every directory on my disk and reports on existing BAK files. I have another macro that erases them, all of them. I run these two macros every night before running my tape backup. There is no point in saving these files.

HERMAN HOLTZ
P.O. Box 1731   Wheaton, MD 20915
301 649-2499   Fax 301 649-5745

Figure 15–2.   Letterhead.

Related to this idea are the so-called "batch" files. These act like macros. They are usually brief files that issue commands or a series of commands. I run my tape backup every night with a simple batch file. The file, in this case, is named "BU.BAT." (All batch files end in the suffix BAT.) The BU.BAT file looks like this:

```
cd\tape
tape backup c:\*.*/s/c/-a
```

To invoke it I need merely type "BU c:." The system then loads the program and runs for about one-half hour, copying all directories and files on drive C to the tape unit and then verifying that each has been copied accurately.

Word processors also have copying commands. I have a letterhead set up in one of my directories (Figure 15–2), and I can copy it by opening up a file and issuing the WordStar command "Control KR c:\util\ltr.hd Enter." But I have created a macro to do all this keypressing for me. The SmartKey macro "-h" brings the same result, along with the embedded commands that direct the printer with respect to fonts, spacing, and other important matters. (Those commands do not show because they are embedded.)

For any command I use frequently that requires a series of keystrokes, I create a macro. But the use of this function is not confined to commands. Macros can also be used to store entire text passages, quotations, bylines, and other frequently used texts, logos, trademarks, or other such items.

There are separate macro/key-redefinition programs, such as SmartKey (a granddaddy of such programs). In some ways they are superior to the macro programs that are embedded in other programs because they work no matter what program you are in. However, you can also use the several alternatives described.

RUNNING HEADS AND FEET

Word processors also allow you to install running heads and feet. I have long used running heads in my writing, especially in lengthy pieces. One excellent reason for using running heads is to enable anyone handling your copy to identify the author and the project. Even in your own office, you may be grateful to be able to tell at a glance what a particular page or stack of pages refers to.

The head normally includes my last name and an abbreviated title, and I position it as the first line of the page, flush left. The running head for this book, for example, is "Holtz—Writing for Money."

You have a choice of four: left-hand and right-hand running heads and left-hand and right-hand running feet. A frequent practice is to use two such heads, one identifying the title of the entire document, the other identifying the individual chapter or section. They are useful to readers of the final document, as well as to everyone working on the manuscript, including yourself.

MISCELLANEOUS ANCILLARY PROGRAMS

Most modern word processors include both spelling checkers and thesauruses, and the latter are helpful not only as sources for synonyms but also as quasi-dictionaries. However, with the sizeable hard disks so commonly supplied in desktop computers today, it is practicable to have a *bona fide* dictionary on your disk, always available at the press of a key or two. I formerly used one that gobbled up a huge 10 mb of my system's memory, but I have since switched to one that uses only about 2 mb and is, in my opinion, a much more attractive and more useful design. It is Definitions Plus!,™ the product of WordScience Corporation (1415 Oakland Blvd., Suite 220, Walnut Creek, CA 94596) and an electronic version of the *American Heritage Dictionary.* It furnishes simple definitions of words and phrases and may be called on at any time, no matter where you are in your files.

Figure 15–3 is an example of the dictionary program window displayed when asked for a definition of the word *definition.* Note that it offers the division into syllables as an aid to hyphenation and identifies its parts of speech and various meanings. In some cases, a second window is furnished (using arrow or pg up/down) when the full range of definitions requires more space than one window furnishes.

Probably few writers consider database management (dbm) programs as germane to writing, but they can be useful to the writer. I use rather simple dbm software, the "flat file" or nonrelational dbm. I haven't felt a need for anything more sophisticated than this, although that is probably

definitions

def●i●ni●tion
noun
  1. a. The act of defining a word, phrase, or
     term.
    b. The statement of the meaning of a
     word, phrase, or term
  2. The act of making clear and distinct.
  3. A determining of outline, extent, or
    limits.
definitional adjective.

Figure 15–3.   Example of electronic dictionary display.

more a commentary on my own intellectual shortcomings or laziness than
on anything else. I have no doubt that a more sophisticated (relational)
database program would be even more useful than I have found my own
dbm to be. In any case, the principles of use are the same: The dbm is a
highly flexible program with which you can, among other things, record
and organize data in such a way that you can iterate and reiterate it as
reports in a wide variety of contexts and models. As one file in my own
dbm, I have data on a large number of trade periodicals. I can print out
reports on this file in many formats and by various parameters, to wit:

  by trade
  by publisher
  by editor
  by editorial requirement
  by office location
  by ZIP code
  by area code
  by type of physical characteristic (e.g., slick magazine, tabloid, etc.)

The number of such parameters is limited only by the number and
kinds of "fields" I have assigned in entering these records into my dbm. I
could easily expand the list if I chose to.

Now suppose you specialize in writing proposals for clients. You could enter résumés into a dbm and be able to summon up for a client the kinds of résumés he or she wants to support a proposal. Or you could list physical plant characteristics and equipment for the same kind of application.

The most attractive feature of any dbm is its great flexibility: It is a form that you can design and redesign according to your own ideas and needs. It is a master tool for gathering, organizing, reorganizing, manipulating, and printing out data of all kinds in all forms. This is one case in which applications are truly limited more by your own imagination and ingenuity then by any other factor.

Let us go on now to talk about the broad field of computer clubs, shareware, bulletin boards, and marvelous new research capabilities available to you without leaving your office.

Chapter 16

Researching from Your Office Chair

Efficiency in research is a secret weapon for the freelance writer. Today's office equipment can confer on you the same capabilities enjoyed by large organizations.

A FEW FACTS ABOUT FAX

By now almost everyone who is conscious and old enough to go to school has heard of "fax"—facsimile machines that use modems and telephone lines to send messages and copies of printed materials back and forth. For those who do not own a fax, there are public fax machines available. A hardware store in my neighborhood, for example, displays a prominent sign in the window announcing the availability of fax service, and I have seen at least one coin-operated fax machine in a hotel lobby beside a public telephone. For me, my own fax machine has become a necessity, an indispensable tool for many uses.

There are stand-alone fax machines, independent units, and they are by far the most popular. You can use them to transmit copies of almost any kind of printed material that is on paper thin enough to be fed through the machine. Some people use a "fax board," an electronic card that fits into a computer and transmits and receives messages and at least some graphic material. It has the drawback that material to be transmitted must be keyboarded or somehow fed into the computer (e.g., by scanning), and when received must be printed out if a hard copy is required.

What the fax board can do, the computer with its own modem can do, usually much more efficiently, especially if the material to be sent is lengthy. The chief advantage of the stand-alone fax machine is that anyone can learn to use it in a few minutes, whereas computer literacy and a certain degree of skill are required to transmit materials from one computer to another. The modern freelance writer needs both a fax and a computer and should be able to use both as communications devices.

THE LESS-WELL-UNDERSTOOD COMPUTER CAPABILITY

Today's computers are powerful communication devices as much as they are anything else. Unfortunately, too many of us, including writers, fail to make full use of this capability. Too many confine their mastery of this marvelous new tool to word processing and related functions such as desktop publishing, which is essentially a graphics-oriented capability. Many, in fact, do not have a modem, the hardware necessary for communicating with other computers.

With a modem attached to your computer, either as an external "black box" or internally as another electronic "card," and suitable communications software, you can dial up other computers via your telephone and gain immediate access to a great deal of valuable information, as explained in Chapter 10. The communication is two-way, via typed messages, but also by transmitting entire files.

CONFERENCES AND MESSAGE EXCHANGES

In general, electronic bulletin board systems (BBS) are organized into "bulletins," "conferences," and "files." Conferences are usually message areas, where you post messages and respond to others' messages. Many callers use them to "confer" on a variety of subjects. Many of these bulletin boards have many conferences organized according to interests such as freelance or independent writing. In these conferences you can exchange information of interest and value. For example, Appendix 3 in this book offers a fairly complete listing of writer's associations. I received most of that list via computer-to-computer communication from Norman

Bauman, a New York writer who was kind enough to supply it to all who
wanted it.

A typical succession of screens on a typical BBS follows. The opening
screen greets me, calls for me to identify myself with the password I use,
and presents me with choices:

Welcome to Generation 5 BBS
SERVING THE MICROCOMPUTER
COMMUNITY
SINCE 1983
300/1200/2400/9600 baud V.32/V.42/V.42

Enter your first name > Herman
Enter your last name > Holtz
Enter your password > . . . . . .
Good afternoon, HERMAN
Welcome to Mailnet Central
Time on: 12:11 pm

(301) 680-9300

This BBS is here to serve the computer community. Over
1.5 GB of files, multiple phone lines, great discussions.
Full privileges extended to subscribers, Shareware/PD
authors and visiting SYSOPs of established boards.

Generation 5, Inc.
12061 Tech Road
Silver Spring, MD 20904
Paul LaZar, SYSOP
680-3600 (voice)

Press any key to continue . . .
NEWS
NEW BULLETINS

I choose to read the messages on a conference identified here as "J;1,"
read messages that happen in this case to be addressed to me, and sign off:

ENTRY - > F M B J P G X H Y NOTE GO > J;1
General discussion
You last visited this discussion on 06/30/91

The last comment in this discussion is: 6510
The last comment that you read was 6507

< <S> > ince last comment or comment number > > S
COMMENT: 6510   THREAD #:
6441

TO :HERMAN HOLTZ   SENT :
06/30/91 10:24:55
FROM :BRUCE BOTTOMLEY
RECEIVED: 06/30/91 12:11:58
REPLIES: NO   REPLY TO: 6507
SUBJECT: Henry V

When you become deeply immersed in any discipline, it becomes difficult to step back a few paces and see the connections to the other
disciplines. I face this in dealing with system engineers and design
engineers. I would liken most physicians to the design engineers. Who is
the systems engineer of the body? (This is not a theological question.)
Read - > (Forward)
(#) Number, (R)espond, < <N> > ext, (T)hread,
(D)elete, (+), (−), (E)xit >

No more comments. Press ENTER to exit.
Read -> (Forward)
(#) Number, (R)espond, (N)ext, (T)hread, (D)elete, (+),
(−), < <E> > xit >

General - > L V U T Q S D J F E B M G P X H > G
CLICK

This is a simple communication, reading messages, entering your own
messages by typing them, and then sending them to be posted on the BBS.
There are different kinds of BBS software, and commands vary slightly,
but in general the commands for basic functions are similar. When you
start, you use the "nonexpert" mode and you get menus to help you
understand the commands for doing different things. Later, when you are
familiar with the commands, you opt for the "expert" mode, and the
menus no longer appear. Following is the menu for the Generation 5 BBS
shown here:

ENTRY MENU
F - Files menu
M - Mail menu (ALL mail is PRIVATE)
B - Bulletins
J - Join a Discussion (ALL public comments)
P - Change your default Preferences
G - Goodbye (logoff & hang up)
X - Expert Mode (no menus)

H - Help
Y - Yell for Sysop (chat)
NOTE - Leave PRIVATE message to the Manager
GO - Go to other available areas

There are, of course, many benefits in this, of which getting a list of writer's associations is only one. For example, I have used these systems to find individuals who would help me make surveys by filling out questionnaires. In some cases I have been directed to excellent sources of information. I have used such subscriber services as CompuServe to get information from their many "forums," both by exchanging information with others (I have recently aided some others in learning how to pursue business opportunities with government agencies) and by drawing on their extensive files. And that brings up another aspect of computer-to-computer communication: transferring files.

DOWNLOADING AND UPLOADING

Transferring entire files to and from your computer is known in the jargon as "downloading" and "uploading," respectively. Some users who appear to be quite at home in reading and posting messages on BBS find downloading intimidatingly complex. It is not really so. It is more complex than simple messaging, but not greatly so.

Modern communications software makes downloading and uploading rather simple. First I call up the list of files:

1 Miscellaneous	2 File Utilities
3 Disk Utilities	4 Printer Utilities
5 System Utilities	6 Video Utilities
7 Keyboard Utilities	8 CP/M Emulators
9 Communications Programs	10 BBS programs
11 Turbo Pascal 3	12 Turbo Pascal 4 and 5
13 C Language	14 Clipper Summer '87
15 Dbase III	16 Programming
17 Games	18 Word Processors
19 Spreadsheets	20 Databases
21 Productivity	22 Text files
23 Desktop Publishing	24 Graphics
25 Clip Art	26 Magazine sources
27 Hypertext	28 Math and Scientific
29 Files for CP/M systems	30 Laser printer utilities

31 Unprotects

32 Text utilities

33 Business

34 Financial

35 Pictures (MAC GIF, etc.)

36 Music and sound

37 Home & personal

38 Menus, shells

39 Educational

40 Windows 3

41 ASP direct submissions

42 Clipper 5

98 Last chance - soon to go

99 UPLOADS

Then I choose to look at list 33:

Filename	Size	Date	Description

OPR10.ZIP 69,340 06/26/91 One Page Resume. Version 1.0.

STARTUP.ZIP 23,214 06/06/94 Small business startup calculator.

DKTMDR25.ZIP 268,246 06/04/91 "Docket Minder" Lawyer's assistant v2.5.

POSTAL91.ZIP 33,795 06/02/91 1991 postal rate display program—not text.

DAYOB.ZIP 223,005 05/30/91 Create, maintain specialized pricing for clients.

SCHWAB24.ZIP 37,376 05/24/91 Charles Schwab commission calculator, v2.4.

FZMLINV.ZIP 95,163 05/22/91 Invoice/Statement program.

BOM.ZIP 79,399 05/21/91 Box Office Manager, version 3.2.

SLS—BK.ZIP 75,513 05/17/91 Sales Book, customer/client contact tracker.

GUIDE610.ZIP 275,300 05/16/91 Home & business legal guide and forms generator.

GP26.ZIP 215,898 05/15/91 General Invoice Sales Tracker. Customer billing.

PMC10.ZIP 29,544 05/06/91 Phone Message Center. Message taking & reporting.

WHOWORKS.ZIP 40,310 04/24/91 Scheduling program.

MRB341A.ZIP 169,707 04/19/91 "Mr. Bill" - billing program. Part 1 of 2.

MRB341B.ZIP 155,808 04/19/91 "Mr. Bill" - billing program. Part 2 of 2.

!SF300.ZIP 203,934 04/17/91 Form generator and manager.

FORMMST.ZIP 142,144 04/17/91 "Form Master" - form generator/manager.

REGIT.ZIP 328,165 04/12/91 Point Of Sale program, v4.0.

REGIT-2.ZIP 67,994 04/12/91 Bar Code Levels, v1.0.

SURVEY33.ZIP 142,839 04/04/91 Survey analysis program.

ZK0890.ZIP 120,484 04/04/91 ZIP code database for ZIPKEY, as of 8/90ZK200.ZIP 93,748 04/04/91 ZIPKEY ZIP code lookup engine.

TCASHFLO.ZIP 113,417 03/15/91 Cash flow analyzer.

GIST59.ZIP 200,972 03/07/91 "General Invoice Sales Tracker."

HOTNET.ZIP 284,593 03/07/91 LAN-based multi-user caller support system.

SUPRFORM.ZIP 208,510 01/11/91 Form generator and manager.

CARS16.ZIP 45,714 01/09/91 Auto expense tracking system.

OPTIMARC.EXE 179,992 01/09/91 OPTIMA MK XVI Management scheduler.

OPTIMA.DOC 5,248 01/02/91 OPTIMA mgt schedule syst.docs upl/auth.

PW-GUIDE.ZIP 60,741 12/27/90 Price-Waterhouse guide to develop business plan.

ORDER.ZIP 243,828 12/04/90 Order entry, invoicing, inventory, accts. rec . . .

FAXCOVER.ZIP 36,997 12/03/90 Prints fax cover sheets on Epson, compatibles.

LOG202.ZIP 59,658 12/03/90 Keep track of hours for billing purposes.

CONTACT.ZIP 170,732 11/14/90 Client tracking system.

PAL21.ZIP 285,421 11/13/90 Appointment tracker/calendar/alarm/tickler.

PF.ZIP 265,052 11/13/90 Form generator.

5PLUS20.ZIP 182,966 11/02/90 "Contact Plus" - client, contact tracker.

BILLING3.ZIP 79,986 11/02/90 Keeps track of time spent for billing purposes.

FILL11.ZIP 164,440 09/27/90 Form filler program.

HEM11.ZIP 93,854 09/13/90 Hours/expense.mileage tracking system (ASP).

FORM 333.ZIP 103,681 08/29/90 Form generator.

I then choose the Optima.Doc file I want:

Enter filename you wish to send from us to you (.ZIP assumed)
optima.doc.
Filename   Size Blks   Transfer time   Total time
OPTIMA.DOC   5248 5   32 seconds   32
seconds.
Total time needed for transfer : 32 seconds
(A)bort transfer, (C)ontinue after transfer, or (G)oodbye after
transfer? G.
Begin ZMODEM file receive of OPTIMA.DOC.

Once the transfer is complete, I am notified that it is, and a copy of the
Optima.Doc File is now in my own computer.

SHAREWARE

Such BBS are mostly free or charge a nominal annual fee. Individual
computer enthusiasts run them as hobbies, companies run them as marketing aids, and many are run in government agencies, usually as quasi-
official BBS. The files are of many kinds, as the representative listings
given here show. A few are completely free—software placed by their
authors into the public domain—but most are so-called "shareware."
That means that the author, who is the copyright owner, offers the
shareware on a free trial basis, asking the user to pay for it if he or she likes
it well enough to keep it and use it regularly. Authors upload their products to as many BBS as they can personally reach, and then encourage
others to proliferate the distribution, so the files on a BBS are almost
entirely files uploaded by subscribers. Commercial software products,
usually sold through conventional retail channels, are barred here. If the
"sysop" (system operator) of a BBS discovers that someone has uploaded a
copy of a commercial program, he or she erases it from the files immediately.

Shareware is, as you might suspect, of widely varying quality, from
abysmally bad to excellent, much of it better than many of the commercial
programs produced by large software companies. There are a number of
excellent word processors, communications programs, accounting programs, database managers, spreadsheets, and others of all categories
offered as shareware. Prices asked by the authors of shareware for their
products are much less than that asked for equivalent commercial software. That, plus the privilege of using it free on a trial basis, makes
shareware quite attractive.

PUBLIC DATABASES

The desktop computer has given rise to a new information industry, the public database, also known as the *online database*. Essentially, a public database is a central or host computer in whose storage areas are information files of various kinds. These are available to any subscriber equipped with a computer, modem, and telephone. You can call and query the system to search out items for you from their database, whereupon the system will do so and either advise you and ask for your disposition or transmit the items to you directly, depending on what you requested. You may then have the items printed out as the data is received or transferred to storage in your own system, to be printed out later. (The latter is the more economical thing to do, since it is much faster than printing out directly, and therefore takes less connect time.)

Fees and fee bases vary widely. Some charge initiation fees, some charge monthly fees or monthly minimum usage fees, and all charge on some basis of "connect time." This is usually an hourly figure, but it is actually calculated and billed on the basis of minutes. Some charge a flat price per item retrieved. You may find other variations in pricing practices, but the main basis is usually connect time.

Following is a small sample of the online databases available. (There are many more than this handful.) It will give you an idea of the diversity of what is available.

- IRS, 1200 Route 7, Latham, NY 12110: Databases in education, engineering, science, and medicine.

- CompuServe, 5000 Arlington Centre Boulevard, Columbus, OH 43220: A well-known public database and service for lay people. (CompuServe is a special case, since it is a combination BBS and public database. It has many "forums," in which individual subscribers with relevant interests such as writing, advertising, and consulting exchange messages, as well as forums that are databases.)

- Dialog Information Services, Inc., 3460 Hillview Avenue, Palo Alto, CA 94304: Access to more than 180 databases on many subjects.

- ITT Dialcom, 1109 Spring Street, Silver Spring, MD 20910: An electronic mail system with access to airlines flight information, news, and many other databases.

- National Library of Medicine, 8600 Rockville Pike, Bethesda, MD 20209: MEDLINE and MEDLARS databases, medical information provided to physicians and hospitals (but available to and subscribed to by others), including diagnostic assistance.

- West Publishing Co., Box 43526, St. Paul, MN 55164: Legal information, including research into case law, precedents, and the like.

PERSON-TO-PERSON COMMUNICATIONS

The methods used to send messages back and forth and to download and upload files between your computer and a BBS or public database can also be used to communicate directly with another private owner of a computer. This may be used for various purposes, such as collaboration with another writer, interviewing individuals via questionnaires (i.e., sending a list of questions and getting responses via fax or computer), and sundry other uses.

A FEW OTHER RESEARCH SUGGESTIONS

There are associations of all kinds—trade, business, industrial, social, and other categories. When I was researching the temporary-workers field not long ago, I called the association of temporary-workers suppliers and got immediate answers to my chief questions by telephone. A few days later, I also received a thick envelope of printed materials amplifying that brief information. Associations are always a resource in research. Don't overlook writers' associations, either; they can be helpful in many ways.

Appendix 1

Copyright: Law and Practice

Copyright law is one of those things about which a great many myths and misunderstandings have sprung up. Here are the basic facts, some of which will probably surprise you.

DOES COPYRIGHT CONCERN YOU?

As a freelance writer doing custom writing—a "writer for hire," in the legal sense—what you write is normally the property of your client. You are therefore unlikely to need to copyright anything you have written unless you write also for commercial publication. On the other hand, you are a professional freelance writer and (presumably) editorial consultant. Clients will expect you to understand copyright law and related practices and thus be able to guide them accordingly when questions of copyright arise. Included here is an admittedly summary coverage of copyright law and practices, but it does present the major points and should furnish a reasonable orientation in the subject. At the least, it should serve to brush away some of the cobwebs that cloud understanding and give rise to many popular myths and misunderstandings concerning what copyright is and what it is not. However, a caveat here: Copyright is a protection that can be and is applied to many kinds of products—musical compositions, computer software, and artistic renderings, for example. These applications of copyright law and practice are necessarily mentioned in these discussions, although our chief concern here is copyright protection as it applies to literary properties.

POPULAR [MISTAKEN] BELIEF NUMBER 1

It is perhaps understandable that many people have the notion that to get copyright protection you must register your literary property with the Copyright Office. That is mistaken: Registration of a copyright is an option, but protection is far simpler to secure than that. In fact, here are the words of the Copyright Office on the subject:

> Copyright protection subsists from the time the work is created in fixed form; that is, it is an incident of the process of authorship. The copyright in the work of authorship immediately becomes the property of the author who created it.

Copyright was always easy enough to apply for and get, even under the older statute, but under the newer law (the Copyright Act of 1976, which became effective January 1, 1978) it became even easier. It never was and is not necessary to register a copyright with the Copyright Office to get copyright protection, at least insofar as a common law or statutory copyright is concerned. Your literary property is endowed with such copyright protection automatically when it is set in its final form, and you may (and should) announce that fact to everyone who reads the work. However, there are reasons for registering a copyright in many cases, as you will soon see.

WHAT IS COPYRIGHT?

Copyright means literally the right to the copy or the right of ownership of the creation. It is available for all kinds of literary works, computer programs, music, drawings, paintings, and similar works of creation. As the author of the work, only you and/or others to whom you grant permission or assign your rights are legally entitled to reproduce, copy, or make other use of your property other than to read it.

The old law provided copyright protection for 28 years and was renewable for another 28 years. In a broad overhaul of the basic theory of copyright equity, the current law provided copyright protection for the life of the author plus 50 years, with no renewals authorized.

WHAT CAN BE PROTECTED BY COPYRIGHT?

The nature and scope of what is protected by copyright is another area of popular misunderstanding. Many people tend to confuse the protection of copyright law with that of patent law covering inventions, trademarks, and tradenames. The two kinds of protection have little in common, other than being provided to protect the originator of a new product. Copyright covers the specific and unique *combination* of words, musical notes, colors, brush strokes, computer commands, and other basic elements that have been assembled and organized to constitute the creative property. It is only that combination of elements that is so covered and protected by the copyright, nothing else. Understand that; it is fundamental to the entire idea.

WHAT CANNOT BE PROTECTED BY COPYRIGHT?

Obviously, you cannot copyright *individual* words, notes, colors, brush strokes, computer commands, and so forth; they belong in the public domain as common property. Other items that are not protected by copyright are less obvious. They include works not yet in fixed form (printed, recorded, etc.), titles, names, short phrases, slogans, listings of ingredients, calendars, and other such brief items. More significantly and less well understood—probably the single most misunderstood idea regarding copyright—is that you cannot copyright ideas or information. No one has the right to reproduce your book or article or any lengthy portion of it, for example, but anyone can use the *information* in it to write his or her own book or article. This begins to get into a hazy area, one that is not well defined because it is extremely difficult to be absolutely precise about it. If what appears to be information is, in fact, the unique creation of an author, it may be possible to prove that the "information" was protected by copyright. Note especially that titles cannot be copyrighted. That does not mean that they cannot be protected, however: Titles may qualify for protection as trademarks or tradenames under patent law. But they are definitely not qualified for protection under copyright law.

MUST THE WORK BE
PUBLISHED FIRST?

It is no longer required that a work must be published to afford it copyright protection, as was the case under the older law. (Distributing a half dozen or more copies of the work was legally "publication" under the old law.) Under the current law, copyright obtains automatically when the work is produced in some fixed form. But publication is still desirable, from a practical viewpoint. For one thing, it announces the copyright to the world. *Publication* is defined as distributing copies to the public by rental, sale, or other transfer of ownership, temporary or permanent. Publication should be accompanied by a notice of copyright, advising everyone of the protection. Here, again, the law has changed.

NOTICES OF COPYRIGHT

There are several ways to inscribe a copyright notice. It can be simply the words "Copyright (year) by (name)." It may say "Copr.," followed by the year and name. It may use the symbol "C" in a circle. The first choice is the best because some foreign nations do not recognize the symbol or the abbreviation and may therefore not respect the copyright. Many publishers, however, use both the words and the symbol. (For phono or sound recordings, use the symbol "P" in a circle.)

The notice should be placed in some prominent position on the product. Fortunately, under the newer law, an inadvertent failure to post the copyright notice does not automatically proscribe copyright protection, as it did under the original law, but the author must take steps to correct the error by issuing copies with the proper notice and/or by registering the creation with the Copyright Office.

REGISTERING A COPYRIGHT

There are a number of forms supplied by the Copyright Office for registering copyrights. For ordinary textual works—single works such as novels, plays, articles, reports, monographs, dissertations, and directories—Copyright Office Form TX is used. For serial publications—newspapers, newsletters, magazines, and the like—Form SE is provided. There are, in fact, a number of forms for various applications and uses, as follows:

Form	Application
TX	For published and unpublished nondramatic written works.
SE	For serial works, works to be published in successive parts with numerical or chronological designations, to continue indefinitely, such as newspapers, magazines, bulletins, journals, etc.
PA	For published and unpublished works of the performing arts—dramatic and musical works—motion pictures, other audiovisual works.
VA	For published and unpublished works of the visual arts—paintings, drawings, sculptures, etc.
SR	For published and unpublished sound recordings.
RE	For claims to renewal copyright rights for properties protected under the 1909 Copyright Act.
CA	For supplementary registration to correct or amplify information given in an earlier registration.

Should You Register?

Since copyright protection—statutory or common law copyright—is so easy to get without the trouble of registering it, why bother to register a copyright? Well, perhaps you should not; many publications are protected by only the statutory copyright cited here, and not by registering that copyright. The question of need revolves around the value you assign to the property: Is it potentially of such great value that it appears to require full protection? Also to be considered is the question of whether there is a likelihood that someone will infringe upon your rights.

Many publications are really not in any great danger of infringement because they are not especially valuable. It is hardly worthwhile to register a copyright in these circumstances. Hence, despite the abundance of copyright notices on literary and other properties, a large portion of these copyrights are unregistered and the protection is purely by common law copyright.

On the other hand, there are some good reasons for registering a copyright regardless of the value you assign to your literary property. One reason is that registration establishes a public record of your copyright claim at a rather small cost. But there is another immediate, practical reason: You cannot seek legal remedies, if you must at some point defend your copyright via legal action (i.e., file or defend yourself against an infringement suit) unless your copyright is registered. However, you may register your copyright at any time. Of course, it will be much easier to prove your claim if you registered your copyright in the beginning.

There are some other provisions of interest, too. If made before or within five years of publication, registration establishes *prima facie* evidence of the validity of your copyright claim, including the statements in your application. If you have registered the copyright not later than three months after publication or prior to the infringement, you may collect statutory damages and attorney's fees from the defendant. Otherwise, you can collect only actual damages and profits.

Procedures

The procedures themselves are quite simple. First, request from the Copyright Office the application form(s) you will need, as explained here. The address of the Copyright Office is as follows:

Register of Copyrights
Copyright Office
Library of Congress
Washington, DC 20559

The form will include an explanation of procedure along these lines: To register a book or manuscript, send the following three elements, packaged together, to that same address:

1. A completed application form.
2. A nonrefundable fee of $10. (This may change, of course. But send check or money order, not cash, for amount specified.)
3. A nonreturnable deposit of:
   - One copy of the work if unpublished at the time of registration.
   - Two copies of the work if published at the time of registration.

The copyright, when issued, dates from the day your application was received by the Copyright Office.

OTHER RELEVANT MATTERS

You will notice, in your reading of various publications, that authors often include brief quotes from other copyrighted publications without any indication that permission for the quotation was granted. This quoting of brief excerpts from copyrighted works is authorized under the doctrine of "fair usage." One reason for and justification of the authorization of this kind of usage is to permit critics and other reviewers to cite the works they are reviewing. (It would be difficult to review a literary work without citing excerpts from it!) Another is to permit scholars and other authors to document and support their own published works, both in text and in footnotes, by citing passages from other related or relevant works.

Unfortunately, we have no good definition of how brief is "brief," so "fair usage" remains a rather difficult area to define, except philosophically. As a matter of practical application, it is best to request permission from the copyright owners before quoting more than a sentence or two, should you wish to quote someone. And always make attribution—identify and credit the source—when quoting anyone, regardless of how brief the quote. This should be done as an act of common professional courtesy, attesting your professional integrity. More important, it is also *prima facie* evidence that plagiarism was not your objective. It also weakens any claims of damages by copyright owners of the material quoted.

In practice, it is usually not difficult to get permission for brief quotes. However, copyright owners may request payment of a fee or royalty for permission to quote, especially if the quotation is to be a lengthy one. This is not at all unusual. Copyright owners may and often do demand the right to know precisely what you will quote and how you will quote or cite it, sometimes even demand the right to review and approve that portion of your own work in which you cite or quote them.

Of course, whether you agree to permit that action is up to you. In all fairness, I can understand another author's fear of having his or her work misrepresented by being quoted out of context to suggest a meaning the author never intended. Still, it is a form of censorship that I personally cannot accept. I have therefore always refused to yield to that kind of demand and found some other way to illustrate or document my work, often by paraphrasing the other author or by simply reporting his thoughts, phrased in my own language. It is my opinion that you ought to make the representation that you will make proper attribution and treat the author's work fairly, and the other ought to accept your pledge. I must add here that I have only rarely encountered either of these kinds of demands, possibly because I have always been quite open in my requests

RELEASE

Permission is hereby granted to Herman Holtz and his publishers to reproduce, cite, comment on, and/or quote briefly from material supplied herewith, with the understanding that full attribution will be made.

_____   _____
(Typed/printed name/title)   (Signature)

_____   _____
(Company/division)   (Date)

Figure A–1.   Sample release form.

of other authors and their publishers and made a firm pledge to be scrupulously fair in quoting them.

You must be sure to get written permission—a signed release—from the copyright owner before using his or her material. I suppose a lawyer would draft a formidable release form for this purpose, but I have not found it necessary to be quite that formal and legalistic. If there has been an exchange of correspondence with the copyright owner and he or she has given specific permission in correspondence, that should suffice. But I use a simple form that I supply with my request, illustrated in Figure A-1, and it has always worked well for me. (On one occasion I encountered a publisher who insisted that I get releases on the publisher's own forms, which were lengthy and heavily legalistic.)

Note that the form illustrated in Figure A-1 was designed for my own use, but I write professional and business books for owners and other entrepreneurs, and so most of the materials I cite, quote, and/or reproduce in my books are materials originating with business firms. The form was designed with that in mind. You can easily adapt it to your own needs with simple changes.

Appendix 2

What the Well-Equipped Writer's Shop Should Have

A few suggestions for reference and guidance.

HARDWARE

It is almost inconceivable that anyone would attempt to provide writing and related services today without a computer, although I would not have made this statement as recently as five years ago. Few new machines, except perhaps the automobile, TV, and VCR, have had such complete acceptance in such a short time.

At the same time, few new products have undergone such dramatic—even revolutionary—development so swiftly. Products produced by the computer industry change so rapidly that almost any hardware I could recommend here would surely be dated, if not obsolete, by the time you read this. Therefore, I will not suggest any specific makes or models but discuss only general types of computers and the other hardware generally used in today's small office.

My own computer is a "386" (i.e., uses the Intel 20386 chip), and was the latest word in desktop computers when I bought it less than two years ago. Today, 386s are still state of the art and are still being bought enthusiastically, but the latest product is the 486, which uses the Intel 20486 chip. For a writer's needs and purposes, the 486 offers no great advantages over the 386. My machine has 2 mb of memory, but I am considering adding two more mb. Most modern machines can be upgraded in this manner, and it is wise to be sure that any machine you buy is amenable to such upgrading.

If you expect to do a great deal of graphics work, perhaps a Macintosh is better suited to your needs. Macintosh enthusiasts insist that the IBM-type PC, despite its overwhelming popularity, is not as well suited to graphics work as is the "Mac." (Those who champion the IBM and clones dispute this, of course.) Some writers solve the problem by having both a Mac and an IBM or clone computer, an effective but expensive solution.

Most computers sold today have hard disks of at least 40 mb capacity or larger. My own provides approximately 65 mb of storage, but hard disks of well over 100 mb are more and more commonly used. Memory and storage space in computers are like money: You never have too much and usually do not have enough. Your needs tend to expand to fit the disk space available.

The computer requires a great deal of support from ancillary equipment to provide a complete system. A modem, the device that permits one computer to "talk" to another via a telephone connection, is a must. You should have a modem of not less than 2400 baud. That is a measure of its speed of transmission. Many modems are offered today with speeds of 9600 baud, but relatively few PC owners have them, and you can still get along well with a 2400-baud model. Modems are inexpensive enough to scrap when and if the 9600-baud model becomes a necessity. You can opt for an internal modem (one on a card that is installed in your computer) or a stand-alone unit. The internal unit is slightly less expensive and is functionally the same as the stand-alone unit.

You should have a fax machine. They have become relatively inexpensive and are all but indispensable for business. There are fax machines available for prices as low as under $400. These "plain vanilla" faxes do not offer all the conveniences of the more expensive models, but they provide the same function and do it as well as the more costly machines.

Your computer should have a backup system of some sort. It is just too risky to be without one. I am now using a tape backup, but you do not really have to add to your equipment to provide the security of backing up your files; you can back them up with floppies. Strictly speaking, you don't need to back up the entire hard disk because much of the data stored on it is programs for which you still have all the original disks safely stored away.

If you make disk copies of all new material you create and all other new material you gather and store in your machine, you can create an effective backup system with a reasonable number of floppy disks. But do it constantly; you never know when something unforeseen could cause a loss of data on your hard disk.

A printer is also essential. By far the best print quality today is provided by a laser printer, a successful combination of laser, xerographic copier, and computer technology. In most copiers, a camera photographs original copy and transfers an electrical analog ("copy") of it to the surface of a selenium-coated drum, to be transferred to paper. In the laser printer, a laser beam is driven by the data bits (electrical impulses from the computer representing the data), and the laser paints an image on the drum, to be transferred to paper. While a 24-pin dot-matrix printer also does a creditable job of printing with letter quality, it does not approach the laser in overall capability. There is also an ink-jet printer that works very much like the dot-matrix printer but squirts tiny jets of ink on the paper. It is considered by many to rival the laser printer for quality of reproduction. However, laser printers have declined in cost to the extent that they are beginning to rival the more expensive dot-matrix printers. Today, laser printers are available at prices beginning under $800.

SOFTWARE

There are many software publishers and a great abundance of software. Just as many small firms began to assemble and market computers under their own labels, a great number of programmers set up shop as independent software publishers. Some produce software they sell to software publishers, and some produce and market software as mainstream commercial products, but many produce the software referred to in Chapter 16 as *shareware*. Shareware is usually the least costly, although competition is having its effects in driving down the prices of commercial software. But shareware is essentially risk-free, since you try before you buy.

You must have a word processor. Any of the leading word processors, including WordStar, WordPerfect, and Microsoft Word, will provide you with many extras. Here is a list of suggested programs and/or features that will make life easier for you:

Word processor	Outliner
Spelling checker	Thesaurus

Dictionary	Grammar checker
Word counter	Indexer
Footnoter	Table of contents gatherer
Communications program	Utilities shell

BOOKS

The following is a short list of books that should be useful to all writers. (Unblushingly, I include one of my own.)

Business Writing by J. Harold Janis/Howard R. Dressner. New York: Barnes & Noble, 1956.

The Careful Writer by Theodore Bernstein. New York: Atheneum, 1965.

The Complete Desktop Publisher by Daniel J. Makuta and William F. Lawrence. Greensboro, NC: Compute! Publications, 1986.

Consultant's Guide to Proposal Writing, Second Edition, by Herman Holtz. New York: John Wiley and Sons, 1990.

Direct Mail Copy That Sells by Herschell Gordon Lewis. Englewood Cliffs, NJ: Prentice Hall, 1984.

The Elements of Style by William Strunk and E.B. White. New York: Macmillian, 1972.

Going Freelance by Robert Laurance. New York: John Wiley and Sons, 1988.

On Language by Edwin Newman. New York: Warner Books, 1980.

Proposal Preparation Manual. Washington, DC: U.S. Department of Transportation, Research and Special Programs Administration, Office of University Research.

Selling Your Services by Robert W. Bly. New York: Henry Holt and Company, 1991.

The Writing Business by Donald MacCampbell. New York: Crown Publishers, 1978.

Writing with Precision (unnumbered revision) by Jefferson D. Bates. Washington, DC: Acropolis Books, 1990.

REFERENCE DIRECTORIES

At least one good reference directory is a must for the writer. One that I can recommend without hesitation is an annual, *The [year] National Directory of Addresses and Telephone Numbers*. This directory is the size of a telephone book, and it offers a great deal more than addresses and telephone numbers. It has lists of all kinds of things, including hotels, airlines, associations, publishers, manufacturers, largest U.S. cities and their principal agencies, federal agencies, and business services. It is sold by mail and is available from the publisher:

General Information
11715 North Creek Parkway South
Suite 106
Bothell, WA 98011
206 483-4555

PERIODICALS

Following is a list of periodicals referred to in Chapter 9, suggested as inexpensive media for advertising your own monographs and other publications.

Benedict J. Fraser
Eagle Success Digest
PO Box 150955
Arlington, TX 76015

Ray Hipp
Entrepreneur Digest
154 West 22nd Avenue
Oshkosh, WI 54901

Bill S. Booth
Infopreneur Publishing
3755 Avocado Boulevard,
   Suite 110
La Mesa, CA 92041

Bruce Young
Mail Order Messenger
PO Box 17131
Memphis, TN 38187

Gerald Carson
Mail Profits Magazine
PO Box 4785
Lincoln, NE 68504

Igal Sudman
HWH Enterprises
230 Don Park Road, Unit 1
Markham, Ontario, Canada
   L3R 2P7

Self Employment News &
   Views
TNT Books
PO Box 681519
Miami, FL 33168

Ray Thomas
Second Income News
PO Box 455
Fremont, CA 94537

Anthony R. Carroll
North American Shopper
204 Newark Avenue
Bloomfield, NJ 07003

Chris Curran
National Opportunist
1123 Edmund Avenue
St. Paul, MN 55104

Conleth C. Onu
PO Box 74398
Los Angeles, CA 90004

Appendix 3

Associations
for Writers

Belonging to any association is a worthwhile idea for anyone who is in the business world, including freelance writers. Belonging to a good writer's association is an even better idea.

Belonging to a writer's association is beneficial in many ways, one of which is that an effective writer's association helps its members get business. However, I would rather let Norman Bauman, a New York City freelance writer, tell you a little more about the advantages of association membership. He has been kind enough not only to furnish most of the material in this appendix, but also to permit me to quote his words directly. Reproduced here is a message from Norman in a writer's conference on a BBS.

There are many other writer's groups, of course, especially in the metropolitan areas, and you should seek out those in your own locality.

* * *

Date: 03-30-91 (22:54) WRITERS Number: 5215
To: ALL
From: NORMAN BAUMAN Read: 04-02-91 (07:30) (Has Replies)
Subj: Writers Organizations

>Can anyone recommend a writer's association, group, guild, etc.
>that would benefit a beginning writer?
Glad you asked!
The National Writers Union [NWU] just sent me their list of local contacts
in California, Massachusetts, New Jersey, New York, Washington DC,
Chicago, Minneapolis and Texas (below). I recommend it.

The most useful advice I can give a writer is to join a writers' organization. I am a member of several writers' organizations, and the work I've
gotten through their job phones, directory listings, and personal contacts
at their meetings has paid back the membership dues and luncheon
expenses many times.

If I had to narrow it down to one organization that would be most useful
for the members of this conference, I would recommend the NWU, which
is a large national organization that welcomes writers at every level of skill
in every specialty.

In NYC [New York City], the NWU is so large that they have several
specialty groups. I am active in the science [and] medical writers' group
and the business writers' group. The business writers have regular luncheons, at which we invite a magazine editor to explain what kind of
writing s/he's looking for. The science writers' luncheons and gatherings
are less formal events to make contacts, get advice, and generally talk
shop, but the organizer prepared a science writers list which she faxes to
the editors and PR firms that often call her looking to hire writers.

There was also the "Wine and Whine" magazine writers' group, which
was a self-help group set up by some writers of self-help articles.

The Boston local compiled a freelance magazine market directory.

Dues are $55–$135, based on income (honor system), and you can
make that back if you get one writing job through the NWU.

We particularly need writers who would improve the NWU's diversity:
e.g., younger writers, minorities. We have only one Republican in the
business writers' group, and he feels outnumbered.

The New York Business Press Editors and Editorial Freelancers Association are also good if you live in NYC, and the National Association of
Science Writers and American Medical Writers Association are good if
you write about that.

The NWU is particularly aggressive in some ways. The NWU Griev-
ance Committee has collected thousands of dollars from publishers
who resisted paying, and offers advice on contracts, agents, etc. NWU
contacts:

NWU National Office
13 Astor Place
NY NY 10003
(212) 254-0279

New York Local
799 Broadway #222
New York, NY 10003
(212) 677-9705

Westchester Local
P.O. Box 292
Eastchester, NY 10709
Sarah White, Chair
(914) 682-1574

New Jersey Local
20 Pine Knoll Drive
Lawrenceville, NJ 06848
Eric Lerner
(609) 883-8878

Boston Local
Box 1073
Harvard Square Station
Cambridge, MA 02238
(617) 492-0240

Western Massachusetts
  Local
PO Box 398
Hadley, MA 01035
Steve Simurda
(413) 586-9354

Washington DC Local
1924 Park Road NW
Washington, DC 20010
Carolyn Weaver
(202) 755-4556
(703) 532-4571

Chicago Local #12
PO Box 3454
Chicago, IL 60654
(312) 348-1300

Twin Cities Local #13
PO Box 80026
Minneapolis, MN 55408
Marc Hequet, Chair
(612) 222-0581

Now organizing Texas:

Noelle McAfee
4405 Avenue H
Austin, TX 78751
(512) 450-0705

Santa Cruz/Monterey
  Local #7
c/o Ray March
PO Box 343
Carmel Valley, CA 93924
(408) 659-4536

Bay Area Local #3
236 W. Portal Avenue
San Francisco, CA 94127
Stacy Frederick
(415) 654-6369

Los Angeles Local
PO Box 11043
Glendale, CA 91226
Minoca Gullon
(213) 281-6901

If you are in DC, and you write about science, you might also be interested in the National Association of Science Writers, which has a strong local DC chapter, the DC-SWA (pronounced Duck-SWA). I don't know their local contact, but the NASW Administrative Secretary, Diane McGurgan, P.O. Box 294, Greenlawn, NY 11740, (516) 757-5664, (516) 757-0069 (fax), can get you everything you need to know. The NASW has just started its own BBS, though they aren't doing much with it yet.

COUNCIL OF WRITERS ORGANIZATIONS, MEMBER ORGANIZATIONS

American Society of Indexers
1700 18th Street NW
Washington, DC 20009
(415) 524-4195

Aviation/Space Writers
  Association
17 S. High Street, Suite 1200
Columbus, OH 43215
(614) 221-1900

Computer Press Association
1260 25th Avenue
San Francisco, CA 94122
(415) 681-5364

Editorial Freelancers
  Association
PO Box 2050
Madison Square Station
New York, NY 10159
(212) 677-3357

Florida Freelance Writers
  Association
PO Box 9844
Ft. Lauderdale, FL 33310
(305) 485-0795

Independent Writers of Chicago
8137 S. Yates Boulevard
Chicago, IL 60617
(312) 374-8850

Independent Writers of
  Southern California
13856 Bora Bora Way #226C
Marina del Rey, CA 90292
(213) 827-0747

Midwest Travel Writers
  Association
PO Box 3535
Omaha, NE 68103
(402) 390-1000 ×290

National Association of
  Science Writers
PO Box 294
Greenlawn, NY 11740
(516) 757-5664

New York Business Press
  Editors
PO Box 5771
Grand Central Station
New York, NY 10017
(212) 297-9689
(212) 697-6248

North American Ski
  Journalists Association
PO Box 5334
Takoma Park, MD 20913
(301) 864-6428

Outdoor Writers Association
of America
2017 Cato Ave. Suite 101
State College, PA 16801
(814) 234-1011

Philadelphia Writers'
Organization
PO Box 42497
Philadelphia, PA 19101
(215) 387-4950

Science Fiction Writers of
America, Inc.
PO Box 4335
Spartanburg, SC 29305
(803) 578-8012

Society of American Travel
Writers
1155 Connecticut Avenue
NW, Suite 500
Washington, DC 20036
(202) 429-6639

St. Louis Writers Guild
PO Box 7245
St. Louis, MO 63177
(314) 965-8191

Washington Independent
Writers
220 Woodward Building
733 15th Street NW
Washington, DC 20005
(202) 347-4973

Women in
Communications, Inc.
2010 Wilson Boulevard,
Suite 417
Arlington, VA 22201
(703) 528-4200

Writers Guild of America,
East
555 W. 57 Street, Suite
1230
New York, NY 10019
(212) 245-6180

Appendix 4

A Recommended Proposal Format

Some RFPs mandate a proposal format, and some companies have a standard format specified for their proposal, either of which you should follow. In the absence of these, the following format is recommended as being straightforward, logical, and suitable for most applications.

1: Front Matter

Copy of Letter of Transmittal

Executive Summary

Response Matrix

Table of Contents

2: Section/Chapter 1: Introduction

About the Offeror: Provide a brief introduction to your firm, a thumbnail sketch of your company and qualifications, reference to details to be found later, and any other opening statement.

Understanding of the Requirement: Provide a brief statement of your understanding of the requirement, in your own language (don't echo the RFP), leaving out the trivia and focusing on the essence of the requirement, providing a bridge (transition) to the next chapter.

246

3: Section/Chapter II: Discussion

This section includes extended discussions of the requirements, analyzing, identifying problems, and exploring and reviewing approaches (with pros and cons of each). Include similar discussions of all relevant matters such as technical considerations, management considerations, schedule, and other important points, including worry items. This is the key section in which to sell the proposed program, make the emotional appeals (promises), explain the superiority of the proposed program, and demonstrate the validity of the proposer's grasp of the problem, how to solve it, and how to organize the resources, and otherwise *sell* the idea. It should culminate in a clear explanation of the approach selected, bridging directly into the next chapter. Include graphics, as necessary, especially a functional flowchart explaining the approach and technical or program design strategy employed.

4: Section/Chapter III: Proposed Project

This is where the specifics appear—staffing and organization (with an organization chart) and résumés of key people, either here or later in this chapter, but at least introduced here by name.

Project Management: Include procedures, philosophy, methods, controls; relationship to parent organization, reporting order; and other information on both technical and general/administrative management of the project. (This may be a separate chapter or even a separate volume, for larger projects.)

Labor Loading: Explain the major tasks and estimated hours for each principal in each task (use a tabular presentation), with totals of hours for each task and totals of hours for each principal staff member.

Deliverable Items: Specify, describe, and quantify as explained.

Schedules: Specify as explained. (Use a milestone chart if possible.)

Résumés: Include résumés of key staff, prepared for the project.

5: Section/Chapter IV: Company Qualifications

Give a description of the company, past projects (especially those similar to the one under discussion), resources, history, organization, key staff, other résumés, testimonial letters, special awards, and other pertinent facts.

6: Appendices

Include here, as appended material, anything you believe will be of interest to some, but not all, your readers.

A FEW MISCELLANEOUS ITEMS USEFUL TO KNOW IN WRITING PROPOSALS

Response Matrix

A response matrix is designed to help the reader verify the total responsiveness of your proposal and so maximize your technical score. In general, it is a table in which are listed the requirements specified in the RFP (and derived from the checklists prepared earlier), assuming the following general form:

RFP/SOW page/par	DESCRIPTION	PROPOSAL page/par	NOTES

A Tip or Two on Graphics

A good illustration requires little explanation, and that is the way to test the quality of any illustration: Does it require explanation, and if so, how much?

Is the illustration clear or is it "clever"? Forget about clever devices and artistic considerations; the purpose of an illustration is to communicate information accurately and efficiently. If the reader has to puzzle over the meaning or study the illustration to understand it, the reader will probably set your proposal aside with a sigh and go on to the next one. Basic rule: Make it as easy as possible on the reader. Cleverness is all too often the death of meaning and understanding, and therefore the death of the sale.

For function charts, use the Why? How? technique to generate the chart and test it. Going from left to right (or from top to bottom, if you prefer that progression), ask Why? of each box, and the answer should be in the next box. Going the other way—in reverse—ask How? and the answer should be in the next box. If the answers are not very clear, consider adding boxes for more detail or changing the wording in the boxes. (Charts, like text, should go through drafts, editing, reviews, and revisions.)

Use of Headlines, Glosses, and Blurbs

Proposals are not exciting literature, and at best they are fatiguing to read in quantities, as customers are compelled to do. Anything you can do to make it easier for the reader will help you in more than one way: (1) It will help you get your own messages across and pierce the consciousness of readers who may be reading mechanically, and without full appreciation, by the time they get to your opus; and (2) you will earn the reader's gratitude, which can do nothing but help your case. There are at least three devices that will help: headlines, glosses, and blurbs.

Headlines

Use headlines—sideheads and centerheads—as freely as you can, as often as you can. Use them to summarize messages, to telegraph what a paragraph or page is about, what the main message is. But use them also to *sell*. That is, use the headlines to summarize promises—benefits—and proofs. Use them to remind the reader of the benefits and reinforce the proofs.

Glosses

A "gloss" is a little abstract in the margin of a page that summarizes the text next to it. Usually, there is at least one gloss on a page, and often there are several. Like headlines, glosses can and should be used to help sell the proposal by focusing on benefits and proofs.

Blurbs

A blurb is very much like a gloss, except that it is not used as frequently, and is thus somewhat broader in scope and, usually, of greater length. A blurb generally appears after a major headline or chapter title. Like headlines and glosses, blurbs should be used to sell as well as to sum up information and communicate generally.

Index